Sex, Consent and Justice

This book is dedicated to my parents, Neeru and Devinder Sikka, my sister, Nisha Sikka, and the myriad colleagues and friends who helped me throughout this process.

Sex, Consent and Justice

A New Feminist Framework

Tina Sikka

EDINBURGH
University Press

Edinburgh University Press is one of the leading university presses in the UK. We publish academic books and journals in our selected subject areas across the humanities and social sciences, combining cutting-edge scholarship with high editorial and production values to produce academic works of lasting importance. For more information visit our website: edinburghuniversitypress.com

Edinburgh University Press Ltd
The Tun – Holyrood Road
12(2f) Jackson's Entry
Edinburgh EH8 8PJ

First published in hardback by Edinburgh University Press 2022

Typeset in New Caledonia by
Servis Filmsetting Ltd, Stockport, Cheshire

A CIP record for this book is available from the British Library

ISBN 978 1 4744 7920 2 (hardback)
ISBN 978 1 4744 7921 9 (paperback)
ISBN 978 1 4744 7922 6 (webready PDF)
ISBN 978 1 4744 7923 3 (epub)

Contents

Preface

I first heard about #MeToo from a friend who, in mid October of 2017, had seen actress Alyssa Milano's blog post and tweet encouraging women to 'shout' their own experiences of harassment and assault using the hashtag 'MeToo'. Milano wrote, 'If you've been sexually harassed or assaulted write "me too" as a reply to this tweet . . . If all the women who have been sexually harassed or assaulted wrote "Me too" as a status, we might give people a sense of the magnitude of the problem' (Milano 2017).

The disclosures came hard and fast. They began with a simple retweeting of #MeToo, but then transmuted into more detailed confessions ranging from the specific, in which women named particular workplaces as well as their assailants, to the more general, which tended to describe the incident(s) but leave other details out. Experiences ranged from quotidian – e.g. being accosted on a bus or catcalled – to ones that were more severe, such as rape, stalking and sexual assault. The widely publicised and shocking cases of actor Bill Cosby and Hollywood producer Harvey Weinstein had propelled Milano to do this (she notes the idea came from a friend of hers and later credits activist Tarana Burke for starting the hashtag years earlier – more on this later):

> I thought, you know what? This is an amazing way to get some idea of the magnitude of how big this problem is . . . It was also a way to get the focus off these horrible men and to put the focus back on the victims and survivors . . . That was basically it . . . I looked down at my daughter, sent the tweet, and went to sleep not knowing it was going to snowball. (Sayej 2017)

This snowballing produced what was initially referred to as a moment (i.e. the #MeToo moment) and later a movement. While I provide more details about the impact and scale of #MeToo further on, it bears signposting here that the #MeToo Twitter space quickly became a locus through which women felt able to dismantle the silence and stigma that surrounded their experience of gender-based violence, challenge the impunity of their assailants, draw attention to the ways in which the criminal justice system had failed them, and cultivate a sense of solidarity with women who had experienced similar violations (Alaggia and Wang 2020; Clarke 2019). Sarah Miller refers to this as a form of 'epistemic refusal', wherein women are encouraged to craft their own 'space for epistemic, ethical, and political community between survivors of sexual violence by denying hegemonic epistemic discourses of contemporary rape culture' and, in doing so, subvert more formal modes of disclosure while also calling for the criminal justice system to do more and do better (Miller 2019: 13).

As the months went on, I followed the movement's progress and grappled with whether or not to disclose my own #MeToo story. I then began to think more carefully about the trends towards consensus on a number of issues relevant to the movement, two of which are particularly relevant to this book – namely, agreement on what constitutes permissible sex and conformity on the ideal outcome of any disclosure. For #MeToo advocates, consent is the primary barometer of sexual permissibility. As I argue throughout the book, consent norms have shaped cultural beliefs and legal standards governing women's sexuality for decades. They see the female body as the site on which the yes and no of consent is inscribed, fought over and maintained. This organising dichotomy, I argue, is at the heart of contemporary approaches to sexual relations as well as #MeToo. While there have been attempts to contextualise and complexify consent, I maintain that it is a rather impoverished model of sexuality – one that fails to leave sufficient room for a more robust, capacious and representative understanding of how sex occurs in practice. I argue that sex is full of greyness, is contextual and norm-busting, and challenges hegemonic assumptions around liberal subjectivity, rational communication, symmetrical power relations and transparent desire (Murray 2018; Baer 2018).

However, consent discourse has never been static either. It has morphed over the decades to include affirmative consent, enthusiastic consent and communicative consent and has given rise to related concepts like sexual autonomy, sexual integrity and sexual citizenship. It was from the study of these divergences that I then began to construct what I believe is a more commodious approach. From these frameworks, the following assumptions became evident: first, that sex is not a discrete act but one that reflects an assemblage of values and norms, discourses, relations, bodies, laws and affects; second, that any analysis of sex must account for power differentials vis-à-vis gender, race, class and sexuality; third, that we need to identify the structures that continue to oppress 'women's everyday lives' and constrain 'their sexual desire[s]' (Calogero and Siegel 2019: 1,697); and fourth, that sex is a boundary-breaking act that is difficult to litigate due to its merging of performance, risk, danger, vulnerability and pleasure (Kitrosser 1996). I call this new approach the 'pleasure and care-centred ethic of embodied and relational sexual Otherness'.

The second observation I made from closely following the #MeToo movement was with respect to how carceral forms of punishment constitute the preferred outcome for most #MeToo advocates (Mack and McCann 2018; Gruber 2019). I found this to be particularly curious given #MeToo's purported objectives such as consciousness raising, social transformation, repair and justice (Gilbert 2017). I felt uneasy about the carceral turn #MeToo had taken (as did Tarana Burke, I return to this later): one that is focused on individual perpetrators rather than structures; punitive punishment instead of understanding and transformation; and state-led processes over grassroots initiatives. Even more confusing was that the very same women who supported #MeToo also purported to support Black Lives Matter (#BLM) even though their visions of justice were often diametrically opposed (i.e. incarceration versus prison abolition). Alison Phipps describes some of what we see emerging from #MeToo as a form of 'white feminism' – one that focuses on sexual violence and patriarchy at the expense of racial capitalism, colonialism and 'alternative forms of accountability and governance that are not based on domination, hierarchy and control' (Phipps 2020: 163).

From these frustrations, I constructed an alternative approach – one that incorporates the 'pleasure and care-centred ethic of embodied and relational sexual Otherness' model of sexual ethics I mentioned above into a robust practice of restorative justice. Restorative justice is an approach to justice that brings survivors and offenders together in order to repair harm. Taken together, I contend that these two frameworks bring us closer to fulfilling the objectives of #MeToo while also allowing an anti-racist and anti-heteronormative conception of justice and sexual ethics to take hold.

Introduction: The Genesis of #MeToo

The #MeToo movement, in its current iteration, represents a significant socio-cultural turning point with respect to what constitutes acceptable sexual conduct and desirable sexual behaviour. Beginning with the publicisation of allegations against Harvey Weinstein, former president Donald Trump, Bill O'Reilly, Larry Nassar, Louis C.K., Aziz Ansari, Jian Ghomeshi, Avital Ronell and Kevin Spacey, thousands of women (and some men) all over the world took to Twitter and social media to 'out' their assailants, tell their stories and, in some cases, seek formal justice.

On a micro level, #MeToo has empowered those with access to challenge both structures and persons guilty of perpetrating and/or facilitating various forms of gender-based violence. However, thus far it has been the more high-profile celebrity-driven cases that have received the bulk of public attention and legal remedy. As such, it remains the case that women (and men) without some form of status, notoriety, money or power have been unable to tangibly harness the movement. In this way, it could be said that #MeToo has served an important normative, pedagogical and cathartic role but perhaps not a material one. At least not yet.

In this book, I take up and explore many of the contradictions and tensions that make up the #MeToo movement and movements that preceded it – particularly those that draw together contemporary understandings of justice, violence, consent, pleasure and desire. In doing so, I draw on historical, explanatory, diagnostic and solutions-based tools to unpack two debates in particular – namely, contemporary sexual norms vis-à-vis what is permissible and desirable sexual behaviour, and what constitutes justice vis-à-vis gender-based sexual violence. On both fronts, I contend that #MeToo has opened the door to much-needed conversations but, in doing so, has ended up expanding problematic conceptions of consent and institutional carceral justice in ways that are no longer fit for purpose. It is here that my model of a 'pleasure and care-centred ethic of embodied and relational sexual Otherness' and restorative justice can do the most work by offering a way forward that is fit for purpose. The central question I aim to answer is that given our current legal framework's inability to serve women ethically or juridically when it comes to violence that is gender-based, what is the alternative?

Chapter 1 of the book begins with a history of rape and sexual assault law examined through the lens of various iterations of feminist thought inclusive of liberal feminism, radical feminism and the three feminist historical 'waves', as well as other modes of thought borrowed from gender and sexuality studies. These include queer theory, intersectional feminism, postfeminism, fourth wave feminism, cancel culture, sex wars and rape culture. Chapter 2 examines the different forms of permissible sex that dominate cultural and legal discourse including consent in its liberal, affirmative, enthusiastic and communicative iterations, as well as the related frameworks of (embodied) sexual autonomy, sexual integrity and feminist materialism. I also provide an introduction to non-integrative modes of sexual expression left out by #MeToo including excess and overwhelm, queer sexuality and BDSM. All of this culminates in the articulation of the new model of sexual relations (a 'pleasure and care-centred ethic of embodied and relational sexual Otherness') which I outline and discuss in detail.

Chapter 3 provides a more detailed overview of the genesis of #MeToo including a discussion of whisper networks and related movements as well as hashtags including #TimesUp and #BelieveAllWomen. Also discussed is a central criticism of #MeToo which is that it can be exclusionary, elitist and heteronormative. In chapter 4, I take up and discuss the possibilities offered by restorative justice as an alternative to the forms of carceral feminism expressed by much of the activism around gender-based violence including #MeToo. After delivering an overview of restorative justice as a practice and epistemology, I examine its various models and often successful uses in a variety of contexts including that of gender-based violence.

The remaining chapters consist of close critical analyses of controversial #MeToo cases using a case-study method and an adapted form of discourse analysis. These cases are Hollywood producer Harvey Weinstein, comedian and actor Louis C.K., Canadian broadcaster Jian Ghomeshi, New York University academic Avital Ronell and comedian and actor Aziz Ansari. The objective of these case studies is to probe how the consent-based approach to sexual relations embraced by #MeToo (inclusive of consent, affirmative consent, enthusiastic consent, communicative consent, sexual autonomy, sexual integrity and sexual citizenship) is expressed and functions in each of these cases. I interrogate whether these frameworks are robust enough to capture the complexity and nuances of embodied sexuality and/or capable of attending to non-normative sexuality and the structures of power in which contemporary sex occurs. I also challenge the role of the carceral state and the efficacy of punitive punishment in each of these cases which is an objective #MeToo continues to pursue.

I also explore the possibilities offered by the 'pleasure and care-centred ethic of embodied and relational sexual Otherness' model of sexuality I have constructed. Specifically, I examine whether and how the principles of pleasure, care, relation, embodied autonomy and respect for the Other that make up this approach have been breached and ask if a restorative justice-led process, with the 'pleasure and care-centred ethic of embodied and relational sexual Otherness' at its core, might have led to an improved, more just outcome for all involved and one that is more in line with #MeToo's stated goals.

The cases of Harvey Weinstein, Louis C.K., Jian Ghomeshi, Avital Ronell and Aziz Ansari were chosen because they are high profile, media driven (both traditional and social) and reflective of the debates that occurred at the height of #MeToo. They were also chosen because of the level of public and media activity they ignited with respect to the subjects of sex and sexuality, permissibility, consent, gender, race and justice. The copious media coverage and the trackability of online conversations produced a rich archive of data suitable for this kind of analysis. Also of note is that these cases include a queer woman and two people of colour, adding a further layer of complexity and historical weight to the discussions that follow.

In terms of shortcomings and absences, these cases, while paradigmatic, reveal deep disparities between those considered worthy of discussion in a book – i.e. rich and powerful men and women – and the millions of cases of harassment and assault that are never discussed or reported. These cases are also American-centric apart from the case of Jian Ghomeshi, who is Canadian, which, while appropriate since #MeToo emerged out of the American context, does not account for the diverse and situated conversations and cases of gender-based violence occurring all over the world. As demonstrated in Chapters 1 and 2, there are many examples around the world (from South Korea, Egypt, Sweden and India to France, Morocco and Brazil) representing a myriad of sectors (from law and entertainment to politics and academia) that have drawn public attention and opprobrium and taken on the #MeToo moniker (Starkey et al. 2019; Stone and Vogelstein 2019).

The two cases that involve men of colour are those of Aziz Ansari, who is of South Asian descent, and Jian Ghomeshi, who identifies as ethnically

Iranian. Race becomes a factor in some of the media coverage – particularly with respect to the way in which sexual behaviours and ideals are sometimes expressed and understood through this lens. The case of Avital Ronell, a queer woman, comes out of academia and was chosen because of the media interest, the contentious nature of the case, and the fact that her accuser is a gay man. It brings to the fore novel quandaries around boundaries, sexual normativity and desire. The Louis C.K. example is more straightforward and was chosen because it is paradigmatic of many cases involving cis heterosexual white men. Yet, it is notable given C.K.'s reputation for being an advocate for female comics as well as for his apology, that even his response was followed by qualifying statements and jokes that undermined any remaining feminist bona fides. The Harvey Weinstein case is the most clear-cut but significant because of its impact on public discourse and the discussions it drove around power and impunity.

Throughout the book, there is some slippage between the terms 'victim' and 'survivor' primarily because of the unique way in which each is deployed in media and academic texts. The use of 'victim' in media, and some legal scholarship that is over ten years old, is relatively consistent, so when referring to those texts I have also used the term. In other areas, particularly in relation to more contemporary research in critical legal studies, social justice work, alternative media and feminist texts, I have followed their lead and used 'survivor'. My general preference for 'survivor' is in line with the established feminist desire to challenge the image of feminine passivity that leads to further forms of 'objectification and the negation of an active and evolving self' (Papendick and Bohner 2017: 3; Lamb 1999; Henley, Miller and Beazley 1995). I am also sympathetic to recent moves to reclaim the term 'victim' by women resisting societal pressure to 'heal', 'get better' and 'move on'. As Campoamor argues, '"Survivor" paints a misleading picture of victimhood and healing, promoting a super-human response that encourages victims to "get over" an unspeakable violation' (Campoamor 2018).

Others, like Tami Spry, reject the survivor identity, arguing that it too is insufficient since it excludes women's voices and embodied experience by defining 'the meaning of the assault in relation to his action rather than her experience; she survived it or was a victim of it. The perpetrator's body is viewed as the locus of action and power' (Spry 1995: 30). Overall, my decision to use both terms with a preference for 'survivor' is a product of all of these considerations as well as practical ones related to readability and flow.

This book, I confess, has rather ambitious goals, ones that get to the heart of contemporary conversations around identity, privilege, entitlement, race, class, sexuality and justice. I admit that the desire to make substantive societal change from on high, however, no matter how well researched and theoretically grounded, is rarely successful. Social and cultural transformation requires getting involved in the muck of sex education, criminal justice, abolition, restorative practices, media rearticulations and forms of public scholarship. More on these projects and where we must go from here can be found in the conclusion. Let us begin . . .

1. Feminist Waves, Movements and Moments

This chapter engages in a historical overview of how sex is constructed and the conditions under which we understand it as desired. Prevailing understandings of appropriate, normative and legal sex leave much to be desired. Whilst what is considered 'acceptable' varies from country to country and jurisdiction to jurisdiction, what is constant are the general parameters of permissible sex. These include heteronormativity (that is, penetrative sex between a man and a woman); a focus on consent (whether verbal and/or implied); and, increasingly, a 'no means no' and/or 'yes means yes' model of sexual communication (Friedman and Valenti 2019; Little 2005; Coy et al. 2016).

Additionally, learned gender norms and sexual myths often work together to co-constitute prevailing sexual practice (Brewster 2013; Sanchez, Crocker and Boike 2005; Wiederman 2005). Media, inclusive of films, television, social media and music, operate in tandem to perpetuate gendered stereotypes and scripts that reflect stereotypical representations of sexual encounters. These include representations which assume that 'permissive sex is the norm, that looks and sexiness count for women, and that men are sex-driven creatures whose cool and tough looks enhance their pick-up skills' (Ter Bogt et al. 2010: 846; Ward and Friedman 2006).

These norms are based on the default male/female binary in which two discrete yet complementary genders exist but, due to the way in which binaries operate, men are seen as superior, powerful and predisposed to rational thought (McKinney and Sprecher 2014; Bing and Bergvall 1996). This sex/gender binary is seen by many feminist scholars to constitute *the* ontology of Western civilisation through its mapping of the central Cartesian Enlightenment dualisms of reason/emotion and mind/body (Tuana 1983; Jaggar and Bordo 1989; Maruska 2010; Bordo 1993). As Stanley and Wise explain:

> reality as characterised by two opposing principles, those of masculinity and femininity (or rather maleness and femaleness) and their working out through science and nature, reason and emotion, objectivity and subjectivity, and so on; the very

> grounds of reality are presupposed in binary and gendered terms . . . And these opposing principles are seen both as symbiotically related and necessary to each other *and* as existing in relations of super- and subordination, with the feminine supportive of the masculine. (Stanley and Wise 1992: 347)

Many feminist poststructural and deconstructionist thinkers have sought to challenge and restructure the systematic undermining and marginalisation of one side of hegemonic binaries inclusive of nature/culture, whiteness/Blackness, East/West, savage/civilized and so on. Revealing and contesting the hierarchy, oppression and practices of Othering that make up these dichotomies, they argue, works to empower both the oppressed terms and the identities they reflect (Rosenau 1991; Derrida 2016; Spivak 1990; Butler and Scott 2013; Kristeva 2002).

In the context of sex, the passive, repressed, undesirous female is situated in a position of subordination and in opposition to the active, desirous male such that full female subjectivity is placed under question. Supposed sex-based differentiation is used to produce and reproduce behavioural difference that 'supports dominance systems by demonstrating that superordinate and subordinate groups differ in essential ways and that such differences are natural and even desirable' (Reskin 1988: 63).

Feminist activism and engagement that challenge this ontology, as well as the structures of misogyny and patriarchy that emerge from it, are present in a number of socio-cultural 'waves' of change beginning with revisions to legal norms and frameworks governing sex in the late 1800s to early 1900s. These transformations, broadly defined, began with amendments in the form of achieved suffrage and basic civil rights that emerged out of the feminist first wave (Banks 1986; Schwendinger and Schwendinger 1983; Smart 2002). At the same time, rape laws and public perceptions around gender-based violence evolved such that rape was rearticulated and codified not as an infringement of male property rights, as in the past, but as the unjust violation of bodily integrity requiring force and nonconsent (Rubenfeld 2013; Backhouse 1983; Anderson 2002). The oft-told story of seventeenth-century Italian painter Artemisia Gentileschi is illustrative of the property model wherein Artemisia, having been raped, had to have her father, a painter for the Pope, press 'charges' because of the way the law was structured, the value attached to virginity, and, cynically, the potential that 'Scandal, being the father of a damaged daughter, would drive down the price for his paintings' (Mohacsy 2004: 155; Spear 2000).

The status of women's bodies as property explains why 'marital rape' was not considered illegal at the time since the marriage contract implied perpetual agreement (consent) to sexual relations (Hasday 2000). The central conceit of the construction of women's sexuality throughout these centuries, however, is one which 'gave currency to ideologies that emphasised the preservation of women's chastity. Effectively, this meant the restriction of women's sexuality to situations controlled by men, especially fathers and husbands' (D'Cruze 1992: 379). I return to more recent iterations of the property model further on but first lay out the central tenets of liberal feminism and interrogate its role in the evolution of consent norms and law as it relates to gender-based violence and #MeToo.

LIBERAL FEMINISM AND THE SECOND WAVE

Liberal feminism reflects the various transformations outlined above and extends into the second wave of feminist activism. It also continues to exist in the form of contemporary lean-in, neoliberal postfeminism. Liberal feminism takes the position that the achievement of gender equity can and should be pursued through the traditional channels of politics and law. Its penultimate goal is to attain full legal rights for women. In accordance with the liberal tradition, liberal feminists argue that 'if the possession of rights is based on a gender-neutral quality such as rationality, and if women can be shown to possess this quality, then women are possessors of rights, and any infringement of those rights is morally unacceptable' (Groenhout 2002: 51; see also Nye 2013; Phillips 1987). As such, formal legal equality constitutes the telos of liberal feminism rather than radical institutional and structural change. Liberal feminists, in 'overemphasiz[ing] the importance of individual freedom over that of the common good', run up against feminists that push for a radical restructuring of a social order that they see as deeply patriarchal (Tong 1989: 11). Liberal feminists, particularly throughout the first and second waves, were overwhelmingly white, straight and middle/upper class demographically and thus rightly criticised for being exclusionary (Mandell and Johnson 1995; Kotef 2009).

In the second wave, during which liberal feminism thrived, there was a concerted push in the Global North for equity in women's everyday personal lives in the form of new workplace, harassment and gender equity laws including those enshrined in the Civil Rights Act (1964 and 1991), Title IX, the Violence Against Women Act, and the Government Accountability Act (Brownmiller 1986; Friedan 2010; Evans 2002). Also part of the second wave was a more fulsome critique of patriarchy and misogyny coupled with actions aimed at 'freeing half the race from its immemorial subordination'

(Millett 1977: 363). Women's liberation from oppressive conditions of 'rape culture', a term radical feminist Susan Brownmiller coined in 1975, was a central goal of second wave feminists. It was believed that through concerted acts of consciousness raising, women would come to realise how pornography, prostitution and a sexualised media culture had produced the very culture of gender-based violence they were working against.

Second wave feminists were also critical of the ways in which heterosexual sex under male supremacy was constructed as normal despite 'intercourse [itself functioning] as an act . . . express[ing] the power men have over women' (Dworkin 2006: 288; MacKinnon 1997; Abrams 1995). Attendant reforms in the 1960s and 1970s included stricter workplace harassment laws; the slow and uneven introduction of rape shield laws (wherein the complainant could not be doubly violated through the condemnatory introduction in court of past sexual behaviour); the dropping of the third party corroboration requirement; longer time limits for reporting assaults; the complexification of the force requirement; the introduction of victim impact statements; and the widespread 'making illegal' of the practice of marital rape. These reforms came together to form what has come to be known as the 'victim's rights movement' (Burgess-Jackson 1999; Seidman and Vickers 2004; Caringella 2008). The objective of victim's rights advocates was to transform societal perceptions around rape and sexual assault including:

> (a) the belief that rape was not a serious and violent offense; (b) the notion that acquaintance rapes or rapes perpetrated by intimates were less serious than and different from 'real rapes' – those that fit a cultural stereotype involving a stranger jumping out from a place of hiding and violently raping a physically resisting woman; and (c) the various 'rape myths' which suggested, among other things, that rape victims were somehow partially to blame for their own victimization. (Bachman and Paternoster 1993: 554–5)

A network of support services attached to the victim's rights movement were also created in the 1990s including rape crisis centres and hotlines, expanded social services, self-help tools, and a transformation in language from 'victim' to 'survivor' which encouraged 'survivors' to speak their truth from a position of agency (Matthews 2005; Derene, Walker and Stein 2007; McSherry and Keyzer 2011).

These changes, however, while being grounded in concrete social oppression, were enacted in ways that had some troubling outcomes for marginalised communities. Specifically, some of the very laws and policies that were aimed at protecting vulnerable women elided their racialised history since, particularly in the US, racial profiling continues to result in the overpolicing of Black communities and incarceration of Black bodies. These changes also tended to focus on the experience of white women over Black women and other women of colour; were carceral in their vision of solutions – thereby discounting the need for major structural change; and resulted in advocates opportunistically allying themselves with anti porn, anti sex-work, and pro death penalty conservatives (Smith 1990; West 1987). Liberal feminism became the default position of many of these activists with radical feminism emerging as its main opponent – first in the 1960s – which guided feminist thought into the third wave and the introduction of the so-called 'sex wars'.

THIRD WAVE FEMINISM

The feminist third wave of the 1990s dealt with the much-delayed inclusion of women of colour and women from the Global South (global feminisms) into the feminist movement while also challenging gender essentialism, which asserts this existence of a universal woman and an innate model of femininity, and embracing sexual difference and empowerment (Mann and Huffman 2005; Gillis, Howie and Munford 2004; Baumgardner and Richards 2010). Younger third wave feminists also began to think about the ways in which race intersects with class, the importance of grassroots activism, and adopted pluralism as their defining ethos (Heywood and Drake 1997; Johnson 2002).

The vocabulary of third wave feminists includes that of 'sexism, reproductive rights, sexual autonomy, fair treatment, lesbian-gay-bisexual-transgender issues [inclusive of queer theory], workplace equity, global awareness and intersections of race, class, and gender' (Kinser 2004: 134). Diverse concerns, including the importance of decolonisation, the interests of immigrant women, and the gendered and gendering effects of cultural production, technology and media, converged to produce a synchretic form of feminist praxis. Some of the third wave's most activist manifestations were filtered through youth culture and feminist popular culture in the form of zines, music, progressive sexual politics and rage (Gillis and Munford 2004).

Third wave feminists shared some of their concerns about sex with radical feminists who in opposition to their liberal counterparts – and prior to the rise of the third wave – worked for emancipation over liberal choice and formal equality, albeit for different reasons. Radical feminists centred women's embodied experiences while also advocating for a view of structural marginalisation in which women were identified as oppressed by a myriad of social formations. These include family structures, sexual norms and the 'burdens' of reproduction, as well as the mothering role (Rowland and Klein

1996). Sex- and gender-based oppression was seen by third wavers as at the root of women's overall subjugation and constitutive of other oppressions including racism and colonialism. As Burris writes,

> We find it self-evident that women are a colonized group who have never – anywhere – been allowed self-determination. Therefore all women who fight against their own oppression (colonized status) as females under male domination are anti-imperialist by definition. (Burris as cited by Nachescu 2009: 40)

These sentiments were echoed by radical feminists like Mary Daly (1999, 2016), Monique Wittig (1985) and Catharine MacKinnon (1987, 1989). They are especially reflective of MacKinnon's work vis-à-vis the so-called 'sex wars'. The 'sex wars' took place over about two decades, beginning in the early 1970s, and pitted late second wave radical feminists against emerging third wave feminists (remember that many radical feminists read sex as a site of oppression and victimisation in which free and equitable consent is impossible under conditions of endemic gender-based inequality).

For example, noted radical feminist Andrea Dworkin, in her book *Intercourse*, wrote that, 'physically, the woman in intercourse is a space inhabited, a literal territory occupied literally: occupied even if there has been no resistance, no force; even if the occupied person said yes please, yes hurry, yes more' (Dworkin 1987: 133). Susan Brownmiller takes this argument a step further by framing the penis as a weapon that carries an ever present potentiality for violence such that rape 'is [seen as] nothing more or less than a conscious process of intimidation by which all men keep all women in a state of fear' (Brownmiller 1975: 5). Pornography and sex work figure prominently in the sex wars, with radical feminists arguing fervently that the grounding of both in relations of inequality and dominance renders them anathema.

SEX POSITIVITY AND THE THIRD WAVE

In opposition to second and third wave radical feminists, millennial feminists advocated for sex positivity in which sex is seen as a site of pleasure and empowerment (Cossman 2019). Women's desire and sexual pleasure, they contend, has been elided by radical feminists through their denial of agency under conditions of inequality. Sex positive third wave feminists like Carole Vance (1984, 1993), Ann Snitow, Christine Stansell and Sharon Thompson (1983) and Gayle Rubin (1998, 2011) make the case that pleasure can be found in dominance relationships; they 'reject sexual repression, favor freedom of sexual expression, and claim that dominant configurations of power do not prevent women from exercising agency' (Glick 2000: 22). This centring of the tensions between coercion and power as well as choice and agency, particularly on the subjects of pornography and sex work, represents the defining feature of the early sex wars (Duggan and Hunter 2006; Showden 2016).

The sex wars also played out in the context of law with radical feminists pushing for anti-pornography legislation in the form of Civil Rights Ordinances that would recognise pornography as a form of sex discrimination. Andrea Dworkin and Catharine MacKinnon used this tactic throughout the US (successfully in Minneapolis), while also pressing for harsher criminal and legal penalties for all forms of gender-based violence, including harassment, and the further criminalisation of sex work (Dworkin 1981; Becker and Barry 2003). In opposition, sex positive feminists made the case that anti-porn activists were not only denying women sexual choice and the creative potential that porn offers, but, in doing so, were reifying and perpetuating the 'women as victim' trope in ways that undermined women's sexual freedom. Many of these tensions played out at Barnard College's 1982 conference 'The Scholar and the Feminist IX: Towards a Politics of Sexuality', which convenor Carole Vance described as a forum that addressed 'women's sexual pleasure, choice, and autonomy, acknowledging that sexuality is simultaneously a domain of restriction, repression, and danger as well as a domain of exploration, pleasure, and agency' (Vance 1984: 443).

In the 2000s and just prior, the third wave fractured into a multiplicity of competing and overlapping feminisms in the forms of postmodern feminism (Hekman 2013; Alcoff 1997), socialist/Marxist feminism (Barrett 2014; Weeks 2011), intersectional feminism (Crenshaw 2015; McKibbin et al. 2013), queer theory (Huffer 2010; Turner and Turner 2000) and postfeminism (Genz and Brabon 2009; McRobbie 2004). Apposite to the subject at hand, queer theory, postfeminism and intersectional feminism have contributed significant insights with respect to sex, agency and choice in ways relevant to #MeToo and beyond. These three feminist formations are particularly significant in relation to how they inform and shape the model of sexual relationality I propose, whether positively (intersectionality and queer theory) or as a form of critique (postfeminism). I turn to these formations in the following sections.

QUEER THEORY

Queer theory, situated in the third wave, offers a rich and dynamic approach to sexuality that, when filtered through a feminist lens, provides an important counternarrative to normative sexual relations by posing questions and oppositional perspectives that disrupt hegemonic sexual and non-sexual norms (Hames-García 2011). Noted queer feminist scholars like Judith Butler (1993b, 2011a), Eve Kosofsky Sedgwick (1993, 2008) and Teresa de Lauretis (1987, 1991) have produced a sexual politics that aims at destabilising reductive thinking. 'Queering', as a verb, is thus linked to activism, the restructuring of relations of power, and what Butler refers to as 'futural imaginings' (Butler 1993a: 228). For Sedgwick, '"queer" can refer to an open mesh of possibilities, gaps, overlaps, dissonances and resonances, lapses and excesses of meaning where the constituent elements of anyone's gender, or anyone's sexuality, cannot be made to monolithically signify one's gender identity' (Sedgwick 2013: 8).

The act of 'queering' has evolved into a tool through which to disrupt, challenge and rethink hierarchy and binary thought (Foucault 2012; Halperin 1990; Warner 2000). Other central tenets of queer theory include:

> attacks on the fixed nature of concepts and identity; assaults on the unitary formulation of man and the knowing subject; the idea that what is accepted as truth is really the change of 'epistemes' over time; the view that there are no universal and timeless truths, but only the interested formulations of those in power; and the desire to see subjugated knowledge revolt. (Wall 2001: 1)

As such, to 'queer' means to upset the existing order and is used in a variety of fields beyond sexuality including the state and academia (Hunter 2006). The insights that queer theory offers aim to facilitate an openness to the future and the myriad potentialities for sexual exploration that exist. Its centring of the sexually discriminated against, coupled with the knowledge that emerges from these marginalised spaces, opens us up to the 'possibilities [that] emerge for denominating and declaring a range of differences and positions arising from the gamut of sexual diversities' (Honeychurch 1996: 341). This repositioning has led to a plethora of tools, techniques and acts of sexual de- and re-construction.

For example, Natasha Hurley, in an insightful article, 'Pornocracy's queer circulations', applies a queer logic to the diagnosis of sexuality under capitalism by arguing for 'pornocracy' as a political structure (democracy + pornography) and as a means by which to understand sex in a way that eschews commodification, unleashes female sexuality, and queers the heteronormative. Hurley writes, 'queerness, in short, resides not merely in the concept's capacity for naming a subversive mode of gendered and sexual sociability but also in its simultaneous aspiration for dampening that very possibility.' What is feared 'most about pornocracy – its redistribution of sex and gender roles – is arguably what makes the concept a site of political possibility consonant with the world-making capacity of sexual life outside of heteronormative' (Hurley 2018: 158).

Feminist queer theory is particularly helpful to this project as is the 'pleasure and care-centred ethic of embodied and relational sexual Otherness' model in that it relies on an ontology in which gender and sexuality are inextricably linked and thus in synch with intersectional feminism (see below), while also providing a set of epistemological tools that prevent 'forms of "dissonance"' from 'emerg[ing] between gendered self-understandings and forms of sexual engagement' (Weed and Schor 1997: 3).

Feminist queer theory's treatment of agency, consent and choice revolves around the erotic, the deviant, subversive pleasure, and engaged subjectivity (Karaian 2013). As Edenfield argues,

> queer approaches are often less polished, more inclusive, distributed very differently, acknowledge spectrums of consent, and often rely on notions of affirmative consent and rhetorics of pleasure. (Edenfield 2019: 50)

Taken together, queer theory represents a critical resource from and through which to articulate the kind of progressive and transgressive sexual politics and relationality our contemporary moment requires. As such, it informs the model of sexual relations I propose further on. #MeToo, I am afraid, has not yet productively reckoned with the resources offered and challenges posed by queer theory and praxis.

INTERSECTIONAL FEMINISM

Intersectional feminism represents another throughline or path forward with respect to the kind of feminist practice around sex and justice I propose. Intersectionality describes the ways in which identity positions (e.g. race, class, dis/ability), structures (e.g. values, norms) and institutions (e.g. governments, schools) overlap to produce oppressions based on interconnection and synergy while also providing a way in which to theorise, diagnose and provide solutions to the tensions that exist around sex and justice (Nash 2008; Crenshaw 1991; Cho, Crenshaw and McCall 2013; Noble 2016; Collins 2004). Beginning in the domain of critical legal studies in the 1990s, Kimberlé Crenshaw, who coined the term, was attempting to account for the experience of Black women who, having been laid off from General Motors (GM) in 1977, were unable to challenge their firing as simultaneously Black *and* female employees. As Parks, Felzien and Jue explain,

> The courts . . . ruled in favour of GM, stating that the plaintiffs could not make a claim based *only* on sex discrimination (since GM had White women as clerical employees), nor could their claim be based only on race discrimination (since GM hired Black men as manufacturing employees). Because of the court's lack of acknowledgement for the intersection of racial and sexual identities, the claims of discrimination were not recognized. (Parks, Felzien and Jue 2017: 127)

The routinised erasure of the ways in which multiple sites of marginalisation impact the lived experiences of Black women has since expanded to capture the experiences of a multiplicity of sexed, raced, classed and gendered identities. Patricia Hill Collins, inspired by the work of the Combahee River Collective (2014), refers to intersectionality as reflecting a structural matrix of domination that centres the experiences of Black women and Black feminist thought. This approach, she argues, 'instead of starting with gender and then adding in other variables such as age, sexual orientation, race, social class and religion . . . sees these distinctive systems of oppression as being part of one overarching structure of domination' (Collins 1990: 554). While contemporary uses of intersectionality have expanded (and arguably been politically diluted), its impact as mode of critical praxis, inquiry and knowledge production remains important. Intersectionality sees inequality and unjust power relations as embedded in our social identities and draws on a mode of analysis that recognises the 'inadequacy of analysing various social divisions, but especially race and gender, as separate, internally homogeneous, social categories resulting in the marginalization of the specific effects of these, especially on women of colour' (Yuval-Davis 2006: 206). As stated, intersectionality has been used in critical legal studies (Ellickson 2000; Anders and DeVita 2014), but also in the disciplines of psychology (Cole 2009; Rosenthal 2016), critical race theory (Delgado 2010; Alexander-Floyd 2010), feminist theory (Carbin and Edenheim 2013; Dill and Kohlman 2012), political science (Simien 2007; Weldon 2006) and science studies (Davis 2008; Kaijser and Dronsell 2014).

In the context of #MeToo, intersectionality highlights the significance and salience of overlapping identities where sex is seen as one of several potential sites of oppression (Rubin 1993). Its focus on local and contextual entanglements, as well as material inequality, draws attention to how identifying in and with multiple marginalised social locations can render one especially vulnerable to inequity, isolation and sexual exploitation (Greene et al. 2019). Intersectional approaches to #MeToo are highly critical of the invisibilising of race in the movement and the divergent standards of social media outrage with respect to how racialised women have been treated. Angela

Onwuachi-Willig outlines a salient example with respect to the vastly different ways in which the public handled the Twitter suspension of actress Rose McGowan when she tweeted the contact information of an online harasser versus how actress Leslie Jones has been treated as one of the stars of the all-female cast of *Ghostbusters*. In the former, a widespread public boycott of Twitter was organised while, for Jones, public and institutional support was visibly lacking. Tweets like that from Black Girls Code director Kimberly Bryant capture this incongruity: 'Intersectionality = when you really want to support #WomenBoycottTwitter but you're conflicted bec[ause] Black women never get the same support' (Onwuachi-Willig 2018: 112). Calls for an authentically intersectional approach to #MeToo requires centring the ways in which sex and sexuality is experienced by women under conditions of unequal social power and filtered through the lived experiences of racialised women specifically. As Leung and Williams contend, in an article chronicling the failures of #MeToo on the subject of race, what is revealed by #MeToo is a history of embedded marginalisation, oppression and disregard. Citing a noted disc jockey in a documentary about the sexual offences of singer R. Kelly, Leung and Williams point out how 'the double standard in the mainstream media of Weinstein and Kelly reflect[s] . . . how society has historically treated African American women':

> The most disrespected woman in America historically has always been the black woman. You know, I always say if you want to get away with murder, kill a black rapper. If you want to get away with sexual assault, assault a young black girl . . . If R. Kelly had been doing this to white women, oh my god. The fact that it is mostly young black girls he preys on, simply nobody cares. (hampton as cited by Leung and Williams 2019: 358–9)

In more progressive strands of #MeToo-affiliated activist movements, intersectionality is harnessed along with queer theory to call for provisional coalition building based not on identity, but on affinity. Intersectionality can thus be utilised as a form of praxis through which to engage in activism rooted in shared experiences of domination and oppression while grappling with the ways in which race and gender motivate and shape sexual violence (Buchanan and Ormerod 2002).

In addition to the criticism that intersectionality has become little more than a buzzword, scholars like Carbin and Edenheim, both poststructural in their grounding, are critical of intersectionality with respect to how it functions as a universalising form of feminism, arguing that it, in practice, occludes difference and thus tends towards neoliberal consensus formation (Carbin and Edenheim 2013). I, however, argue that intersectionality is more akin to a materially grounded discourse and form of practice that should be seen 'as having value for progressing feminist debates, particularly in relation to research, policy and practice' in ways that inspire activism (McKibbin et al. 2015: 102). Taken together, feminist intersectionality offers a progressive and holistic theoretical lens through which to understand the complexities of identity and social location set against oppressive structural conditions but which 'demands that its adherents challenge oppression through struggles for social justice' (Heaney 2019: 3).

POSTFEMINISM

Postfeminism, much like intersectionality, bleeds into the fourth wave feminism of the 2010s but really takes hold in the late 1990s and early 2000s as expressed in popular media (Tasker and Negra 2007; Coppock, Haydon and Richter 2014; Whelehan 1995). This form of anti-feminism makes the case that the goals of feminist equality have been realised and, going forward, women can 'have it all', thereby giving lie to the argument that there are patriarchal structures, unequal power relations and misogynistic norms in place that work against women's emancipation and which severely curtail their exercise of agency (Cossman 2003). The operating terms of postfeminism are that of agency, individual empowerment, personal responsibility and choice which, as Angela McRobbie argues, manifests itself in popular media representations of female characters (*Bridget Jones*, *Sex and the City*, *Legally Blonde*) as simultaneously successful, intelligent, beautiful, desiring and desirable (McRobbie 2004).

In its more radical form, postfeminism eschews and repudiates feminism by acting as a form of anti-feminism. It does so by (1) embracing expressions of traditional femininity and gender roles (as if they are freely 'chosen'); (2) emphasising 'self-surveillance, monitoring and discipline', particularly as they relate to normative beauty standards resulting in the 'dominance of a "makeover" paradigm'; and (3) 'the marked resexualization of women's bodies' supported by 'an emphasis upon consumerism and the commodification of difference' (Gill and Scharff 2013: 4). Postfeminism is thus decidedly neoliberal in its treatment of the subject as rational, calculating, agential and disciplined (Gill 2007). As Gill argues, 'just as neoliberalism requires individuals to narrate their life story as if it were the outcome of deliberative choices, so too does some contemporary writing depict young women as unconstrained and freely choosing' (Gill 2008: 433). In relation to sex, postfeminism is sex positive in its embrace of a feminine sexuality replete with an 'up for anything' sexual subjectivity in which pole dancing, sexual exhibitionism, self-objectification and adventurous sex are seen as desirable in so far as they are freely chosen.

Postfeminist positionalities, however, fail to address the very unequal conditions under which choices are made; the inherently disempowering nature of objectification; the ways in which 'a cultural habitat of images may be internalised to form a pernicious disciplinary regime', spanning sex, beauty and the body (Gill 2008: 436; Kilbourne 1999); and the potential reproduction of the 'male heterosexual fantasy based on the assumption that she is doing so for herself' (Evans and Riley 2013: 273).

Bringing us back to sex and #MeToo, the postfeminist position is decidedly in opposition to #MeToo's central tenet of disruption and the belief that a mass movement addressing inequalities in power, asymmetrical gender relations and institutional misogyny is needed. As such, postfeminism, in sharing liberal feminism's antipathy for disruptive change, presumes that the pursuit of legal reform and new workplace policies are sufficient in rooting out the 'few (anomalous) bad apples' – the likes of which include Harvey Weinstein and Bill Cosby. This is consistent with postfeminism's grounding principle that the objectives of feminism have been achieved.

A prime example of postfeminism rearing its head in relation to #MeToo is in relation to a much reported on letter actress Catherine Deneuve and other prominent French women wrote and signed in 2017 conveying their concerns that #MeToo has gone too far. The letter, amongst other things, makes reference to the death of romance; the shaming of male sexuality (in support of what they refer to as 'the right to bother'); and their communicating concern with how #MeToo, echoing the early sex wars, is disciplining desire and perpetuating women's disempowerment by framing them as lacking the agency to say no (Burgess 2018; Pipyrou 2018).

To wit, Deneuve et al.'s attendant call for due process and the letter's homing in on the problems inherent with 'trial by media' relies on the assumption that the law is an impartial arbiter. As we know, this is not always the case – particularly with respect to the suspicious, infantilising and uneven way in which it has historically treated women alleging some form of gender-based violence (Beaumont 2016; Brysk 2017). Anita Hill's testimony at Clarence Thomas's Supreme Court hearings and the high-profile coverage of the trial adjudicating the alleged rape of Patricia Bowman by William Kennedy (of *the* Kennedys) in 1992 are just two examples. This postfeminist perspective considers #MeToo to have implemented 'a new sexual Puritanism in which women are considered delicate and unapproachable, easily offended and most likely to fear the man that propositions them, whatever his manner' (Quixley 2018: 2).

Additionally, the kind of acceptable, nay desirable, flirting that the letter decries losing might be the experience of some women, most likely the rich, white and privileged, but is decidedly not so for most women – particularly women who are materially poor and marginalised in other ways (race, sexuality, body size, dis/ability, etc.) (Andersen 2018). Similar postfeminist-adjacent arguments around agency, feminist gains and the potential for women to lie have been made by writers like Katie Roiphe (1993, 2018), Caitlin Flanagan (2018a, 2018b) and Bari Weiss (2018).

#MeToo and #TimesUp, the celebrity-funded programme to pay for the legal costs of women experiencing workplace harassment, are both somewhat postfeminist in their reliance on individual acts of cathartic confession online, but also decidedly not so in their simultaneous engagement with collective action in the form of legal action, women's marches and grassroots activism (Gieseler 2019). Transforming systems of power and patriarchy is, in some of its more radical permutations, #MeToo's penultimate objective. Calls for #MeToo to collaborate with more radical feminist organisations like Feminism for the 99 Per Cent (F99) and the Global Women's Strike are aimed at drawing in a more coalitional form of political praxis and thus disidentifying it with the neoliberal aspects of postfeminism by linking #MeToo to 'struggles against predatory capitalism, sexism, and racism by grounding its activism in lives of . . . women of colour in the Global South and North' (Emejulu 2018: 272). It is also consistent with what has come to be known as digital feminism – to which I now turn – in considering the ways in which online spaces and movements are fostering forms of #MeToo-related attachment and solidarity at and between the margins.

FOURTH WAVE FEMINISM

Fourth wave feminism rides the crest of internet culture and, while continuing to challenge patriarchy and misogyny through organising, activism and critique, does so in a context of a media-saturated world. This new media ecology offers potentialities for networked activism and engagement, but also risks engaging in slactivism – a politics of clicking 'likes' rather than actively participating in engaged coalitional politics IRL (in real life). Despite this, the fourth wave's embrace of intersectionality, the politics of privilege, fat justice, racism and trans rights politicises feminism in new ways (Maclaran 2015; Rampton 2015). Vogel's description of the fourth wave is especially apt; she describes it as having 'more or less the same goals of the third – reproductive justice, trans inclusion, sexual-minority rights, intersectionality, and the deconstruction of privilege – while utilizing social media and other burgeoning technologies to spread their activist message' (Vogel 2014). Sometimes referred to as digital feminism or cyberfeminism (Haraway 2004; Braidotti 2003), fourth wave feminism buttresses the significance of the kinds of digital activism #MeToo engages in. It does so through its critique of rape culture using an intersectional lens and drawing on digital media to challenge gender norms and sexual violence (Chamberlain 2017; Rivers 2017). Keller, Mendes and Ringrose point out how fourth wave feminism, as expressed by #MeToo specifically, has worked to cultivate 'a feminist consciousness amongst hashtag participants, which allows them to understand sexual violence as a structural rather than personal problem' (Keller, Mendes and Ringrose 2018: 238). It thus has the potential to be a place 'for those who are otherwise omitted' to 'build "margin-to-margin" solidarity networks that are inclusive (dos Santos Bruss 2020: 8).

Criticisms of fourth wave feminism include its use of the internet in ways that (1) commodify feminism by focusing on the image and the fetishisation of the hashtag, and (2) rely on 'cancel' or 'call out culture' to perform structural change (Munro 2013; Andersen 2018). 'Cancel culture' is a phrase that emerged out of Black Twitter and evolved to refer to the purported social excising of mostly male media content producers due to sexual and non-sexual (i.e. racist, ahistorical, ableist, heteronormative) statements and infractions. While this has led to the juridical 'cancellation' of the likes of Harvey Weinstein and Bill Cosby, it has not resulted in a substantive cultural annihilation of most entertainment figures like Charlie Rose, Matt Lauer and Louis C.K. Since the last's infractions are less severe on the gender-based violence spectrum, and given the conservative backlash against #MeToo, the 'fear of being cancelled' has become a shibboleth of those opposed to #MeToo's extrajudicial goals and who refer to its supporters as the 'social justice warriors (SJW) of the #MeToo movement' (Dutton 2020; Bauer 2019).

Supporters of cancel culture as a communicative act make the case that it is more akin to historical acts of public shaming that 'builds the bonds of a community, as members can agree or disagree with certain values or what counts as acceptable, express a joint disgust at certain behaviours, and use language developed by the collective to evolve a public morality and ethic to live by' (Chi 2019; Beard 2020). More nuanced critiques of #MeToo and cancel culture include discussions of whether/how to enjoy the art of problematic men and the role 'earning and forgiveness might play'.

A notable case of this going well is the public apology given by television producer and media creator Dan Harmon to writer Megan Ganz, whom he had harassed for months. Harmon's apology included an acknowledgement of harm, including the statement that he 'damaged her internal compass', as well as a clear admission that her rejection of his advances would never have resulted in similar kinds of retaliation were she male (Martinelli 2018). Ganz has since accepted Harmon's apology, calling it a 'master class in how to apologize', and stating later how relieved she felt 'just hearing him say these things actually happened' (Framke 2018). The fact that much of this occurred online is significant and reflects the fourth wave's centring of digital media in its manifestation of feminist praxis.

It is important to highlight the role digital technologies play in fourth wave feminism. For these feminists, online modes of communication provide the means through which to produce feminist solidarities and encourage mobilisation despite the persistence of entrenched austerity, under and unpaid labour and misogyny (Rivers 2017). Social media, according to proponents of the fourth wave, has allowed younger feminists to form nodes of 'connective action' with widespread reach (Munro 2013). #MeToo is just one example of this, while others include the Everyday Sexism Project and One Billion Rising. For fourth wave feminists, digital communication makes it possible for transnational collectives with diverse interests and intersectional identities to work towards equality and justice together. Moreover, according to Afzal and Wallace (2019), it is the empowerment and safety provided by online groups that have encouraged survivors to speak out. While concerns about slacktivism and/or clicktivism remain, it is important to point out how sites of digital engagement can address unequal power relations (Harlow and Guo 2014; Butler 2011a). The Harmon case is also paradigmatic of the kinds of restorative justice practices I refer to further on and can be juxtaposed with apologies that have fallen short (e.g. those from Aziz Ansari and Louis C.K.).

Taken together, this short overview of feminist waves, movements and moments provides an important snapshot not only of feminist practice and activism, but also of the sites of controversy, tension and change that have brought us to where we are today. Before closing this chapter and moving towards a discussion of sexual relationality, a short diversion is necessary in order to ground what has come to be known as the *contemporary sex wars* and which was hinted at in the section on postfeminism with respect to Catherine Deneuve and writers like Bari Weiss and Katie Roiphe. To reiterate, today's sex wars, colloquially referred to by Brenda Cossman (2019) as Sex Wars 2.0, are playing out under conditions in which there are much broader avenues of recourse and stricter laws around sexual harassment and assault. In opposition to previous sex wars, Sex Wars 2.0 focuses on litigable and/or morally wrong sexual action and assault – i.e. where do we draw the line? Because I have already discussed the critiques made by writers who argue this position, what I expand on here is the role of the 'culture wars' in enabling our contemporary 'sex wars'.

Those who argue that #MeToo has gone too far, representing one side of the contemporary sex wars, are articulating their argument in the context of wider 'culture wars' pitting identity politics (i.e. social location), including feminism, up against more conservative ideologies (Bernstein 2005; Moghadam 2019; Heyes 2012). Identity politics, loosely defined, refers to the active mobilisation of individuals around a shared, often marginalised identity position (i.e. gender, race, class, sexuality, dis/ability or caste), whether claimed or proscribed. As Sonia Kruks explains, 'What makes identity politics a significant departure from earlier, pre-identarian forms of the politics of recognition is its demand for recognition on the basis of the very grounds on which recognition has previously been denied . . . what is demanded is respect for oneself *as* different' (Kruks 2001: 85). Identity politics reflects the fact that people's social location within social structures shapes how they experience the world as well as their ability to achieve certain life outcomes. With respect to gender, what identity politics pinpoints as the crux of the problem is the fact that a woman must navigate the world within a culture and society that objectifies, denigrates and treats her as 'less than'. Gender then becomes an organising identity around which to push for change. It is this coalescing around difference and injustice based on gender that detractors of #MeToo argue is problematic for the reasons listed above – namely, that it overstates the problem, reifies feminine passivity, undermines women's agency, assumes male guilt, and militarises/de-romanticises sexual relations. A further critique of identity politics from the materialist left asserts that #MeToo's reliance on individual acts of cathartic confession is 'sealed off from the structures of patriarchy in which acts of sexual violence are rooted' and thus 'Outrage becomes the mechanism through which, first, the corrective scene takes place *over and against* these patriarchal structures and . . . any critique of the movement or its rhetoric is rejected as not properly belonging to the scene of address' (Burgess 2018: 360). A more productive way forward, left critics argue, is to eschew a 'politics of sentimentality', performance and neoliberal individual action and, instead, embrace a politics of class around which a more radical and inclusive social movement can emerge (Berlant 2000; Ghadery 2019). The fear, according to Jo Littler in conversation with Nancy Fraser, betrays a concern that 'a fixation on cultural dimensions of recognition and identity politics' is operating at 'the expense of economic egalitarianism' (Fraser 2019: 862).

Two further variations of the identity politics conversation as it relates to #MeToo comes from the political right by writers and media fixtures like Jordan Peterson, Tucker Carlson and Julia Hartley-Brewer. They focus on skirmishes around (1) the existence of so-called 'trigger or snowflake culture' – which is purportedly made up of overly sensitive millennials for whom political correctness has gotten out of hand; and (2) arguments around the persistence of a debilitating 'rape culture' that has severely and violently restricted the free, just and autonomous existence of women. In relation to the former, the introduction of trigger warnings about difficult material around race, sexuality and gender-based violence in university classrooms has got critics especially up in arms, as has the public shaming of personalities, comedians and celebrities who have tweeted or stated something that is 'racially insensitive' or misogynistic (Kyrölä 2019; Campbell and Manning 2018). Andrew Hunter Murray, in an article titled 'Generation snowflake?', chronicles the statements of influential right-wing political group Turning Points USA, whose comments perfectly capture this ethos:

> The group's [then] communications director, Candace Owens (herself a millennial), told *Telegraph* readers unsmilingly that, 'Students have gone soft.' Worse still, the snowflakes were even coming for the famous British Sense of Humour. 'The Left has killed comedy,' she darkly warned. The group's founder, Charlie Kirk (aged 25), agreed: 'Monty Python would not be allowed in this politically correct culture.' (Murray 2018: 44)

The deplatforming of speakers from public and college events, as well as media platforms like Twitter and Facebook, has become the site of an especially fractious debate wherein the right to free speech clashes with the right for marginalised communities to feel safe. This is particularly relevant when those speakers are, for example, homophobic; present misleading arguments that tie race to intelligence; challenge the 'womanhood' of trans women; are active in anti-immigrant groups; or stand accused of misogyny and gender-based violence (Rogers 2020; Smith 2020). Arguments that women have been too quick to take offence at sexual jokes and/or advances, or that their marches and demands for 'safe spaces' and gender-neutral language are a step too far, reflect the expansiveness of this iteration of the culture wars. As Anna Sicari argues, what detractors fail to recognise is that while the degree and seriousness of 'assaults[s] [may] differ, they are all forms of systemic abuse within a patriarchal institution, and they are all daily experiences that largely go ignored' (Sicari 2018: 200).

The second part of the culture wars that is germane to this study of #MeToo, sex and consent is what has come to be known as 'rape culture'. The systemic and structural character of this kind of gender-based violence, it is argued, has produced an analytic diagnosis of a social order (our social order) that enables rape through a permissive 'rape culture':

> We live in a culture that demands public ownership of the body. We live in a culture where rights to abortion, birth control, sex education, and bearing children . . . are under near-constant attack . . . though the form and intensity vary, any oppression you care to name works at least in part by controlling or claiming ownership of the bodies of those oppressed . . . In this sense, rape culture works by restricting a person's control of her body, limiting her sense of ownership of it, and granting others a sense of entitlement to it. (Troost 2008: 171)

This holistic and systemic critique of rape culture, as it relates to the wider culture wars, is front and centre when it comes to #MeToo. It includes microaggressions like street harassment, the sending and solicitation of explicit pictures via social media, middle-school clothing regulations, fraternity-engendered hypermasculinity, and criminal acts like sexual assault, stalking, domestic violence and rape (Keller, Mendes and Ringrose 2018; Phillips 2016). Taken together, it is argued that these compounding acts create a permission structure such that women live in a state of fear, are consistently hypersexualised, and thus begin to internalise the misogyny they are subject to. The blaming of women and their revictimisation is often the outcome of rape culture which, according to Maxwell (2014), has led 'to rape myths that women are aroused by being sexually dominated or that women like to be talked into having sex. These notions are "sexist rhetoric" that harm the victims and undermine their credibility' (Armstrong and Mahone 2017: 110). Many advocates of #MeToo make the case that it is this wider, systemic critique, much of which is intersectional in its outlook, that gives the lie to the argument that identity politics is distinct from or inimical to coalitional politics that aim at structural change (King 2017; Sorensen 2018; Haider 2018; Yudice 2018).

The tensions outlined above around #MeToo as a movement and a moment, coupled with my description of the socio-historical context that gave rise to it, provide a snapshot of what is a complicated and transnational phenomenon of shifting iterations. What I have attempted to do here is to offer a synthesised narrative of the various feminist waves, feminist 'camps' and a number of pertinent conflicts and controversies (e.g. the sex wars, identity politics, pornography and rape culture) that have given rise to #MeToo. Chronicling these historical twists and turns is necessary in order to better understand the significance of how sex is currently regulated, constructed, gendered and raced, as well as the conditions under which it is entered into. The next chapter provides an outline of the various kinds of legal, normative and cultural frameworks that regulate what constitutes permissible sex. It also provides a wealth of insights around gender scripts, relationship dynamics, legal norms, and race and class dynamics necessary to understand the analysis that follows.

2. Consent Cultures, Alternatives and a New Approach

There are six significant approaches to sexual relations that provide the historical and theoretical scaffolding necessary for understanding the framework I propose and the subsequent case studies. They are: (1) the consent model; (2) communicative consent; (3) enthusiastic/affirmative consent; (4) sexual citizenship; (5) sexual autonomy; and (6) feminist new materialism (FNM). In this chapter, I examine each of these frameworks by providing a historical overview and explanation as well as a critique.

It should be noted that because #MeToo is largely US-centric and English-language dominated, most of the mainstream social and traditional media conversations and legal precedents are as well. However, examples taken from Canada and the UK, and countries in the Global South, are also taken up in this chapter in light of the diffusion of #MeToo around the world. My decision to include these examples reflects a desire to challenge the Eurocentrism of conversations about sex, consent and #MeToo through what Lukose calls a 'politics of location' that sees non-white raced, sexed and classed identity positions in the Global North as naturally at the forefront of this work. Women from the Global South have cultivated their own 'radical space[s] of articulation forged in and through anti-colonial resistance, nationalism and the struggle for women's emancipation' (Lukose 2018: 45). #MeToo and #MeToo-adjacent movements that aim to deconstruct and rearticulate sexual norms and laws around gender-based violence in the Global South are both rich and robust and should be recognised (Lin and Yang 2019; Paiva 2019; Brajanac 2019). A salient example is the #NiUnaMenos social media campaign in Argentina around abortion which preceded #MeToo but mobilised around it in order to talk 'about the Argentine feminist agenda on mainstream media . . . by framing the issue as a form of discrimination and violence against women' (Garibotti and Hopp 2019: 186). Also of note are the changes to rape laws in India (the Criminal Law (Amendment) Act, 2013) that further shifted the burden of proof from the accused to the accuser after massive protests against the rape of a fourteen-year-old lower caste girl by police in 2012 (Dutta and Sircar 2013; Lodhia 2015). This was led by a feminist-driven legal campaign that ended up in the Supreme Court and is seen as marking 'the beginning of a slew of legal reforms that would address domestic violence, sexual harassment, and rape' in India (Roy 2016). I will leave the carceral dimension of these changes in India and the objectives of the #NiUnaMenos campaign for now except to say that the focus on incarceration and stricter punishment remains persistent around the world.

Each framework discussed below is first described heuristically as an ideal type. I begin with a careful (re)construction of each socio-sexual norm in order to 'render [the] subject matter intelligible by revealing or constructing its internal rationality' (Aron 2018: 244). Ideal types facilitate the analysis of 'historically unique configurations or the individual components in terms of genetic concepts' (Weber as cited by Jayapalan 2001: 103), meaning that it allows consent, for example, to be discussed as a genetic, generalisable concept before examining how it is expressed in practice. While this approach reflects a sociological as opposed to a legal methodology, the law still figures prominently as a social institution that co-constitutes sex. Note that the US focus in what follows is also a function of the case studies – all of which are from the US save one (the Jian Ghomeshi case, which is Canadian). As such, for clarity and relevance, most of the historical, juridical and cultural background is America-centric as well.

CONSENT TO SEX

In the US, the consent model of sexual relations is normatively, culturally and legally described, in 10 US Code 920 – Art 120, as 'a freely given agreement to the conduct at issue by a competent person' (Legal Information Institute 2020), while the Canadian legal code defines consent as 'the voluntary agreement of the complainant to engage in the sexual activity in question', under subsection 273.1(1). This subsection also sets out situations under which consent is not or cannot be given (e.g. abuse of power, incapacity, lack of agreement) (Department of Justice 2020). It is important to point out, however, that in the US states definitions of sexual consent vary widely with North Carolina, for instance, holding fast to a law that states that consent cannot be withdrawn once sex has begun (Willingham 2019). On the subject of nonconsensual sex (i.e. rape) state statutes tend to vary on things like penetration, use of force, capacity to consent (i.e. its presence or absence), and whether or not the sex is demeaning (National Research Council 2014). These laws cannot conflict with federal rules but can surpass them. Notably, Illinois, New York and Colorado have or are close to having affirmative 'yes means yes' consent laws on the books while the majority, particularly those in the middle of the country, do not (Consent Respect 2020; Alabi 2019). Additionally, universities and colleges in the US must have the capacity to handle sexual violence reports under Title IX, according to which gender-based violence is considered a form of discrimination (Anderson 2015; Know Your IX 2020).

In Canada, it is the federal government that has jurisdiction over criminal law which the provinces must then carry out (Criminal Code – General 2012). Current Canadian laws regulating sexual relations retain a robust conception of affirmative consent on a federal level (Bill C-49) and, since the early 1980s, have subsumed rape under broader sexual assault laws (Barranco 2016). With respect to post-secondary institutions, individual provinces are responsible for instituting consistent college and university sexual violence policies, with provinces like Ontario mandating that each university or college have a clear set of rules and support structures (Lopes-Baker et al. 2017). These differences become important in the case studies as they relate to the jurisdictions in which accusations are made or charges brought against the accused. This brief overview represents a snapshot of a much wider and more complex ecology of laws, rules and norms in both countries. It also provides the legal context necessary to understand larger themes discussed in the case studies, including criminal reform, carceral feminism and restorative justice.

Sexual consent laws and norms follow from the general rejection of the property model, referred to in Chapter 1, in which a woman's bodily and sexual autonomy is considered the property of her father or husband. Before elaborating on the specifics of consent law, a short aside is needed in order to explain the relevance of the property model today. The property model of sexual relations persists in a more updated form in which legal scholars like Donald Dripps (1992, 1993, 2008) make the case that penetrative rape should be seen as a form of violent theft – a property violation that involves force and nonconsent. Dripps's solution to what he terms the crime of sexual appropriation separates acquaintance rape from forceful rape, wherein the latter (his focus) reasserts violence as the central violation since

> Physical violence in general does far more harm to the victim's welfare than an unwanted sex act. Physical violence in general expresses a more complete indifference, or a more intense hostility, to the victim's humanity. (Dripps 1992: 1,800)

Acquaintance rape and consent

Acquaintance rape, of the type #MeToo generally focuses on, is seen as a lesser but not trivial offence best dealt with separately because of what Dripps contends is the inherent difficulty in litigating guilt under consent-centric rules and distorted gender norms. These norms permeate the perceptions of juries who, when 'confronted with a sexually active woman, sees not two morally equivalent hedonists, but a stud and a slut' (Dripps 2008: 971). Notably, this property model allows for sex work to be considered validly chosen work and relies on a preponderance of evidence rather than a reasonable doubt directive for so-called 'real rape'. This, potentially, renders guilty verdicts more likely since it lowers the burden of proof (Burgess-Jackson 1999).

Others, like Robin West (1993), point out that this approach fails to acknowledge unequal power relations by eliding structural inequalities (and bargaining positions) and instrumentalises sex into a form of transactional proceduralism that does not reflect how sex actually takes place. It also, West argues, omits that rape is more often 'experienced, and typically described, as more like a spiritual murder than either robbery or larceny' (West 1993: 1,442). The property model also negates the fact that non-penetrative sex, or sex agreed to under conditions of economic and/or cultural pressure, can be illegitimate (Bryden 2000; Phillips 2013). Dripps's transactional approach can also be overly proscriptive since it ignores the complex dynamics of desired dominance-submissive sex as well as forms of coercion that go beyond violence.

Finally, a persuasive critique offered by Reece is that Dripps fails to acknowledge that what requires addressing in the real rape myth is the 'violent stranger in the alleyway' trope, since most rapes and assaults are committed by acquaintances, not strangers. Also important for Reece is a fulsome debunking of the myth that women lie about rape and attending to misperceptions that underlie beliefs about sexual miscommunication, such as that inviting someone into one's home wearing provocative clothing implies sexual desire (Reece 2013; Conaghan and Russell 2014). Concerns around #MeToo reflect the criticisms of Dripps's property model with respect to the impact of sexual myths, the reality of sexual relations, and the embeddedness of unequal interpersonal, gendered and structural power relations that shape sexual negotiation. On this basis, because #MeToo as a movement is more concerned with acquaintance, as opposed to stranger, rape, the active deconstruction of sexual and gender myths, and consent over force as the defining feature of gender-based violence, it would probably judge the framework articulated by Dripps as wholly insufficient. From my perspective, if one element is to be taken from this approach it is its critique of consent as establishing a difficult legal bar in terms of proving *mens rea* and what counts as consent communication.

Contemporary approaches to consent

Returning to the consent model, consent is arguably the most assented to and widely accepted socio-legal framework from which sexual relations are judged both legally and socio-culturally. Contemporary approaches eschew Dripps's property theory in favour of one that relies on an ethic of permissibility and agreement. However, because sexual norms are socially constructed, they are subject to change. As such, our understanding of consent has evolved over time and contains limit cases, corollaries and discriminatory exclusions that require more attention than can be given here. For example, while age of consent and statutory rape is not the subject of this book, it is notable that the variability and heteronormativity of age consent laws fail to attend to whether or how a particular age qualitatively confers consensual capacity, or to consider how these rules have been used to regulate non-normative sex. 'Age of consent laws', as Judith Butler asserts, 'vary according to whether sexual practice is deemed heterosexual or homosexual' and since 'legal codes [tend] to be heterosexual . . . the lack of a differential regulation between straight and not straight is less a sign of equal treatment, than of the unthinkability of non-heterosexual law' (Butler 2011a: 407).

Putting age aside, the general definition of consent in the context of sex and law is best articulated by those scholars who are able to indicate how consent is reflected in legal principles as well as in social practice. Colloquially, consent implies cooperation of free will communicated by words or actions by one party to another. It assumes that one has the freedom to act and the moral responsibility to do so as well as the ability to rationally enter into agreements and fulfil certain duties and obligations (Hunter and Cowan 2007). It promises social order, governability and a self-possessed identity capable of exercising agency consistent with principles of the liberal contract (Gan 2013; Baehr 2004; Okin 1994).

However, it will be useful to keep in mind for later chapters that, functionally, there is a distinction between factual consent (reflecting one's state of mind), its expression as a social fact, and legal consent, which refers to the 'rules which define situations in which a person is legally deemed to have consented whether or not this is factually the case' (Wallerstein 2009: 320; see also Westen 2017). There is a surfeit of conceptual slippage between these definitions in much of the discourse around #MeToo wherein socio-cultural norms and law meet and sometimes clash. This slippage is reflected in cases in which the relationship between one's state of mind and its expression is 'fuzzy', as in the Aziz Ansari example, or in situations in which sex is engaged in for reasons other than desire (i.e. sex work, duty or to make one's partner happy). In the Ansari case, other elements including celebrity, gendered pressures and expectations, and internalised sexual norms serve as mitigating factors and must be considered when making sense of these complicated cases (since consent does not take place in a social vacuum). I return to this issue in the section on affirmative and/or enthusiastic consent.

Historically, legal conceptions of sexual consent evolved from the use of force ('the force requirement'), wherein force, *in and of itself*, denoted a lack of consent. We can trace this back to English common law in which rape was defined as 'carnal knowledge of a woman forcibly and against her will' (Blackstone 1830: 209). At this point in time, rape required corroboration, a prompt complaint, demonstrable resistance and chastity, amongst other things (Anderson 2010). While my focus is largely on consent from the 1960s on, it is important to consider consent's evolution from a framework rooted in property to one potentially triggering criminal prosecution and defined by the absence of free agreement.

The liberal model of consent

The liberal model of consent (see Chapter 1 for an overview of liberal feminism) has been critiqued by feminists for its assumption that consent can be freely given, that we are all free autonomous agents capable of exercising choice, and that choice is a purely rational act. As a result, socially embedded inequalities, relations of power and gendered positionalities are ignored. As Jan Crosthwaite argues, in a trenchant critique, liberal principles and ideologies are 'androcentric – male-centered – and inherently sexist' (Crosthwaite 1987; Hunter 2019). The justification for this position, and others like it, include: (1) consent's inability to disarticulate theory from practice (rendering it unable to move beyond formal equality to a more robust conception of equity and justice); (2) its replication of the mind/body binary in which the body's materiality and agency is divorced from rational action (and is thus seen as secondary, not to be trusted, feminine); (3) its perpetuation of heteronormative and ethnocentric structures by fixing normative Western heterosexuality as the default; and (4) its racialising elision of liberal consent's imbrication in a history in which consent was not afforded to enslaved women and distorted with respect to enslaved men (for whom consensual sexual relations with white women was thought to be impossible) (West 2000; Fischel 2010; Leung and Williams 2019). Feminist critics of the liberal model also express concern that it further dichotomises the free/forced binary in ways that overlook the complexity of lived sexual experience – meaning that sex is more complex than a verbal yes or no. As Heinämaa argues, it is important to recognise that the body is itself 'invested with cultural meanings' and 'sense-forming aspects' that render it a central 'source of meaning' relevant to the enactment of consent during sex (Heinämaa 2012: 227). The significance of bodily communication will become clearer in the section on affirmative and communicative consent.

Importantly, this traditional understanding of consent assumes that it has been given if no force was applied, meaning that consent is assumed at the outset to have been granted unless explicitly and forcefully denied (Baker and Oberman 2016; Spohn 1999). This places the onus on women to act as the gatekeepers of sex and as the party that is to be blamed if overt action is not taken to prevent sex from occurring. This gives rise to the 'why didn't you fight back?' argument made manifest through embedded assumptions about how heterosexual sex takes place. In law, this originally meant that in court women had to demonstrate forcible resistance. Changes to these laws were ushered in by feminist advocacy in the 1980s, later accompanied by rape shield laws, in order to overturn rules mandating that women had to have demonstrably fought back (meaning that the use of force had to be physically inscribed on women's bodies) (Byrnes 1998).

Consent and #MeToo

While there are several diverse and competing definitions of consent relevant to the study of #MeToo, the operating definition I use sees sexual consent as constituted by a changing socio-legal permission structure used to determine whether sex is permissible or not. Consent, as Wertheimer argues, thus acts as a 'morally transformative act' rendering the impermissible permissible and the illegitimate legitimate (Wertheimer 1996: 92; West 2010). As such, the conferring of consent, according to Frank and Nyholm citing Wertheimer, requires that:

> (1) consent must be an act of some kind, in other words, it 'is performative rather than attitudinal' . . . (2) consent can be 'explicit or tacit, verbal or nonverbal'

> . . . And (3) consent can only take place when 'certain background defects' (i.e. coercion or lack of competence) are absent. (Wertheimer as cited by Frank and Nyholm 2017: 309)

Unequal occupational roles in professional settings, socially entrenched gender norms and other structural inequalities are additional aspects that, in some jurisdictions, help to determine whether consent is freely given. Yet, it remains the case that the consent model continues to reflect hegemonic gender myths and assumptions around ideal heterosexual relations. The most insidious of these is reflected in the desirous active man and passive acquiescent woman myth wherein the insatiability of men's sexual needs and female reticence to engage in sex are accepted as natural. This perceived feminine passivity is doubly harmful when it feeds into the related narrative of forced sex as something women (secretly) want while also placing responsibility for stopping unwanted sex on women. As Hunter and Cowan contend, these myths, and the laws that codify them, erase 'women's sexual freedom and active desire (through the portrayal of women's normal sexual agency as essentially secondary and responsive), but at the same time [demand] a very high level of sexual responsibility [from] women' (Hunter and Cowan 2007: 62).

It is important to point out that whether sex and sexual advances are autonomously consented to and wanted/desired is a question that assumes idealised conditions which are rarely met. Yet, as with most socio-legal norms, context and bare reality often supersede principles of action. The radical feminist analysis of consent discussed in Chapter 1 articulates an important critique that highlights the structures of patriarchy and heterosexism under which decisions to consent are made. As such, free choice is seen as a mirage papering over base oppression through overt and covert forms of violence. For radical feminists like Shulamith Firestone, 'it is the constructs of "female chastity" and "male honour", "wifely duty", "filial piety", "maternal instinct", etc., [that] are also ways of managing women's consent to their subordination to men' (Firestone as cited by Thompson 2001: 25; see also Firestone 2000). This critique, in an adapted form, has re-emerged with respect to #MeToo wherein context, unequal relations of power, and coercion are seen as barriers to women's equality and their exercise of free choice (Clarke-Vivier and Stearns 2019). What distinguishes #MeToo from the arguments made by radical feminists is that the focus on structures is coupled with a doubling-down on consent and a critique of sexual norms. This, I maintain, does a disservice to women by undermining their right to pleasure and the actualisation of desire. Robin West discusses this in the context of the 'reasoned deciding' versus 'subjective desiring' self wherein 'many women and girls and some boys and men likewise . . . often or routinely consent to sex when they neither desire, want, welcome, or ultimately find it to be physically pleasurable' (West 2020: 5). This argument has been used by #MeToo advocates to call for sexual empowerment codified in strong consent laws and norms rather than by a radical feminist rejection of the whole system.

What is wrong with consent?

Turning back to the problems with the consent model, feminists and other scholars of sexuality and queer studies have concerns about the contractualist aspect of consent which they juxtapose with frameworks that strive for co-determination and communication. For example, Holland et al.'s work on gendered disembodiment and the material body makes the case that the exercise of male power has produced a kind of gendered disembodiment characterised by rational discipline and detached desire which women are also forced to live out (Holland et al. 1994). This critique of consent raises further questions about its connection to the putative reification of the Cartesian split between the mind and body that constitutes Western Enlightenment thought (Derrida 2016; Butler 2011a; Hekman 1991). Consent thus forces women to separate bodily desires, emotions and embodiments from their rational capacities: 'It thereby fosters a solipsistic pursuit of one's own sexual interests and thus a merely strategic relationship towards the other, rather than a dynamic communication about desires, needs, and fears' (Loick 2020: 419). This perspective is in keeping with the historic connection of flesh, emotions and bodies with women and the marginalised wherein they are seen as secondary and less than. Unruly bodies, particularly Black bodies, become constructed as 'the source of an irresistible, destructive sensuality', absent 'a subject position' and expressive of dangerous Otherness (Spillers as cited by Musser 2018: 8).

Consent, understood in this way, also risks reducing sex and sexuality in other ways. For example, an important aspect of contemporary queer and some third and fourth wave feminist thought on consent requires unpacking its resistance to juridical regulation (Barnard 2020; Harris 2018; Musser 2018). Research in this area suggests that sex is a unique kind of activity that pushes beyond the limits of normative systems and must be understood through the lens of excess, flows, desire, hesitation and risk. Much of this work relies on the writing of Michel Foucault, who articulated a critique of sexual regulation as part and parcel of disciplining socio-political mechanisms that aim at bodily control over pleasure and novel forms of subjectivity and creativity (Foucault 1990, 2012, 2019). Foucault's position on sex and consent intersects with his work on repression and the exercise of power through the institutional production of knowledge vis-à-vis appropriate sexual practices that discipline our behaviour. The production of discourses about sex (or sex as a discourse) is thus deployed as part of the modern biopolitical order which works by placing

> into operation [an] entire machinery for producing true discourses concerning it. Not only did it speak of sex and compel everyone to do so; it set out to formulate the uniform truth of sex. As if it suspected sex of harbouring a fundamental secret. As if it needed this production of truth. As if it was essential that sex be inscribed not only in an economy of pleasure but in an ordered system of knowledge. (Foucault 1990: 69)

Luckily, according to Foucault, this discursive ordering has also led to the 'proliferation of specific pleasures and multiplication of disparate sexualities' (Foucault 1978: 49), which 'brings out corporeal potentials that have remained unrealised' (or silenced) by these technologies of power (Lyng 2004: 43). Consequently, consent, as a discourse, can be read either as inscribing heteronormative sexualities into and on to bodies, and critiqued as a form of sexual hygiene that operates by excising unfit forms of desire, *or* as providing a basis for the realignment of sexual subjectivity and agency. As an aside, Foucault, in his own life, had some troubling views on the subject of a child's capacity to consent to sex by advocating for a strict 'perpetrator's force plus victim's resistance' model such that were a child not to resist, sex *could* be permissible. In the context of #MeToo, a Foucauldian critique would express concern about the risk of overcorrecting and the use of consent discourse to restrict sexual practices viewed as immoral. Queer theory, building on this framework, draws attention to the ways in which what is defined as wrongful, nonconsensual sex can be overly capacious and disguise an underlying hostility to sexual variation, which is something Janet Halley discusses in the context of 'sex panics' (Halley 2000).

Understood in this way, consent, consistent with #MeToo and according to queer theory, leaves little space for discussions about non-normative sex – for instance, what Robin West describes as 'hot, desired, transgressive sado-masochism' (West 2008: 138). It is important to emphasise the queer critique of these dominant sexual scripts and discourses that aim at the 'forcible materialization of a "regulatory ideal" [heterosexuality]'. For Judith Butler, to materialise the body's sex is 'to materialize sexual difference in the service of the consolidation of the heterosexual imperative' (Butler 1993a: 2). The centring of consent is thus inherently suspect because of its presumption of 'normality'. The female-focused valence of #MeToo, both in theory and in practice, is also potentially problematic in that it tends to exclude men, trans women and nonbinary subjects and ignore how these groups and individuals might conceive of consent differently. Aside from the examples of actor Terry Crews, who accused a prominent Hollywood executive of sexual assault, and the accusations made against Kevin Spacey, it is notable that the conversations around consent and #MeToo-specific transgressions overwhelmingly involve affluent, white, cis, Western women (Kornhaber 2019; Mumford 2017).

Queering consent

There are, however, two interpretations of consent relevant to discussions of #MeToo that draw on Foucauldian theory and sexual non-normativity in ways that are potentially radical. I find these readings particularly important in developing a model of sexual relationality in which consent continues to play some role. The first is with respect to BDSM (bondage, discipline, sadism and masochism) which, putting its more dangerous iterations aside, necessitates that both parties consent fully, clearly and often – often requiring the use of a safe word. Grasped in this way, consent, according to Banerjee, Merchant and Sharma, shifts from harm reduction to being about pleasure and desire while placing responsibility for giving and receiving consent on all parties. As such, unconscious desire becomes an important part of sexual practice (Banerjee, Merchant and Sharma 2018; Bennett 2018; Ortmann and Sprott 2012). BDSM is often discussed as representative of what is possible with respect to embedding a culture of consent into society more widely. In opposition, Margot Weiss has critiqued some of this framing as de-eroticising in that it aims at normalising the non-normative by expanding its remit rather than challenging its underlying assumptions (Weiss 2008). Concerns about simply 'tinkering around the edges' through the performative co-optation of sexual subcultures and practices come up again and again around discussions of sexual norms. I return to a discussion of BDSM in the context of negotiated consent and sexual autonomy, for which it is used as both a limit case and ideal exemplar, a little later on.

More recent Foucauldian interpretations of consent have drawn on his work on moral subjectivity, sexual ethics and care of the self to articulate a conception of sexual relations that is based on care for the Other. By examining, challenging and potentially replacing heteronormative and exploitative power relations with a more robust sexual subjectivity, Foucault makes space for a model of sexual relationality in which the desires, pleasures and ethicality of the Other take centre stage (Carmody 2003; Foucault 1987). While wobbly on what this might mean in practice, care for the self and the Other, when coupled with critical self-reflection, involves the 'consideration of desire [that] also opens the sexual encounter up to interrogation and accountability before sexual interaction begins' (Pastor 2014: 26). This ethos brings us closer to the communicative consent and/or sexual autonomy models but remains important in the context of consent qua consent in that it speaks to how even the most seemingly transgressive sexual modalities retain elements of consent at their core.

AFFIRMATIVE/ENTHUSIASTIC CONSENT

The central ethos of affirmative consent (AC) and enthusiastic consent (EC) is constituted by an active move, driven by feminist legal theory and feminist critiques of rape, towards a model of sexual relations that constructs a new ethic of sexual subjectivity based on full sexual citizenship for women. Some of the limitations of the consent model articulated above have been purposefully worked on and attended to by affirmative and enthusiastic frameworks such as removing residual ambiguities and instilling choice and autonomy into sexual practice. The earliest iteration of a concrete AC policy was Antioch College's 1990 change to their student code of conduct which was pilloried in the press, and even on *Saturday Night Live*, as an act of outlandish overreach. Currently, due to increased interest in AC and EC in light of #MeToo, there are a plethora of overlapping and even competing definitions of each in circulation. The most comprehensive and inclusive one I have found, and which I rely on in my own work, can be found in California's Education Code:

> 'Affirmative consent' means affirmative, conscious, and voluntary agreement to engage in sexual activity. It is the responsibility of each person involved in the sexual activity to ensure that he or she has the affirmative consent of the other or others to engage in the sexual activity. Lack of protest or resistance does not mean consent, nor does silence mean consent. Affirmative consent must be ongoing throughout a sexual activity and can be revoked at any time. The existence of a dating relationship between the persons involved, or the fact of past sexual relations between them, should never by itself be assumed to be an indicator of consent. (California Education Code 67386(a)(1) 2020)

The tenets of note in this definition, aside from being affirmative and consensual, are that (1) parties must be conscious, thereby addressing instances of intoxication; (2) sex must be voluntarily entered into and enlightened as to the possibility of coercion; (3) the responsibility to procure AC falls on the shoulders of both parties (and is thus dispersed rather than asymmetrical); (4) consent must be verbally articulated; and (5) to (7) AC is revocable, ongoing and assessed so that past relations cannot be used to assume consent is present in future ones (Schulhofer 2015; Cole 2019). This definition and its attendant assumptions are broadly in line with those articulated by #MeToo since, amongst other things, it removes responsibility for consent from women, thereby obviating victim self-blame, and renders force an even less relevant factor in litigating sexual assault (Me Too 2020; Consent Respect 2020). As sex education teacher, author and #MeToo proponent Jaclyn Friedman suggests,

> Teaching affirmative consent does something profound: it shifts the acceptable moral standard for sex, making it much clearer to everyone when someone is violating that standard . . . Affirmative consent, when taught well, also removed heteronormative assumptions from sex ed. If we're each equally responsible to make sure our partner is enthusiastic about what's happening, gender stereotypes – such as that women are passive and men are aggressive – about sexuality begin to break down . . . Consent education does something else transformative: it tells girls that sex is supposed to be for them. (Friedman as cited by Abdulali 2018: 45–6)

With respect to terminology, I use AC and EC interchangeably. However, it should be noted some EC advocates contend that EC is distinct from AC in that it specifically requires an enthusiastic confirmatory 'yes' to be part of the consent act (Taylor 2018; Knutson and Miller 2018; Farmer 2018). EC can thus be understood as a variation of AC wherein consent is not only required but must be vigorously asserted. As such, desire on the part of all parties engaged in enthusiastic forms of consent is necessary, sexual passivity is ruled out, and an ethos of symmetricality is made obligatory in order to attend to the asymmetries of power constitutive of many heteronormative sexual relationships. EC is often shorthanded through the slogan 'yes means yes', rather than 'no means no', and advocates maintain that this approach will result in the realisation of enjoyable sex for all involved. As Friedman avers, EC means that 'if you want to have sex, you have to be in a state of continual enthusiastic consent with your partner' (Friedman 2010). For the purposes of this book, however, I argue that the differences between EC and AC are small enough to keep them in the same category since their operating assumptions remain the same – namely, the universal requirement for 'clear, voluntary, and direct mutual [sexual] communication' (Hasinoff 2016: 60). EC's addition of enthusiasm to the consent act layers on a kind of qualifying coda to AC but does not change its central precepts in any substantive way. The advocacy and support group RAINN (Rape, Abuse & Incest National Network), for example, use the term 'positive consent' to refer to the same phenomenon. In areas where a distinction is relevant, however, it has been made.

There are several iterations of AC-specific laws working their way through state legislatures in the US and some states already have references to AC on the books. New Jersey, for example, has its own state law requiring 'freely given affirmative permission to the specific act of sexual penetration', as have a handful of other states including Wisconsin and Illinois (Witmer-Rich 2016: 60; Sandoval 2019). All told, fifteen jurisdictions mention affirmative consent in their rape statutes but, as Tuerkheimer argues, 'all diverge substantially in their treatment of consent' with some requiring 'implied acquiescence' and others more 'affirmative manifestations' (Tuerkheimer 2015: 449).

In Canada, communicated voluntary consent has been on the books since 1992 and has since been supplemented with requirements addressing possible abuses of power, the capacity to consent, and the obligation that 'reasonable steps' have been taken to ensure consent is freely given (Gotell 2008). It has been argued, however, that the high AC/EC standards most commonly held by #MeToo activists are still not met by Canadian law, with more needing to be done on defining what is meant by 'reasonable steps' (to procure consent) and on what grounds sexual history can be judged as 'relevant' and probative in a court of law (Gotell 2008; Vandervort 2019). AC and EC regulations have, however, become de rigueur in university and college sexual conduct codes in the US, with California and New York being the first, in 2014 and 2015 respectively, to require that college campuses adopt AC/EC standards. Like in the US, Canadian university campuses and sex education curriculums have also made AC part of their pedagogy and codes of conduct. Significantly, with AC, silence cannot be taken to indicate permission, but nonverbal acts that imply active agreement can. In the context of law, this means that mistaken belief cannot be used as a defence, nor can silence be presented as representing de facto consent (Gotell 2008).

One of the most salient critiques of AC/EC is that they fail to adequately acknowledge the pervasiveness of gender norms and scripts that shape the sexual behaviour of women who are socialised to be compliant and accommodating. These norms and expectations harken back to the critiques of patriarchy and heterosexism launched by radical feminists for whom 'a femininity constructed through a perfectly compliant and accommodating relation' is believed to be entrenched requiring transformational change (Howson 2006: 68). Simply codifying behavioural change is therefore seen as insufficient as it does not address the structures under which a clear yes, representative of transparently communicated desire, can be expressed, understood and enacted.

There is also the related danger that this approach risks reifying the mind/body split in which the agential, rational actor in total control of their faculties and able to freely consent is juxtaposed to and with traditionally feminised bodily desire and emotional knowledge wherein desire is made manifest in the act itself (Alcoff 2018). Embodied sexual communication is rather messier than the AC and EC models allow and, philosophically, renders bodily engagement with an Other as intertwined with having 'feelings of a certain sort, to act on them, to identify with their warmth and energy'. As such, 'If a tactile-kinesthetic body were merely something an incorporeal thinking subject had at its disposition, then the thinking subject would be divorced from the being who was in love. The appropriate description of the situation would be not that one was in love, but that one's body was' (Johnstone 1992: 31). Inarticulate, physical desire made manifest through an embodied form of communication that is in flux, impulsive and disruptive is not accounted for by EC and AC. This fixing of the body retains a masculine form of subjectivity that brings with it concerns about 'the reproduction of gender norms and an inability to understand how sexual desires, identities, experiences, and relationships [are] fundamentally social and dependent on interpretive processes and . . . exceed reasoned communication' (Fahs and McClelland 2016: 400; see also Nash 2014).

Finally, as in the basic consent model, EC and AC can also be overly prescriptive which can result in an overextension of the law in the case of committed, ongoing relationships in which enthusiasm may not always be forthcoming and constant affirmation incongruous. Engaging in sex for reasons other than pure wantedness is also not unusual as in the case of sex work, where enthusiasm is often performed, or to avoid rejection and conflict, or even to affirm self-worth. This renders some acts of EC and AC superficially performative and potentially criminalises everyday motivations for engaging in sexual relations (Burmakova 2013).

Some of these concerns have been taken up and mitigated by more contemporary models that build on AC and EC, such as communicative consent and sexual autonomy – both of which aim to redistribute power more equitably and address issues of embodiment and desire in new ways.

COMMUNICATIVE CONSENT

Communicative consent, also referred to as communicative sexuality, is a robust framework first fully articulated by Lois Pineau (1989), but subsequently written about by others for whom securing consent is a practice analogous to everyday conversation (Cahill 2001; Flynn and Henry 2012; Gibson 2016; Schulhofer 1998; Willis and Jozkowski 2019). The kinds of conversations about sex Pineau envisions are ones that are characterised by intersubjectivity, openness, respect and empathy – ones that demand a context and mode of relationality that is 'non-manipulative and non-paternalistic . . . [thereby] combin[ing] the appropriate knowledge of the other with respect for the dialectics of desire' (Pineau 1989: 231–5). In practice, this means that entering into just sexual acts requires that consent must be procured through communication with an Other, that said communication is constituted by 'a continuous process of mutual decision-making' (Croskery-Hewitt 2015), and that responsibility for the pleasure and well-being of the Other is equitably distributed.

In the legal context, communicative consent demands that for sex to be ethical and legal, clear communication about wanting to have sex (including what kind of sex) must have taken place. This might include a discussion of contraception, the kind of sex one prefers, or the kind of practices one does not want to engage in. An individual accused of assault would thus have to prove that communication did occur and said discourse would be interrogated in order to ascertain whether the sex was freely entered into. Importantly, communicative sexuality, were it to be integrated in law, would also necessitate that all parties have good reasons for engaging in sex which must be proved if enjoyment is not the central motivation (thereby leaving room for sex work to be considered both legal and permissible). Moreover, this approach flips the norm of reasonability which is no longer about whether the initiator has good reasons to believe consent was given but, instead, whether it is reasonable for 'women to consent to something that they have little chance of enjoying – hence it is not reasonable for individual men (or, therefore, the law) to expect that women consent to aggressive non-communicative sex' (Powell 2010: 89). This constitutes an important readjustment of power relations both inside and outside the legal system.

Philosophically, communicative consent is Kantian in that it requires that the ends of the Other are respected, that individuals enter into relationships with formed epistemic obligations and desires, and that ensuring mutual pleasure is the responsibility of all involved. Pineau goes as far as to argue that this approach 'makes consent female' and, in pursuit of historical equity, we must now turn to 'what is reasonable from a woman's point of view' as providing 'the principal delineation of a criterion of consent that is capable of representing a woman's willing behaviour' (Pineau 1989: 221). Chamallas highlights how communicative consent endorses an ethos of mutuality and welcomeness or desiredness reflected in the question of 'whether the target would have initiated the encounter if she had been given the choice' (Chamallas 1987: 836). While this latter interpretation may risk reducing 'the communicative' to the biologically feminine, communicative consent is notable in that it moves the goalposts for what constitutes pleasurable sex. The ongoing expression of wantedness and desire, consistent with the communicative model, is aimed at reclaiming female sexuality and empowerment not through the postfeminist assertion of individual agency, but through a form of agency that expresses itself intersubjectively. Finally, communicative sexuality leaves room for nonverbal cues to be considered as acceptable as a form of communication (i.e. as part of the 'communicative package') and asserts that for sex outside of pleasure to take place, it must be agreed upon (i.e. for pregnancy or to make one's partner happy) (Marino 2019).

Another advocate of the communicative consent model of note who takes a slightly different position is Stephen Schulhofer (1998, 2015), whose approach is more modest than Pineau's. Schulhofer sits somewhere in between consent, AC, EC and communicative consent but is worth discussing here because of his focus on the strong requirement of communication and the number of times his work comes up in examinations of legal reform. Schulhofer defines communicative consent as 'a person's freely given agreement to engage in a specific act of sexual penetration or sexual contact, communicated by conduct, words, or both' where consent takes place through communicative acts 'inferred from the totality of the circumstances' (Schulhofer as cited by Gruber 2016: 684). Schulhofer takes a holistic view of the circumstances under which sex can occur such that even silent acquiescence can form part of communicative practice (Schulhofer 1998). His is seen as a practicable approach, what he calls 'socially realistic' in that it places trusts in citizens and their common sense. This framework, however, has come under critical scrutiny by legal scholars for a number of shortcomings; I outline their arguments below.

Communicative consent is qualitatively different from EC and AC in that it is a process-oriented framework aimed at changing sexual ethics and practices rather than a performative one (where 'performative' is understood descriptively) in which the 'yes means yes' of EC and AC represents a signpost of permissibility but which ignores underlying inequalities in power and proscribed gender norms. There are no countries or jurisdictions in which communicative consent is explicitly part of the law but it has been proposed in the context of law reform by groups like SWOP (Sex Workers Outreach Project) in Australia (SWOP 2018), and almost became part of law in the province of Tasmania in 2003. The province of Victoria, also in Australia, has a clause in its criminal code about communicative consent as it relates to jury direction (Cockburn 2012).

This strong focus on practices, norms and behaviours, as in AC and EC, necessitates education and large-scale behavioural change that is both daunting and promising. In its most optimistic reading, communicative consent gets us beyond problematic assumptions and behavioural expectations related to gender. It also centres mutuality and focuses on an activity, communication, that is reputationally democratic, egalitarian and oriented towards a philosophical ethos in which 'Reaching and understanding [is understood as] . . . the process of bringing about an agreement on the presupposed basis of validity claims that are mutually recognized' (Habermas 1998: 23). What could be better than that?

By way of critique, some scholars argue that the allowance given by communicative consent for nonverbal cues leaves too much room for misinterpretation. Anderson, for example, points out that 'study after study indicates that men consistently misinterpret women's nonverbal behaviour. They impute erotic innuendo and sexual intent where there is none' (Anderson 2005: 1,417). Others, however, like Hannah Frith, maintain that this is not the case, arguing that men are perfectly capable of reading bodily cues (Kitzinger and Frith 1999; Adams-Curtis and Forbes 2004).

There are also a host of other possible drawbacks of the communicative approach – many of which stem from a critique of language itself. For instance, the idea that discourse perfectly reflects reality (internal desirous states) is tenuous at best since communication requires interpretation and an understanding of context in situ (Ogden and Richards 1923; Carey 2008; Phillips and Oswick 2012). As such, the implication that 'yes' and 'no' merely reflect 'reality' overlooks the fact that 'communication is always somewhat ambiguous, it requires both interpretation and coordination' (Harris 2018: 158). The world-building aspects of communication reflected in a more robust conception of communicative sexuality would also have to consider the role of ambiguity, intent, desire, fear, manipulation and power.

Also of note is the role of socio-political and historical context inclusive of gender norms and expectations, inequalities of power, heteropatriarchy and misogyny – all of which work together to form structural impediments to the kinds of egalitarian communication this model demands. Also overlooked by this approach are (1) the racial dynamics of consent – namely those who have been historically denied the power to consent (i.e. Black women) and who have been subject to the majority of arrests (racialised men); (2) the construction of those thought to always be consenting (i.e. sex workers); (3) the very real (gendered) sexual gatekeeping that remains despite moves towards discursive equality; (4) the elision of how desire works in practice (i.e. sometimes in pursuit of dominance play and non-normative sexual practices); and (5) the discounting of queer sexualities wherein consent can be more complicated than a simple yes/no and in which heteronormative behavioural norms are challenged through the production of 'new normative centers . . . [in which] queer actors assert the right to self-define [sex] outside of societal strictures' (Lamont 2017: 629; see also Welch 2012; Friedman and Valenti 2019; Braun et al. 2009; Bennett 2018). It is also important to remember that, historically, consent statutes have been used to incarcerate gay men as well as trans and nonbinary individuals, leaving very little trust that these frameworks will work as envisioned (Fischel 2016).

Aya Gruber makes some salient points about the shortcomings of communicative consent (in addition to AC and EC) also worth mentioning. These include that communicative consent can (1) be overprescriptive; (2) be empirically inconsistent with reality, since the verbalisation of consent is simply not the norm; (3) be repressive of 'risky' but desired sex; and (4) encourage the overreporting of miscommunication such that discursive acts become the subject of litigation (Gruber 2016, 2019). Finally, Patricia Marino draws attention to what I think is a slightly tenuous but interesting argument that communicative sexuality, in the course of sex, does not adequately consider how sexual acts occurring at one point in time, and communicated verbally or nonverbally as consensual, are related to consent to future acts. As Marino argues, 'it is wrong to think that your communicating that enjoyment is grounds for thinking you've consented to further acts' (Marino 2019).

Taken together, these three iterations of consent, pro forma consent, affirmative/enthusiastic consent and communicative consent, I argue, represent significant but insufficient models of sexual practice. They have been manifested in law but are particularly salient vis-à-vis #MeToo. I contend that these frameworks are lacking first and foremost because they fail to adequately come to terms with structures of power and gender norms that give rise to institutions that condone behaviours that #MeToo seeks to address while also retaining significant practical and philosophical shortcomings. The most important of these is their support of a liberal model of agency, the assumption that intention is wholly transparent, their overreliance on a normative conception of sexuality, and their holding fast to a disembodied and rational conception of desire – all of which, I argue, render them not fit for purpose if the purpose is to construct and disseminate a capacious set of sexual norms and practices that are generative, responsive, empowering and transformative.

SEXUAL AUTONOMY AND SEXUAL INTEGRITY

Some of the most pioneering research in sexual ethics, law and norms comes out of work in the area of sexual autonomy and bodily integrity. As a philosophical concept traditionally associated with Kant in the first instance, autonomy is about having the capacity to decide and act according to one's rational judgement (Kant 1996, 2001). *Sexual* autonomy, however, does not quite fit with the Kantian model since sex, for Kant, is the antithesis of rational autonomy and, as such, 'a degradation of human nature' (Kant 2001: 163). Nevertheless, sexual autonomy retains elements of the Kantian ethic of self-determination and works to ensure that individuals have both the freedom to act and the knowledge needed to do so (Lacey 1998a; Schulhofer 1992; Herring 2005; Tracy et al. 2012).

Protecting liberal sexual autonomy is bound up with the exercise of 'meaningful and transformative choice' (Munro 2008: 949), rooted in 'conscious reflection about preferences and a deliberate choice of one's goals' (Schulhofer 1998: 106). Thus, to use one's sexual autonomy means that one can act on one's desires and interests freely. Positive sexual autonomy allows individuals to shape and control their sexual lives and make choices based on reasons they deem significant. Its roots are liberal in that it assumes the separability of individuals from one another and highlights the right to self-determination. Other terms and frameworks associated with sexual autonomy are moral self-government, sexual self-expression, the realisation of life plans, bodily integrity, sexual equality and personhood (Cornell 1998; Nedelsky 2011; Lacey 1998a). Under this approach, sex work is permissible if freely chosen, as is engaging in sex for reasons other than desire including making one's partner happy and having sex out of a sense of duty. Sexual assault, of the sort #MeToo has mobilised against, will have been committed if actions have been taken that infringe on a person's ability to 'act freely on their own unconstrained conception of what their bodies and their sexual capacities are for' (Schulhofer 1992: 70). Thus, any action that impairs the exercise of autonomy is seen as harmful, whether it is rape or any other form of sexual assault. Significantly, liberal sexual autonomy abandons the physical force requirement for one in which other forms of coercion – and this may include negging, which is significant in the Aziz Ansari case – are also seen as legally impermissible, albeit to different degrees. On the point of law, the question of what determines guilt revolves around whether a sexually autonomous person would have consented to the sexual act. Additionally, using that basic parameter, the operative question would be whether the accuser would have initiated sex themselves if given the choice (Burgess-Jackson 1999; Chamallas 1987). As stated, however, the integration of sexual autonomy into criminal law is less widespread. In the US, while there have been legal interpretations and juridical decisions that make note of sexual autonomy (e.g. Kortner v. Martise (Conn. dated 10 June 2014) and the case against Hunter Moore in the state of California as it relates to revenge porn), no explicit integration of it as an enforceable tenet has been codified and enacted (Rubenfeld 2013).

The criticisms of sexual autonomy to do with whether or not it is achievable in practice. This depends, of course, on how sexual autonomy is interpreted, that is, how high the bar is. It is not possible, for example, to ensure the sexual freedoms of everyone equally since they are likely to conflict with one another and because the context in which sexual autonomy is sought is always unequal. As such, many of the same problems around consent, inclusive of AC and EC, extend to the more liberal instantiations of sexual autonomy. This includes how to enact and/or transform these principles into concrete legally binding rules and social norms. The difficulty this poses is not only mired in questions of codification and legislative action, but also relates to how closely this definition of autonomy reflects the realities of people's daily lives and the capacities of average people. Women's socialisation into roles that focus on 'care-giving, self-sacrifice, and the satisfactions of domesticity', in opposition to 'men [who] are encouraged to sample the range of more public opportunities that their greater independence allows', poses significant barriers to the substantive exercise of autonomy (Abrams 1999: 818).

Radical feminist Catharine MacKinnon's characterisation of how gendered norms and expectations work to undermine the autonomy of women from the bottom up is clarifying: 'When you are powerless, you don't just speak differently. A lot, you don't speak.' You 'are deprived of a life out of which articulation might come' and 'prevented from having anything to say' (MacKinnon 1987: 39). These concerns are salient in discussions around #MeToo which, in addition to advocating for affirmative consent, has taken on an autonomy-centric philosophical position in that its ultimate objectives are founded on principles of self-sovereignty and sexual choice. The question of sex work is important as it relates to whether sexual autonomy is truly being exercised by women involved in the profession. Radical feminists would likely say no, while postfeminists and third wave feminists would tend to augur a yes. Thi is based on, for the latter, an embrace of autonomous choice rooted in sexual pleasure, self-awareness and a rejection of conceptions of false consciousness and, for the former, the entrepreneurial driven rejection of female victimhood and support for an 'always up for it' sexual subjectivity (Agustín 2007; Gill 2007; Crawford 2007).

Also of note are the raced, classed and ableist structures under which the exercise of sexual autonomy is made even more challenging. Arguments along these lines are articulated by radical feminists, Marxist feminists, critical race theorists and disability scholars. Each, in its understanding of autonomy, lays out the myriad ways in which the actualisation of sexual autonomy is subject to the disciplining power of institutions, laws, economic structures and social hierarchies. With respect to race, it remains the case that the autonomy of raced women is shaped by racist and heteropatriarchal hierarchies that condition how autonomy is expressed. Stereotypes about sexual availability, for example, are made manifest in studies of sexual harassment which produces what Hernandez (2000) calls a form of sexualised 'racial commodification' that limits the autonomy of women of colour facing harassment in the workplace. The familiar criticism of liberal instantiations of sexual autonomy as heteronormative is also applicable here (Bloom 2015).

Disability scholar Bethany Stevens writes about how the barriers to sexual autonomy for disabled people are both structural and attitudinal by demonstrating how 'medicalization, policy, and law work in concert to perpetuate ableism – the system of social power that simultaneously exalts and enforces normalcy, as well as excludes and devalues disabled people' (Stevens 2011: 14; see also Bernert 2011; Liberman 2018). However, it is also true that sexual autonomy has the potential to be expressed in a more radical manner through the renewal of desire, pleasure and possibility

(Warner 2000; Bailey 2019). Additionally, how one defines choice, and in particular 'free' choice, is culturally variable. A postcolonial critique of the Eurocentric biases of traditional conceptions of autonomy as an ideal has been articulated by Reiss (2002) and Comaroff and Comaroff (2001), who make the point that even under a progressive conception of sexual autonomy, a colonising lens continues to determine sexual norms (Weeks 2012). It is out of these critiques that the notion of embodied autonomy emerges as a more nuanced, postcolonial, feminist, materialist, anti-neoliberal and anti-racist sexual model.

EMBODIED SEXUAL AUTONOMY

The model of sexual autonomy I am most interested in, and which is reflected in the framework I ultimately propose, takes on a feminist and materialist (as opposed to solely discursive) valence. It has been referred to alternatively as embodied autonomy, relational autonomy, sexual integrity or sexual citizenship (Mackenzie 2006; Herring 2009; Diprose 1994). The telos of each of these approaches is constituted by a movement away from the atomistic liberal model of autonomy and towards one that highlights an ethic of care, interdependence and bodily enactment. Embodied and relational autonomy grounds autonomy and consent in the 'mutuality of relationship and responsibility between individuals' (Lacey 1998a: 121), while also incorporating the 'bodily and affective aspects of sexual life more directly in issue' (Lacey 1998a: 118).

It is worth expending a few sentences articulating the critique of liberal sexual autonomy from a feminist perspective specifically as it is this critique that best explains what materialist approaches to autonomy aim to accomplish and their motivations for doing so. Feminist scholars like Seyla Benhabib and Carole Pateman, for example, contend that liberal models of autonomy rely too heavily on a disembodied and individualist conception of the self leading to the 'privatization of women's experiences and to the exclusion of its consideration from a moral point of view' (Benhabib 1992: 152). Equality, reciprocity and socio-cultural specificity are norms that, for Pateman, should replace those of transaction, zero sum negotiation and transparent intelligibility (Pateman 2016). The specifically feminist positioning of relational and embodied autonomy is a point I would signpost as important in the context of #MeToo.

A few further notes on embodied and relational autonomy worth highlighting include that its focus on affect and embodiment makes emotion, hope, care and desire the locus from which to gauge the permissibility of sexual relations. This is significant in the context of #MeToo since it offers a way in which to explore new sexual possibilities by challenging heteropatriarchal and heteronormative sexual norms and practices while also forming a basis from which to evaluate the 'just-ness' of a sexual act (Sedgwick 2003). As Nedelsky puts it, 'I see autonomy as the core of a capacity to engage in the ongoing, interactive creation of our selves – our relational selves'. Thus any infringement of this should be subject to critical, legal, examination, (Nedelsky 2011: 45).

Joseph Fischel, in his book *Screw Consent: A Better Politics of Sexual Justice*, makes the case for a model of sexual autonomy rooted in determination which he describes as relational, hedonic and cognisant of context, social structures and background conditions (Fischel 2019: 108–9). His 'thick' version of relational autonomy is connected to an ethic of care, self-creation and affect while also centring pleasure and the socio-material affordances that must be in place to realise sexual choice. Fischel's approach acts as a corrective to the disembodied assertion of rational autonomous action discussed above. The embodied valence of this model of sexual autonomy highlights the social networks, bodily engagement and world-building that goes on during all acts of intimacy. Building on queer, feminist and disability studies, Fischel centres erotic pleasure in his approach to sexuality and advocates for reforms that foster a more 'democratic hedonic sexual culture' (Fischel 2019: 140). Most importantly, his framework advocates for a social order that 'more equitably distributes its possibilities for pleasure and intimacy' and which can be facilitated by the state but is not determined by it (Fischel 2019: 128).

Now, one might say yes, this is all well and good, but how does this work in practice – in law, in the bedroom, in the workplace and so on? In order to distil relational and embodied autonomy into more concrete terms, I like to think of these kinds of approaches to sexual relations as being of 'bodily relational autonomy' co-constituted horizontally by relational reciprocity and liminal trust and engagement with others, and vertically by a focus on psychic and bodily experiences and potentialities (e.g. affect – where sexual intentionality is also seen as embodied and lived). These axes of relation can then be set within a framework that is attuned to the oppressive structures that might impair the realisation of relational and embodied autonomy including that of racism, sexism, ableism, classism and capitalism.

For this ethic to be incorporated into law, it would require a foundational socio-cultural as well as politico-legal change to our values, norms and assumptions. As Fischel states, 'Suggesting that we repeal, reform, or revise sex laws says nothing about the kinds of nonlegal, cultural, creative, aesthetic, grassroots, intersectional, and global forms sexual justice politics can and should take' (Fischel 2019: 93). Transformational change will have to occur on a number of levels including what we count as evidence, what we understand to be reasonable, and what we think of as acceptable and desirable behaviour.

With respect to evidence, I identify with Martha Nussbaum and Marilyn Friedman who point out that emotions are indeed 'forms of evaluative judgment that ascribe to certain things and persons outside a person's own control great importance for the person's own flourishing' and thus can serve as a basis from which to evaluate autonomy (Nussbaum 2003: 22). As such, emotions can form the basis from which to evaluate and judge sexual assault, rape, harassment and a whole host of violations that have been taken up and publicised by #MeToo. Thus, a sexual act should be considered as violating if actions are taken that make it impossible for one's counterpart(s) to co-determine sexual relations. Consent will play a role in this but only as part of a larger constellation of actions and engagements, both verbal and nonverbal, set within a context in which power, desire and relationality are considered.

Legally this would mean that consent is not the only factor that must be studied with respect to permissibility. The consideration of social context, power, patriarchy and history as well as of the content and quality of communication prior to sex, both bodily and verbal (and in a non-idealising fashion), is also needed (Ball 2005; Mackenzie and Stoljar 2000; Herring 2009). Yet even then, were these principles integrated into law, we would come up against the fact that our legal system seems perpetually unable or unwilling to deal with how racism, patriarchy and ableism permeate its codes and precedents. As Crenshaw argues, 'systems of race, gender and class domination converge' (Crenshaw 1991: 1,246) in our legal institutions such that, in the case of rape, specificities are ignored including the terrible history of 'the use of rape as a weapon of racial terror' which continues to shape jurisprudence even today (Crenshaw 1989: 161).

When it comes to #MeToo, relational embodied autonomy recentres the question of permissibility and desiredness away from consent and on to a form of politics and law in which the delimiting of one's sexual choices is seen as morally and legally wrong. When actions, sexual and otherwise, are undertaken under conditions of uncommunicated inequality, coercion and violence, sexual autonomy is undermined. It is the capacity to engage equally in acts of world-building and 'self [and world] creation' that is seen as critical in the actualisation of embodied autonomy (Nedelsky 1996; Yeatman 2000). This would render acts of violation against women by the likes of Harvey Weinstein and Bill Cosby unequivocally impermissible along with, if interpreted in a strict sense, other infractions including the actions of Aziz Ansari and Louis C.K., as well. Whether the latter's acts would be considered criminal, however, is unlikely. However, both Ansari and C.K. would be considered as morally suspect regardless of whether or not there was consent and irrespective of the survivor remaining in the situation. This is because, under embodied relational autonomy, it is the 'structural asymmetry of . . . that unpleasantness that is rightfully [seen as] the political problem' (Fischel 2019: 178–9). I think this is a particularly important point – namely, that what embodied relational autonomy allows for is the necessary critique of social arrangements that are functionally dysfunctional and one-sided as it relates to sex, pleasure and desire. The key conclusion is that they do not have to be.

Before moving on to the discussion of feminist new materialism, which offers a way in which to approach sexual relations wherein the body takes on even more significance, a short aside about sexual citizenship is necessary. Sexual citizenship offers an explicitly political model of sex in which the ability and the right to consent from a place of freedom and self-determination is key and where the experience of sexual gratification is understood as a central component of democratic morality (Rubin 1998; Evans 1993; Richardson 1998). Its two central tenets include ensuring 'varying degrees of access to a set of rights to sexual expression and consumption' and facilitating 'access to rights more generally' (Richardson 2000: 107). As such, enabling the expression of female sexual citizenship through institutional, legal and socio-cultural reform is essential. In its most progressive manifestation, sexual citizenship takes into account the right to express sexual desire as a human right and has been extended to include sexual minorities under the guise of 'queer citizenship' (Richardson 2004; Jagose 1996).

However, as in other models, sexual citizenship is far from transformational, as it often aligns with the same institutionally driven political tactics as liberal feminism. Specifically, sexual citizenship emerges out of a privatised framework since citizenship is itself aimed at the realisation of individual rights as opposed to collective and relational forms of action, transformation and engagement. Interestingly, #MeToo, in invoking the language of sexual citizenship, at least partially attends to this critique since it is grounded in the ethics and practice of a feminist social movement. Despite its mediated manifestations, #MeToo has connected survivors to networks of solidarity. As Clark argues, 'a hashtag's narrative logic – its ability to produce and connect individual stories – fuels its political growth. The online telling and connecting of personal stories distinguish hashtag feminism from earlier forms of feminist personal politics' (Clark 2016: 789).

Sexual citizenship also tends to understate the significance of coercive structures of power including gender norms, class structures, racism, heteronormativity and ableism as constraining factors in its actualisation. Additionally, the rootedness of citizenship in the nation-state whose operating logic is mired in a history of defending gender hierarchies and persecuting sexual minorities raises the question of whether this is the framework best placed to attend to the problems raised by #MeToo (McFadden 1992). As Desiree Lewis writes, citizenship is, and will probably continue to be, accessible only 'as long as [subjects] uphold certain ideas about democratic freedoms and social progress' consistent with 'being productive and worthy [sexual] citizens under neo-liberalism' (Lewis 2020: 2; see also Puar 2018). This is a salient political critique based on a suspicion of the co-opting power of institutions coupled with the biopolitical responsibilising of the self to act and perform as a proper sexual citizen worthy of rights and recognition (McWhorter 2004; Taylor 2014). Finally, as Olga Burmakova argues, sexual citizenship risks 'overplaying the extent to which information [and education] about sexuality is democratically distributed', which again demonstrates how these political models fail to attend to and facilitate the actualisation of equity, access and knowledge in light of entrenched sociocultural sexual norms (Burmakova 2013).

Collectively, these various permutations of sexual autonomy and sexual citizenship offer some compelling insights from which to form a robust model of sexual relations that can attend to the contradictions, transgressions and outright harms brought to the fore by #MeToo. First and foremost is the acknowledgement of the embodied – that is, more than solipsistic – nature of sexual relations and the importance of self-definition and agency *within a framework of relationality* where desire and pleasure are seen as sacrosanct. There is, however, one final, more philosophical model I would like to briefly bring into the discussion – and that is feminist new materialism.

FEMINIST NEW MATERIALISM

Feminist new materialism (FNM) offers a novel model of sex based on a radically thought embodied approach to sexual relations. Like embodied autonomy, it addresses the criticism of consent models that rely on the litigation of subjective mental states before and during sex while also attending to how human beings shape meaning through encounters with each other (Barad 2007; Braidotti 2006; Haraway 2004). What differentiates FNM from embodied autonomy is that it makes a radical ontological and epistemological intervention into the realm of sexual norms. The boundaries between inside/outside, nature/culture and self/other are challenged by FNM, thus allowing for an exploration of 'movement, vitality, morphogenesis' where the 'world is not determined; rather it is constantly in the process of its making' (Pitts-Taylor 2016: 4).

Vivian Sobchack makes the case that FNM tries to grapple with the fact that 'despite current academic fetishization of "the body", most theorists still don't quite know what to do with [the] unruly responsive flesh and sensorium' (Sobchack 2004: 59). While contemporary applications of FNM tend to focus on redistributing agency to nonhuman matter – animals, objects, institutions and technologies – it has also been used to examine the subjectivity of the corporal body as it relates to sex. Questions including how subjectivity is enacted and conveyed through expressions of the mindbody during sex draw attention to its situatedness and the difficulty in anticipating desire, pleasure and boundaries in the cut-and-dried ways we might prefer.

Some of the most interesting work in this area has come out of reforms to sex education. Sarah Garland-Levett, in her article 'Knowing-in-being: Traversing the mind/body dualism to dissolve sexuality education's "knowledge/practice gap"', makes the case for a posthuman ethic of knowledge wherein agency emerges in the act of doing. Sexual ethics are thus relational and bodily knowledge is presented as the locus of knowing. She thus advocates for a kind of wholism to be placed front and centre in sex education. By not reducing sex and sex education to either discourse or the corporeal, Garland-Levett uses a desire-focused, unsanitised, anti-didactic and non-outcome-oriented teaching philosophy that addresses some of the constraints of the consent model by 'Drawing on the knowledges that young people identify as meaningful . . . [which] legitimates their potential as sexual subjects' (Garland-Levett 2018: 9).

This includes the discussion of emotions, relationships, power structures, pleasure and gender roles such that 'erotic or embodied knowledge would be acknowledged as an unknowable, changing and constitutive force in sexuality phenomena' (Garland-Levett 2018: 14). A project by Ringrose et al. puts these principles into (creative) practice via a programme in which students are asked to challenge phallocentrism and harmful forms of digital pornography by engaging in conversations around desire, sexual ethics, mattering and toxicity while drawing, sculpting (vaginas) and creating art. This process, the authors attest, 'shift[s] dominance of the phallic referent through revaluing feminine anatomy (not as essentialised, but as differentiated) and encourage[s] resistance to phallic force relations in digital sexual cultures, specifically by responding to and re-mattering girls' experiences' (Ringrose et al. 2019: 260).

As these examples show, FNM offers a pedagogically driven, bottom-up way in which to challenge the subjectivism and patriarchal gender norms in contemporary approaches to sex, desire and permissibility. However, FNM, with some good reason, has also been criticised for being too idealistic, overly esoteric and, as such, lacking in practical means by which to codify and institute its principles into legal practice – or even to establish new norms in a measurable way (Lemke 2015; Braun 2011).

Concrete ways in which to incorporate a race and class analysis into this approach are also lacking. Yet, this turn to the sensory and the everyday is important and can potentially provide a framework through which to rethink sexual relations. From this approach, I take the key insights of relationality, emergence and bodily affect which help inform the new model of sexual ethics I envision.

CONCLUSION, SOME ADDITIONAL REMARKS AND A NEW MODEL

In this chapter I have presented several models of sexual relations ranging from consent *tout court*, affirmative and enthusiastic consent, communicative consent, (embodied) sexual autonomy and integrity, sexual citizenship and feminist new materialism. Each offers a framework from which active, passive and in-between activists and advocates of #MeToo can place their energy. Currently, mainstream #MeToo support has taken to advocating for affirmative and enthusiastic consent with particular importance placed on the need for clear bodily communication to work in conjunction with manifest verbal statements (Brodie 2019; Wilz 2019; Friedman and Valenti 2019). As Rebecca Solnit, writer and feminist activist who is said to have 'predicted' #MeToo, puts it, #MeToo signals the drawing of a line in the sand wherein, going forward, women's voices in all spheres of life will demand to be heard, recognised, and taken seriously. 'This #TimesUp/#MeToo moment', she writes, 'is a revolt for which we have been preparing for decades, or perhaps it's the point at which a long, slow, mostly quiet process suddenly became fast and loud' (Solnit 2018). Affirmative and enthusiastic consent can be seen as the penultimate signifiers of this shift against the endemic social disregard of misogyny and gender-based violence. Women, as expressed through this movement, have become loud, emphatic, agential and assertive.

In this optimistic reading, all of the men outed, shamed, charged, convicted and/or fired as a result of #MeToo have had their comeuppance. From this, space has been cleared for a sexual and potentially legal transformation to take place wherein AC/EC becomes the juridical and socio-cultural norm. Yet, for all of the reasons I have pointed to in this chapter, ranging from its liberalism, solipsism, elision of power relations, structural constraints and failure to deal with the power of gender norms, the hope placed in AC/EC, I contend, is largely misplaced.

THE CARCERAL

There are two further points which speak to this misplacement and help set up the chapters that follow. The first was brought up previously in relation to the carceral-centricity of most of the models of sexual relations discussed thus far. I argue that there is a conspicuous disjuncture that exists between each of these approaches wherein, save for some readings of embodied sexual autonomy and perhaps FNM, the end result of the violation of new sexual consent and autonomy norms will be handled by the police, courts and attendant legal proceedings – albeit under reformed circumstances. My contention, however, is that this is not the only or even the most desirable outcome. Most carceral forms of feminism are founded on highly troubling and ahistorical beliefs around recidivism, justice and survivor enfranchisement (Blatier et al. 2016; Hakimi et al. 2018). #MeToo has taken on an especially carceral position with respect to what is to be done with offenders wherein 'policing, prosecution, and imprisonment' is seen as the best method through which to resolve gender-based violence (Press 2018).

A preliminary conclusion I have reached in light of this is that AC/EC and most, if not all, of the permutations of consent I have outlined above are epistemologically consistent with a carceral approach to justice – which is to say that state-led and juridical methods of dealing with sexual assault and rape are entailed by the norms and behaviours set out in consent-driven models. They are thus ontologically consistent and cohere with one another as they relate to outcomes and values. The violation of consent, whether that refers to an emphatic 'yes means yes' or a slightly less strict definition, sexual self-determination and communicative consent are all premised on a permissible/impermissible binary that works well for the law but fails to capture the complexity of sexual relations. This, however, is not to suggest that survivor-based claims of violation are unfounded or un-litigable. Rather, it is to submit that perhaps we (and by extension #MeToo) have been going about this the wrong way and that dealing with sex- and gender-based violence requires a more nuanced and flexible conception of sexual relations and a significantly less carceral approach to justice. The next chapters are dedicated to setting out this argument.

EXCESS AND OVERWHELM, QUEER SEXUALITY AND BDSM

Briefly, however, before turning to this alternative framework, I would like to set out an important argument that builds on the contention that sex is a unique form of behaviour, action and intention that is resistant to the forms of legal regulation we have been trying to mould it into for centuries. The imbrication of desire, pleasure, risk and variation renders sex, by its very nature, too much for the law and, by extension, underserved by some of the discourses that constitute #MeToo. The two words I have found that best express this resistance are *excess* and *overwhelm*.

Understood through these frameworks, sex is constituted by a non-integrative excess or an excess of signification – which is to say that its meanings and effects are resistant to causal, uniform and linear descriptions called for by the law (Alcoff 2018; Hunter and Cowan 2007). The erotics of sexual excess has been written about at length by psychoanalytic thinkers and queer theorists for whom deviancy, repressed desire and marginality are taken up as they relate to sex specifically, where each is seen as potentially productive (Dean 2003; Goss 2019; Matthis 2018). Brenda Cossman, in her overview and discussion of the affirmation of the sexual abject, describes the excess of sexual relations in the following way:

> In [Leo] Bersani's work, sex involves an annihilation of the self, an undoing of controlled selfhood. He writes of the 'sexual . . . jouissance of exploded limits', in the ways 'that sexual pleasure [which] occurs whenever a certain threshold of intensity is reached, when the organization of the self is momentarily disturbed by sensations or affective processes somehow "beyond" those connected with psychic organization'. (Cossman 2003: 871; see Bersani 2009)

This description of sex in connection with affect, intensity, pleasure and 'annihilation of the self' gets to the crux of sex's desirous inscrutability. Fischel points out the danger of #MeToo continuing to disregard these realities in favour of models that are based on dominance, control and hierarchy. He writes that we need a sexual practice that 'facilitates access for people less privileged by power to risk more and then to "demand better" . . . and, in doing so, "democratize sexual culture"' (Fischel 2019: 382).

Liminality and overwhelm, the other frameworks that depict sex's resistance to easy regulation, capture the elements of risk, discomfort and excitement that render sex libidinally potent in both meaning and intensity. With respect to the liminal-libidinal, Lunceford writes persuasively about the imbrication of shame and excitement that is constitutive of sex wherein

> Bodies in various states of erotic representation in relation to each other, whether gazed upon, touched, or otherwise engaged with, are always in a state marked by the mixed expression of arousal and discomfort. (Lunceford 2012: 143)

This interplay of centripetal and centrifugal sexual forces is further characterised by Saketopoulou as a 'polyamorous psychic economy' that is perpetually in a state of overwhelm, transgression and pleasurable dysregulation. I quite like this description since it gets right to the heart of what #MeToo and other frameworks of sexual regulation and description have failed to grapple with – namely, sex's relation to surprise and its 'too-muchness' which limits the feasibility of fully transparent communication, linearity and equitable relations of power (Saketopoulou 2019).

Law, marriage, heterosexuality and the criminalisation of eroticism are some of the myriad ways in which this excess is regulated. Put in Derridian terms, sex disrupts law's closure and has been historically dealt with in kind (Derrida 1992, 1999). With respect to race, the connection between excess and racialised Otherness is that they are both framed as sexually excessive and in need of restraint. The hypersexualisation of Black men and women, wherein the former is to be feared and the latter perpetually available, is consistent with further forms of Otherness construction through which perceived sexual excess is named and regulated. This 'continued emphasis on Black bodies as inherently aggressive, hypersexual, and violent', and the attendant 'concern with taming and controlling Black males' (Ferber 2007: 11; Collins 2004), works in tandem with the historical hyperregulation of sexual minorities for whom state-led regulation and self-imposed bioregulation is experienced through violent and non-violent practices of 'exclusion, disempowerment and unrecognition directed at homo-variant others' (Grant 2018: 701; see also Cooper 2006).

Third wave feminism, queer activism and BDSM are three notable movements that have been at least partially successful in capturing this dysregulation without focusing solely on the law (Kukla 2018; Bauer 2014; Ivanski and Kohut 2017). Sex positivity is an ethico-political position that formed as a reaction against radical feminist criticism of pornography and sex work. It explicitly 'advocate[s] for the liberalization of female (and queer) sexuality through transgressive sexual acts' with an eye towards sexual liberation via the destigmatisation of female pleasure and sexuality (Ivanski and Kohut 2017: 216; see also Glick 2000). Sex positivity calls for diversity in sexual expression wherein 'all consensual expressions of sexuality are [seen as] valid' (Kimmes et al. 2015: 289). It also draws on the language of sexual autonomy and self-determination to make the case that without positive freedoms, women will continue to be left to re-experience sexual shame and persist in the practice of sexual self-censorship.

Queer theory, while similar to some forms of sex positive feminism vis-à-vis sexual expression, focuses explicitly on the free expression of sexual identity or identities and has arguably provided even more space to cultivate practices of sexual negotiation that are novel, non-normative and pleasure-centred. Queer practices, as Carlström and Andersson maintain, produce 'non-normative communities that can counter societal norms of heteronormativity, monogamy, and vanilla sex' using practices that are self-reflexive, generative and community-based (Carlström and Andersson 2019: 18). Non-binarised queer sex 'exceeds' the traditional and the homonormative by opening up space for dissent while also acknowledging the existence of 'spectrums of consent' by drawing on 'notions of affirmative consent and rhetorics of pleasure' (Edenfield 2019: 50; Mortimer-Sandilands and Erickson 2010; Taylor and Blaise 2017).

Finally, theoretical and ethnographical research on BDSM describes how BDSM participants have managed to capture and incorporate sexual affective excess while also retaining a model of pro forma communicative consent. Some have even put forth BDSM-based consent guidelines, inclusive of safe words and the articulation of clear boundaries, as a standard to replicate in everyday sexual practice:

> Communication and negotiation is an integral part of the majority of kink/BDSM interactions . . . Participants in kink or BDSM activities usually set aside time to communicate before their interactions, and these discussions can cover anything including STD status and safer sex methods that will be used, the type of play/interaction that will take place . . . (Kattari 2015: 887)

BDSM demands a level of trust and self-awareness in order to balance the 'exuberant intimacy' it encourages within a universe that is safe and accessible (Truscott 1991; Bauer 2014).

Cumulatively, however, while these three movements offer some salient and insightful ways in which to balance autonomy, self-determination and consent with sexual pleasure (such that danger and pleasure are not seen as mutually exclusive), their integration into everyday life and legal jurisprudence is another matter. To begin with, forms of sex positivity have been around since the 1960s and, as a general movement towards pleasurable sex for all involved, are not particularly objectionable. Yet, in its more radical manifestations, sex positivity demands a fundamental restructuring of gender norms and sexual mores that could yet gain cultural traction but, in the end, still may not go far enough. Second, queer iterations of sexual overwhelm are also conceptually and analytically compelling but remain inimical to a legal framework in which binaries, hierarchies and hard and fast rules are par for the course. Finally, BDSM is a localised subcultural movement and grouping whose norms and mores may work on a local level (i.e. as it relates to specific sexual practices) but are unlikely to 'fit' with the sex of everyday life. Scholarly and activist iterations of #MeToo have drawn on each of these frameworks to push for socio-legal changes in the form of codified AC/EC and sexual autonomy, the explicit challenging of sexual and gender scripts in law (and especially in the courtroom), and a much more progressive view of sex (Fileborn and Loney-Howes 2019; Hsu 2019; Newman and Haire 2019; Brittney Cooper 2018). The failure of the carceral to address and mitigate gender-based violence, I contend, is at least in part a result of its inability to grapple with the experience of sex as an *embodied*, *relational* and *boundary-resisting* act.

A NEW APPROACH

It is from this that I propose an approach that borrows from the best parts of the models articulated above including their focus on communication, autonomy, relationality, embodiment, pleasure and transgression. I consider these to be leading 'key words' which, when taken together, form the building blocks of a more capacious, just and exploratory conception of sex that attends to the concerns raised by #MeToo as well as to the shortcomings of the criminal justice system. This approach also addresses the realities of sex as a practice that pushes up against and explodes normative regulation. Because sex is contradictory, ever changing, 'excessive', risky and bound up by unequal power relations, I argue that it requires less of a hard and fast framework and more of a conjunctural set of principles or a sexual assemblage (drawing from FNM). The risk of this approach is that it violates every scholarly and norm-driven impulse to define, set out principles and articulate boundaries. Yet this tradition of doing so, as evidenced by #MeToo and abysmal criminal justice clear-up statistics and survivor satisfaction rates, has not worked (Gray and Horvath 2018; Mayer 2018).

My project aims to find a way to think about sex that is discursive – that is, articulatable and definable – but also attends to bodies, matter and the non-rational. Put another way, I argue that we must think of sex simultaneously as a discourse – that is, something we construct and thus can reconstruct – and as a material practice (McCracken 2013; Haraway 2001). This is a very difficult balance to achieve and ill-suited to our current legal institutions. It is the co-construction of our criminal justice system with the models of consent, autonomy and communication I have described that helped to produce the violations exposed by #MeToo and our fractured sexual culture. As such, instead of definitional rules, it may be necessary to think about sexuality as a culture and ask both what it is and what we would like it to be. #MeToo brings to the fore a myriad of often justifiable complaints about rape culture which is constituted, in the context of sex, by unequal power relations, unfair gender roles and scripts, and the decentring of women's agency and pleasure (Harding 2015). Miller and Biele describe rape culture as present when 'sexual violence is sanctioned, at worst taught, and at best excused' (Miller and Biele 1993: 51), and which emerges out of a context in which 'sexual violence is a fact of life, inevitable as death or taxes' (Buchwald, Fletcher and Roth 1993: x). While the merits of describing our current society as consistent with this definition are contested (since it potentially leads to a form of feminism that is carceral and dictated from above), what I suggest is that its saliency in the cultural zeitgeist points to and is illuminative of the contradictions I have discussed throughout this chapter. These contradictions – or perhaps we can refer to them as 'ever widening disjunctures between idealisations and reality' – are rooted in the fact that each of the models of sexuality, no matter how deliberate, well-defined, normatively progressive, egalitarian and inclusive (mind and body, intersectional, etc.), has been unable to successfully cultivate a fulfilling and mutually favourable sexual culture.

As a response, the model I propose can be described as a '*pleasure and care-centred ethic of embodied and relational sexual Otherness*'. It is a mouthful, and could probably be made more pithy by an apt creator of sharp neologisms, but it is the most robust and capacious phrase I could come up with that adequately incorporates and reflects the myriad interrelated elements at hand. This framework, while largely socio-cultural, also has the potential to address issues of justice, offence and harm which I take up in the next chapter and in the case studies. It also contains within it a solidaristic ethic of care and Otherness that is foundational. By ethic, I mean a set of values that are 'internal and literally embodied . . . derived from the practice of intentionally turning toward immediate experience in a very special way' (Grossman 2015: 18). It is this immediacy of embodied experience, I argue, that must take centre stage.

A useful way to think about sex in terms of a 'pleasure and care-centred ethic of embodied and relational sexual Otherness' is, ontologically, as a sexual assemblage. I define sexual assemblages as made up of bodies, technologies, norms, laws, intensities and flows that, by definition, assume no prior unity or stability. They only become legible as an experience that can be reflected upon and judged through intentional stabilisations of messy interactions (Barad 2007, 2014). As such, assemblages reflect 'emerging tension and problems' and produce 'partially connected theories' through which entities acquire their form, efficacy and meaning by virtue of their position within a relational configuration (Anderson et al. 2012; Bennett 2005; Latour 2005). Because they centre the body, sexual assemblages refuse to be subordinated to 'consciousness or to biological organizations' since bodies, particularly in interaction, are by definition illogical and discordant (Grosz 1994: 165). Moreover, assemblages, and the humans, nonhumans, norms, institutions, assumptions and values that constitute them, are not seamless – they change, are anti-didactic, and are thus more consistent with the idea of sex as a practice that is similarly constructed. It is when we engage in forcing a momentary stabilisation of the sexual assemblage and disentangle its various elements that we can then consider whether it fits with the admittedly non-normative model of a 'pleasure and care-centred ethic of embodied and relational sexual Otherness' I propose.

Before delving into an even more detailed explanation of this model, it is important to point out that sexual assemblages challenge the simple binaries of nature/culture, yes/no, autonomous/dependent and communicative/silent on a meta-level. Vis-à-vis #MeToo, this brings with it considerable difficulties as it relates to what the law and movements like #MeToo value the most – namely, verifiable truths and transparent and accessible knowledge. Yet, I contend that a 'pleasure and care-centred ethic of embodied and relational sexual Otherness' is capable of providing a basis on which to build an ethic of sex that is desirous, pleasurable, anti-racist and anti-homophobic, while attending to and being cognisant of the larger social order and the need for a means by which to adjudicate truth claims.

In the first instance, a 'pleasure and care-centred ethic of embodied and relational sexual Otherness' calls for pleasure and care to be central. Crucially, under this definition, pleasure can be expressed either verbally or bodily, can include pleasurable subordination, and must encompass sexual practices that are nonheteronormative. Moreover, pleasure need not be interpreted solely as immediate bodily pleasure, thus allowing for sex that takes place as a matter of routine or functionality (to conceive, for example). It also leaves space for sex that is not necessarily pleasurable but agreed to (as in the case of sex work) which, I contend, should be assessed separately from the kind of sex that takes place in the context of intimate partner relations. Significantly, pleasure can encompass more than arousal to include excitement, intensity, drama and even danger since, as Franke maintains, it is 'the proximity to danger, the lure of prohibition, the seamy side of shame that creates the heat that draws us toward our desires, and that makes desire and pleasure so resistant to rational explanation' (Franke 2001: 207). Finally, consistent with the previous discussion of overwhelm and excess, the definition of pleasure operative here should be understood capaciously in order to make room for not just non-representational exuberant sex but also pleasant sex and 'bad' but ethically permissible sex (which speaks to the Aziz Ansari case), and to balance the realities of sex with the need for norms upon which to gauge wrongness. This complexity involved in disentangling these threads from any sexual assemblage is, I contend, best served not by traditional policing and adversarial litigation, but with practices of restorative justice.

Definitionally, apart from pleasure, this more formative conception of sexual ethics must incorporate relations of self-care wherein self-care is understood not as self-indulgent acts of consumerism, although it can encompass this, but as a relational and reflexive mode of being. It delimits 'the normative principles to which care is articulated, such as sensitivity, trust, generosity, empathy, and commitment . . . [for] desire and pleasure' and features 'responsibility, responsiveness and attentiveness, configured in differently gendered ways as caring for, taking care' (Cooper 2007: 245–6; see also Held 2006; Calogero and Siegel 2019). Another useful way of thinking about self-care through this lens is in terms of pleasure activism in which sexual self-care acts as a form of reclamation that takes on a political valence in that it allows women in particular to reclaim their sexual selves from repressive structures and move towards relations that are just and mutually pleasurable (Rodriguez and Piepzna-Samarasinha 2019).

Also part of this approach is an ethic of communication that, if deemed necessary by the parties involved (e.g. in the case of BDSM and sex work), sets the baseline of agreement, establishes boundaries and, if necessary, attends to problematic power dynamics. In everyday sex, this ethic may not feature as a core part of the enacted sexual assemblage if, for example, sex is occurring between a committed couple for whom a pattern of sexual reciprocity has been established. This communication need not be burdensome or legalistic or even just verbal. Embodied communication expressed through a myriad of bodily cues is perfectly acceptable. I would challenge arguments expressing concern about miscommunication and the inability to recognise cues as largely misplaced given Kitzinger and Frith's important empirical research on the subject. Through interviews and conversational analysis, they demonstrate that 'both men and women have a sophisticated ability to convey and to comprehend refusals, including refusals which do not include the word "no"' (Kitzinger and Frith 1999: 295; see also Ehrlich 1998).

Otherness in this model encompasses two primary dispositions. First, Otherness as a value reflects structures and beliefs that seek to regulate non-normativity and, with respect to respectable sexuality, tends to 'give hyper-focus to the [perceived] misdeeds of women, queer persons, persons of colour, and other marginalised individuals' (McCann 2018: 186). As such, sex from this vantage point of Otherness is more than just discrete acts and laws that seek to regulate said acts while also being constituted by both of these things. What makes sexuality unique (or 'Other') is that it involves two, or more, individuals engaged in an emergent and co-constituted act, namely sex with an Other, that involves '*poignant* body sensations . . . is *excessive* of normal functioning, of work rationality and purposefulness, and even of containment; and, finally . . . is *enigmatic*, being based on the mystery of the desired other's unconscious intentions and the mystified longings they call forth in our embodied mind' (Stein 2008: 46–7). This element of Otherness takes account of sex as an activity as well as its diverse permutations (wherein boundaries are drawn between what is and is not permissible) and the social desire to curtail anything considered outside of the norm.

The other aspect of sexual Otherness embedded in the 'pleasure and care-centred ethic of embodied and relational sexual Otherness' I propose reflects our epistemic obligation to the Other. Elizabeth Anderson refers to this as an act of mutual recognition that affirms attraction in the first instance but also the humanity of the Other. Anderson articulates this in line with the conception of the gift, an important sociological concept that focuses on mutual recognition and supports a non-instrumental conception of sexuality as 'a shared good. The couple rejoices in their *union*, which can be realized only when each partner reciprocates the other's gift *in kind*, offering her own sexuality in the same spirit in which she received the other's – as a genuine offering of the self' (Anderson 1995: 154). Where I part ways with Anderson, however, is on the subject of sex work, which she contends 'destroys' this reciprocity.

The final elements of the framework of a 'pleasure and care-centred ethic of embodied and relational sexual Otherness' are those of embodiment and relationality. Consistent with the explanations given above, an embodied approach to sex requires a healthy scepticism towards AC and EC's insistence on a clarity of intentionality and desire often associated with a 'yes means yes' conception of sexual relations. It also rejects the 'sacred status' customarily extended to the liberal, self-sufficient and sovereign subject (Chen-Wishart 2006: 231). Embodied sexuality, to be clear, is multidimensional and affective, requiring an understanding of the ways in which sex is social, gendered and driven as much by the body, in terms of pleasure and desire, as by the mind (Paechter 2006; Alldred and David 2007).

Sociality or relationality (re 'relational sexual Otherness' – as per the definition) necessitates, in the first instance, that for robust, engaging and mutually beneficial sex to take place it must occur under conditions that are flexible, malleable and dynamic. Also required is an understanding that

> persons are socially embedded and that agents' identities are formed within the context of social relationships and shaped by a complex of intersecting social determinants, such as race, class, gender, and ethnicity. (Mackenzie and Stoljar 2000: 4)

This is the dimension of my framework or definition (a 'pleasure and care-centred ethic of embodied and relational sexual Otherness') that engages in how relations of power and experiences of marginalisation shape whether, how and under what conditions sexual relations take place. It draws attention to the fact that sex often occurs in a context of inequality that will need to be negotiated by participants. With respect to adjudication and assessment after the fact (if there is an allegation of assault), each case will have to be assessed in context, which is something reparative and restorative justice allows for. Relationality also asserts that in order to develop one's autonomy, an Other is necessary since self-creation can only occur in context and through a process of co-determination. This requires a shift in thinking such that interdependent and reciprocal relationality takes centre stage. Relationality's open and generative ethos is in keeping with the limit testing realities of sex and provides an opening to explore the kinds of transgressive sex more normative models make difficult.

Taken together, the elements that hold together this particular assemblage of sexual relations, namely a 'pleasure and care-centred ethic of embodied and relational sexual Otherness', can be distilled into a number of bullet points. Note that I do this reticently, as this is a rather reductive approach, but it is useful as a form of shorthand for the case studies. Thus, I would think of these as a set of heuristics meant to serve as a quick and accessible means by which to assess and judge specific instances of sexual violation.

A pleasure and care-centred ethic of embodied and relational sexual Otherness:

1. Understands that all sexual acts are formed out of assemblages, i.e. bodies, technologies, norms, laws, intensities that are judged through 'cuts' made by individuals (where these cuts shape how they are judged, are contingent on context, and are value-laden);
2. Agrees that sex must centre mutual pleasure and care for self and Other while leaving room for transactional sex (i.e. sex work) and everyday sex;
3. Prima facie accepts sexual practices that push 'queer' boundaries and understands sex as an unbounded practice best characterised by the French word *jouissance* which captures its risky, excessive, energetic and frenetic dimensions (Laplanche 1976; Stein 2008);
4. Requires an ethic of communication manifest, for example, through the discussion of boundaries. This can be communicated verbally or via bodily cues;
5. Centres an orientation to the Other understood as the Other with whom you are co-constituting the sexual act, general sexual Otherness, and the Other whom you have an epistemic obligation to recognise as an ethical subject;
6. Reflects how sex is an embodied, as opposed to solipsistic, practice that is also relational, co-determinative (rather than individualistic) and contextual – thereby requiring an accounting of unequal power relations.

These six principles form the foundation on which I examine the forthcoming #MeToo-related case studies with respect to the values, conventions, sexual and gender scripts, and legal norms expressed through traditional and social media coverage, litigation (if there is any) and the specific acts themselves. Doing so requires making a robust case for the 'pleasure and care-centred ethic of embodied and relational sexual Otherness' as an ideal (as in optimal) model of sexual relations that borrows from several of the approaches discussed above but also attends to their shortcomings. This includes challenging the solipsism of liberal subjectivity, accounting for unequal power relations, making room for sex work, avoiding over-proscription, and accounting for how sex takes place in everyday life.

As an ideal-typical framework, this framework, as in all models, is rarely perfectly enacted. It can, however, act as a lodestar of sorts adjacent to, but not a substitute for, legal norms. One of the core theses I am proposing in this book is one of anti-codification wherein justice is achieved through restorative and reparative alternatives. It is to these alternatives I will shortly turn. The central question I hope to answer is that, given our current legal framework's inability to serve women legally or ethically when it comes to gender-based violence, what is the alternative? As I have demonstrated, none of the models of sexual relations discussed above, whether it is consent, AC/EC, communicative consent, sexual autonomy and so on, is able to fully express human sexuality as it operates in practice – which is challenging when they form the foundation of law. In the next chapter I provide an overview of #MeToo, beginning with whisper networks, before moving on to discuss and explore the ability of restorative justice to address survivor harm, repair frayed (community) relations and identities, reach an outcome that is survivor-centred, and attend to and transform the root causes of gender-based violence – none of which our current legal system has been able to do.

3. #MeToo Past and Future

In this chapter, I provide further background into the genesis of MeToo as a movement and a hashtag. In doing so, I touch on earlier iterations of MeToo-adjacent movements and phenomena including so-called whisper networks, #TimesUp, the controversy around #BelieveAllWomen, and who #MeToo leaves out.

#MeToo began in 2007 with activist Tarana Burke's 'empowerment through empathy' programme aimed at young, racialised and marginalised survivors of sexual assault. For Burke, MeToo provided a collective space for young women to share their stories and gain power and heal through community. In an interview with *The Nation*, she argues that there

> is nothing as powerful as knowing that you are not alone. The sooner young women understand that they are not an anomaly, the sooner they can begin their healing process. This is at the heart of the MeToo movement. Survivors reaching out to those who don't understand they are survivors – and helping them to feel whole again. (Burke as cited by Adetiba 2017)

The iteration of #MeToo we are most familiar with, however, began with actress Alyssa Milano, who in 2017, in response to the allegations of assault from dozens of women against Harvey Weinstein as well as the video of President Donald Trump describing how he felt free to 'grab women by the pussy', encouraged women to take to Twitter and share their experiences of sexual harassment and assault using the MeToo hashtag. Soon thereafter, #MeToo went viral with millions of self-identifying women around the world sharing stories of being catcalled, gaslit, assaulted, stalked, harassed and raped by men (Rodino-Colocino 2018; Pellegrini 2018). As the hashtag and media interest intensified, allegations against other high-profile men from Hollywood (Kevin Spacey, Jeffrey Tambor), legacy media (Charlie Rose, Matt Lauer), the restaurant industry (John Besh, Mario Batali), sport (Larry Nassar) and politics (Roy Moore, Al Franken) emerged.

#TimesUp, which I discuss further below, was organised by several Hollywood actresses in light of #MeToo to help marginalised women access the funds they needed to protect their interests in the workplace. Awards ceremonies like the Oscars featured women activists spearheading the movement, which created even more awareness. As I write this, according to *Vox*, 262 celebrities, politicians, CEOs and others have been accused of sexual misconduct since that first tweet (*Vox* 2020).

Yet, there were – and continue to be – concerns from the political right and left about the #MeToo movement on a number of levels, including that it might encourage overpolicing and juridical overreach in ways that infringe on privacy and enforce heternormative sexuality. Other fears include that due process is not being afforded to those accused (e.g. the case of Al Franken), that #MeToo will disproportionately impact racialised men, and that the majority of women are still being left out of the conversation (Onwuachi-Willig 2018). These tensions are still being fought over in the media and online and I discuss many of these criticisms in subsequent chapters (Dadas 2020; Greene et al. 2019; Airey 2018). Overall, #MeToo remains a strong and increasingly institutionalised media and political phenomenon whose impact on society continues to be felt.

WHISPER NETWORKS

#MeToo can also be read as an extension of older so-called 'whisper networks'. These networks consisted of communicative, largely occupational chains that writer Jia Tolentino describes as 'unofficial information channel[s] that women use to warn each other about men whose sexual behaviour falls on the spectrum from creepy to criminal'. They are accusatory rather than evidentiary but function as 'relatively orderly reporting methods, regulated by the direct accountability of a social ecosystem: if I give you false information, then my credibility and relationships will suffer' (Tolentino 2017). As such, whisper networks, as well as the allegations that constitute #MeToo, are qualitatively distinct from rumour and gossip since their impact is significantly higher for both the accuser and the accused.

Rumour and gossip can be qualitatively distinguished from whisper networks on a number of levels. As DiFonzo and Bordia argue, 'Rumours are unverified and potentially useful information statements in circulation that arise in ambiguous, threatening and potentially threatening contexts that help people make sense and manage threat' (DiFonzo and Bordia 2007: 27). Which is to say that rumours tend to be public, have a sociological function (e.g. the potential to propel social change), but lack any obligatory proof (Spacks 2012; Fine 2007). Gossip, on the other hand, 'is evaluative social chat about individuals that arises in the context of forming, changing or maintaining social networks, and functions to inform, bond, exclude, enhance status and convey social norms' (DiFonzo and Bordia 2007: 28).

Gossip is often gendered and relegated to the private sphere while also functioning as a mechanism of in-group connectivity (Spacks 2012; VanHaitsma 2016).

The first publicised whisper network, as chronicled in Tuerkheimer's article 'Unofficial reporting in the #MeToo era', was the 'Glass Ceiling Club', a group of female investment bankers who, in the 1990s, met to share information about men to avoid – particularly on the trading floor (Tuerkheimer 2019b). Another case involves renowned architect Richard Meier, who had been the subject of a whisper network with women sharing information about his abuse for decades (Monk 2020). *The New York Times*, in a 1990 article about university assaults, wrote about how rape victims, feeling 'helpless with the judicial system', had carved their 'rapist's names on the bathroom wall' in an attempt to educate 'students about potentially dangerous situations early' (Ellis 1994: 14). In each of these cases, what is notable is that communication about these men occurs largely face to face, with some degree of anonymity, and a level of community boundedness in terms of who has access to the information.

For #MeToo, the boundedness of its networks is exponentially more lax and anonymity is difficult to maintain (there is often a digital and rapidly sharable ledger). Consequently, the number of women, and some men, involved tends to be higher. A paradigmatic case involves writer Moira Donegan, creator of what has come to be known as the 'Shitty Media Men' list, who identified herself to *New York Magazine* in 2018 as the author of a list which collated, into a public Google spreadsheet, 'allegations of assault, harassment, and "creepy behaviour" of male coworkers' in Hollywood which allowed 'viewers to [anonymously] add their own accusations to the spreadsheet' (Liu 2017: 939). The fallout of the document's existence, as well as the identity of its author, led to a surge in think pieces, academic articles and socio-political intrigue, with responses ranging from unmitigated support to admonishment for the lack of due process afforded to the men on the list (Jaffe 2018; Cavalieri 2019; Young 2020).

A similar controversy in India erupted around the production and digital circulation of a list of male academics to avoid, called LoSHA (List of Sexual Harassers in Academia). The list itself was curated and published in a private Facebook group by Raya Sarkar, a queer, anti-caste Dalit activist. When the list went public, the same arguments were circulated around the anonymity of the accusers and the lack of 'due process and natural justice' afforded to those accused, as well as concerns around the 'lumping together of different degrees of harassment without nuance' (dos Santos Bruss 2020: 4; Gajjala,

Vemuri and Sarkar 2019). What is most notable about this example of a digital whisper network is that, unlike the 'bad media men' list, and despite the fact that it also features and centres the experience of women inhabiting an elite space, the activism around LoSHA aims specifically at the experiences of the most marginalised women (Dalits). LoSHA has since been engaged in forms of feminist activism focusing on 'critiquing Brahmanical (and other) heteronormative patriarchies on a systemic level and allow[ing] subaltern positionalities to become authors of their own narratives and connect in solidarity and care' (dos Santos Bruss 2020: 8). Its place within what has come to be known as Dalit-Adivasi-Bahugjan (DAB) feminism and its queerness distinguishes this list from Moira Donegan's.

What is most important about these lists is that the arguments for and against them are synonymous with those that are attached to #MeToo generally. They include fears of false allegations, job loss and social opprobrium as well as tensions between slander and free speech, the right to challenge allegations, the anonymity of the accusers (i.e. not being able to confront one's accusers) and the absence of tangible evidence and proof (Burgess 2018; Pastras 2018).

In an article for the *National Review*, a politically right-wing news magazine with conservative views on #MeToo, Hernroth-Rothstein summarises these concerns by asserting that, 'If a person is the victim of a crime, that crime should be reported and the accused should have a right to face his or her accuser. This to avoid a trial-by-mob, and to keep people from losing their jobs and having their reputations ruined by a hashtag rather than proof and due process.' As such, she argues, 'if sexual harassment is a crime, it should be fought not with hashtags but with the full force of the law.' She concludes that 'we should criticize the justice system when it fails, but we must follow due process when it comes to crimes, because if we don't, everyone will suffer' (Hernroth-Rothstein 2017).

These critiques of whisper networks and #MeToo rely on a vision of sacrosanct individual liberties and due process and often support punitive and carceral justice. Interestingly, there has been some movement towards the position that women (and society) should forgive their assailants – particularly famous ones who, ostensibly, just 'made a mistake'. Notably, this expectation of forgiveness is rarely the outcome of reparative action, a heartfelt apology or an authentic mea culpa that includes some kind of engagement with the movement, but, rather, reflects the opinion that the movement has gone too far (Kurtz 2018; Goodman 2018; Williams 2019). This has been asked of women involved in high-profile cases where the men are accused of some form of violence or sexual trespass, whether it be Louis C.K. and Aziz Ansari on one end of the spectrum or Matt Lauer and Charlie Rose on the other. Other questions include: will they (the accused) be invited back into polite society? Will they be permitted to resume their jobs? And, this is a long one, are their 'cancellations' illustrative of a kind of mob justice that undermines traditional modes of redress and results in a process void that does not serve the survivor or the accused? (Tuerkheimer 2019a). Writer Emily Yoffe, in an article about the case of journalist Jonathan Kaiman who was accused of sexual badgering, pressure and general misbehaviour, articulates this perspective succinctly when she states: 'We are now in a time when the uncertain circumstances surrounding one regretted sexual encounter and another hazily remembered (and fiercely disputed) intimate encounter are sufficient to destroy the accused's life' (Yoffe 2019).

More politically progressive women have also communicated concerns related to fairness and due process, like actress Catherine Deneuve who argues that the movement is little more than a puritanical witch-hunt inimical to French norms (Willsher 2018). Those in support of the movement argue that the law has always been gendered, classed and applied unequally and point out the myriad ways in which women have been gaslit by authorities. One reason for this is because their accounts and allegations are often inconsistent with prevailing cultural scripts around how a victim should act (Baker 2001; Pipyrou 2018; Quixley 2018). Not only are the survivor's behaviour, clothes and past relationship with the assailant put under scrutiny, but, as Larcombe argues, it is done so in a way that, particularly in the context of rape, litigates proper 'resistance and . . . [forces survivors to] re-experience domination and the (attempted) denial of her reality and subjective sense of self' (Larcombe 2002: 146).

Internet justice can be seen as the last resort of those consistently let down by the law, society and increasingly hostile online spaces. As such, I refer to these online confessional-cum-nodes-of-resistance as functioning as a form of *cathartic justice* that stands in opposition to the Foucauldian conception of the confessional as a site of discipline and dominant subjectivity (Foucault 1980). That is, digital spaces can function as a reparative, communal, agential and consciousness-raising tool. The heterogeneity of #MeToo's early posts are illustrative of this initial inclusivity. As Bennett contends, it is largely the case that the more diverse the mobilisation, the more personalised the expressions, drawing on 'communication technologies that allow individuals to activate their loosely tied social networks' (Bennett 2012: 21).

In the most optimistic reading, these digital spaces afford #MeToo survivors room to recoup lost agency, gain support, engender action, and become part of a community that encourages the vocalisation of trauma (Gong 2015; Gash and Harding 2018). According to scholars like McDonald, 'The #MeToo movement has encouraged victims to break their silence about the abuse they have suffered' through social media platforms that empower 'individuals by giving them a voice. It thus provides a forum where people can disclose their sexual assault, connect with allies, and secure resources' (McDonald 2019: 79).

This reading of the #MeToo hashtag is in keeping with the feminist practice of 'displac[ing] and provok[ing] the spectator, making him or her aware of the process of experience . . . [and] precluding the spectator's identification with the illusionary and ideological functions of representation' (Bonner 2019: 41). Put another way, it challenges those viewing the posts to address and make sense of said statements with a kind of urgency and immediacy aided by their short, in-your-face and dispositive format.

It should be emphasised that, empirically, the rates of false allegations vis-à-vis gendered violence is negligible (Johnson and Taylor Jr 2018; Lisak et al. 2010). Moreover, due process is technically only required in relation to state action and officially criminalised behaviours – not harassment (Cossman 2019; Gersen and Suk 2016). #TimesUp, the associated movement that aims to provide legal and monetary support for survivors to pursue redress through the courts, is important here. Started by female celebrities in early 2018, #TimesUp's objective is to directly address issues around fair pay, harassment and workplace equity not only in the rarefied spaces of Hollywood, but also amongst service workers, immigrant women and, generally, those left out of #MeToo (Di Leonardo 2018; Fiebrich 2019). This focus on litigation, however, has been criticised for not addressing the root causes of rape, harassment and other forms of gender-based violence like misogyny, patriarchy, gender norms and institutional gender bias, and for relying on a justice system that itself embodies many of these same values and norms.

#BELIEVEALLWOMEN

One of the most fraught slogans from the #MeToo movement, out of which a lot of controversy has emerged, is that of #BelieveAllWomen, or, in its first instantiation, #BelieveWomen. This hashtag has become a locus of tensions as it relates to claims of sexual assault and misbehaviour made by women against prominent men. The use of the 'believe women' hashtag was originally meant to act as a discursive jab aimed at characterising how rape and sexual assault survivors had been treated – namely, as suspect, unreliable, and whose testimony lacked the power, reason and veracity to be believed on its own merits. The cases of Bill Cosby and Harvey Weinstein drew the double standard around the belief accorded to victims in all other sexual crimes into stark relief. A flurry of media debates followed each case, with Emily Lindin (2017), a writer for *Teen Vogue*, arguing that given the past casting of women as liars, she was not particularly concerned with the prospect that a few innocent men could be falsely accused. More conservative columnists like Bari Weiss, on the other hand, took the position that this was not acceptable, arguing that the

> 'believe all women' vision of feminism unintentionally fetishizes women. Women are no longer human and flawed. They are Truth personified. They are above reproach. I believe that it's condescending to think that women and their claims can't stand up to interrogation and can't handle skepticism. I believe that facts serve feminists far better than faith. That due process is better than mob rule. (Weiss 2017)

The fear that these hashtags could end up deifying women and, in doing so, rob them of the agency to lie, to be deceitful and to commit crimes is both persuasive and troubling. Even progressive feminists like Rebecca Traister felt these hashtags about women and belief were a bit clumsy and might result in the trivialising of women's testimony (Traister 2020). However, Monica Hesse, in *The Washington Post*, characterises the transformation of #BelieveWomen to #BelieveAllWomen as 'a bit of rhetorical gaslighting' meant to render absolutist a slogan that is intended to rectify the past recasting of women as unworthy of their own due process (Hesse 2020). Both hashtags gained even more traction during the hearing of now Supreme Court Justice Brett Kavanaugh and the testimony given by Professor Christine Blasey Ford, who made allegations of sexual assault against him. These hashtags were also trending during the height of the allegations made against Joe Biden by the less performatively pristine Tara Reade. Feminist Susan Faludi, in an op-ed for *The New York Times*, argued that the transmogrification of #BelieveWomen into #BelieveAllWomen is not only quite recent, but is actually used mostly by critics of #MeToo in order to absolutise a nuanced sentiment. She writes: 'This is why "Believe All Women" is not an amplification of "Believe Women," but its negation . . . Believing women is simply the rejoinder to the ancient practice of #DoubtWomen' (Faludi 2020).

It is notable that the preceding public and mediated conversations about believing women are monopolised entirely by white voices, lending even more evidence to the critique of #MeToo as a specifically white feminist project. Tarana Burke, as the Black founder of the MeToo campaign and hashtag, however, chose to co-found and lend backing to the BelieveSurvivors hashtag and, with a host of progressive groups like Planned Parenthood, led a protest, walkout and Twitter campaign against Justice Kavanaugh's Supreme Court nomination. In a public letter to Blasey Ford, Burke and others wrote,

> This letter is our love offering to her so that she has a constant reminder that there is enormous support for her and other survivors like her . . . We heard her. We saw her. And we believed her. (Me Too 2019)

Yet, Burke has also been clear she does not advocate for the a priori and unquestioning belief of everything a woman says. In this way, she attends to the concerns brought up by Weiss and Traistor. For Burke, 'when we say we believe survivors, it's not believe them without investigation. Believe them without interrogation. We have set a precedent in this country of not believing . . . thinking that women in particular are lying when they come forward with these allegations' (Burke as cited by Wexler 2018).

Taken together, these tensions, particularly over the past three years, have coalesced around several discursive threads inclusive of (1) the extent to which women have been and should be believed; (2) the historical dismissal of women's voices; (3) the impunity with which some men have used their power against women; and (4) the impulse to protect and uphold due process at all costs. This has led to a bit of a stalemate on the extent to which women as a marginalised group should have their allegations 'believed' at face value, which is odd given the extremely low rate of false allegations and the need for a historical corrective of past injustices (Jackson, Bailey and Welles 2019; Jordan 2004). Aubri McDonald draws attention to the normalisation of sexual assault and the endemic scepticism survivor allegations engender. #Believewomen, she argues, acts as a prognostic frame that propagates the discussion of possible solutions and, in its most generous reading, simply embeds a normative symmetry into the true/false binary (McDonald 2019). However, #BelieveWomen and #BelieveAllWomen are also indicative of wider social apprehensions about how power, sexuality, gender and veracity function in an adversarial legal system and culture in which complex actions often become reduced to a 'he said, she said' back and forth.

It bears repeating that in spite of the salient and persuasive demand for due process for the accused, this right only extends to formal legal proceedings. Our use of this kind of language speaks to an obsession with a form of 'law talk' that extends beyond the courtroom. As Lesley Wexler argues, 'participants in the #MeToo conversation often deploy legal definitions of victims and perpetrators, reference legal standards of proof and the role of legal forums, [and] draw explicit or implicit comparisons to legal punishments.' While this might empower survivors within the system to name, self-identify and self-advocate, it also risks 'crowd[ing] out non-legal conversations and concerns' while also perpetuating the 'mistaken belief . . . that a specific law governs a situation when it does not' (Wexler 2019: 343–4). This is particularly applicable in relation to #MeToo conversations in digital spaces wherein law talk dominates but is not always apposite vis-à-vis the requirements of due process, corroboration and evidentiary proof.

As I have discussed previously, and will do so further in the chapter on restorative justice, it bears repeating that the premise of believing women and their allegations of rape and sexual assault cannot be extricated from the history of false accusations made against Black men under slavery and the way in which rape law was used as a brutal form of policing. Not only were allegations of rape instrumentally used by white women caught in illicit relationships with Black men, but, as Donovan argues, attendant '[s]tories of animalistic African Americans raping white women [also] provided a powerful rationale for racial violence' and overpolicing (Donovan 2010: 14; see also Hodes 2014). The 1921 massacres in Tulsa, Oklahoma, for example, were instigated by the false accusation of sexual assault by a white woman against a young Black man, as was the lynching of Emmett Till and the unjust incarceration of the so-called Central Park Five (Pickens 2013; Smiley and Fakunle 2016). A common rejoinder to the prospect of more punitive rape laws is the concern that, as with stricter laws in other areas, it is racialised men who will be disproportionately charged and convicted due to systemic overpolicing and a history of harsher sentencing (Nathan 2018; Singleton 2017; Wriggins 1983).

The racialisation of false rape allegations has also troublingly fused itself to partisan news coverage and digital disinformation including the now debunked claim by a Russian-German thirteen-year-old girl who claimed she was raped by Muslim refugees in Berlin (Withnall 2016). While the motivations of the original claim are unclear, this allegation was politicised and, as in a host of other rumour-based cases, used by anti-immigrant groups to argue for mass deportations, an end to asylum, and the casting of racialised immigrants as inherently dangerous (Beinhorn and Glorius 2018; Tok 2018; *Der Spiegel* 2018).

One-off examples like the 2014 *Rolling Stone* article chronicling the purported gang rape of a young woman at a University of Virginia frat party, which subsequently fell apart on the facts – leading to the story being retracted, provide fodder to those sceptical of the #BelieveWomen mantra and also of #MeToo (Erdely 2014). While they are rare, the publicisation of these stories tends to take on an aura of 'proved injustice' that undermines the objectives of #MeToo as it relates to its demand to be believed.

#METOO: FOR WHOM?

A central criticism of #MeToo that comes up again and again is that it is exclusionary in terms of who its representatives are and the kinds of stories that have been highlighted and followed up on – namely, those of white, well-off celebrities like Gwyneth Paltrow, Rose McGowan, Alyssa Milano and Angelina Jolie. Our media ecosystem, itself driven by stories of celebrity, drama and intrigue, focuses on the experiences of these women while failing to take up the stories of nonbinary women, disabled women, Black women, women of colour and immigrant women (Gill and Orgad 2018; Onwuachi-Willig 2018). The real founder of the hashtag discussed above, Tarana Burke, in an interview with *Time Magazine*, decried the disproportionate focus on the famous and powerful, arguing that 'The women of color, trans women, queer people – our stories get pushed aside and our pain is never prioritized . . . We don't talk about indigenous women. Their stories go untold' (*Time Magazine* 2019). Ashwini Tambe, in an article for *Feminist Studies*, echoes this criticism by calling out the media's centring of white women's pain in place of the 'workplace experience for women of color – whether we are talking about enslaved women or the vast majority of women in low-wage service professions' (Tambe 2018: 199). The intersections of gender-based violence with race and class are left out of the dominant #MeToo movement, which has spawned hashtags like #UsToo, started by lawyer and journalist Sophia Nelson, to address this disparity.

My own concerns with #MeToo as a movement and in the context of this book have less to do with procedural issues and inter-movement conflict and more with the cultural, juridical and normative assumptions around sex, sexuality, gender, race and justice it reflects. In troubling these aspects of #MeToo, it becomes necessary to interrogate what it assumes about each of these categories and identity positions. I do this through concrete examinations of five case studies of high-profile #MeToo controversies using the 'pleasure and care-centred ethic of embodied and relational sexual Otherness' as a regulative ideal of sexual relations and restorative justice as a framework of ethical practice. In the next chapter, I assess and make a case for restorative justice as an important alternative to carceral forms of feminism in cases of gender-based violence inclusive of those that fall under the umbrella of #MeToo.

4. #MeToo and the Case for Restorative Justice

In this chapter, I make the case for restorative justice as a viable alternative to traditional legal and carceral means by which to address gender-based violence. In doing so, I take up acquaintance rape and assault which are indicative of many of the most publicised #MeToo cases. While I have already touched on the carceral nature of #MeToo, it bears repeating that this ethic of retribution is in keeping with second wave feminist activism that pushed for harsher sentencing and a whole host of victim-rights reforms and programmes in the 1980s and 1990s. I contend that carceral or 'governance' feminism fails to grapple with a sexist system or work towards actualising the kinds of 'nonlegal, cultural, creative, aesthetic, grassroots, intersectional, and global forms sexual justice politics can and should take' (Fischel 2019: 93). Moreover, as Mack and McCann argue, carceral feminism, in its reliance on punitive justice, hides how the state has used and continues to use the fear of sexual violence to justify its own use of force (Mack and McCann 2018). Moreover, it is anachronistic, in light of #MeToo's purported social justice and anti-violence objectives, that punitive incarceration is seen as a feminist solution. This is particularly the case since some of #MeToo's most ardent advocates are the same people who are also mobilising for the Black Lives Matter movement (BLM) whose central platform includes decarceration and police and prison abolition (Illouz 2020; Greene et al. 2019).

This contradiction, coupled with the incongruity between dominant conceptions of ideal sexual relations (consent, communication, autonomy, etc.) and carceral criminal justice, calls for a more robust and capacious sexual ethic and modality of justice. While I have articulated and justified the former in the preceding chapter, in this chapter I want to formulate a case for restorative justice as a more apt and suitable model of redress given the realities of sexual relations, the failure of current criminogenic models, and the objectives of #MeToo. I argue that the 'pleasure and care-centred ethic of embodied and relational sexual Otherness' captures the overwhelm and non-integrative excess of sex, attends to many of the criticisms of other models, and helps make a case for restorative justice that is more in tune with #MeToo'.

I begin this chapter with an introduction to restorative justice inclusive of a brief history as well as an explanation of its objectives, various models and current application with a focus on acquaintance gender-based violence. This theoretical and practical overview is followed by a discussion of sexual violence, the politics of victimisation, and the role of social justice, racialisation and sexuality. Throughout, I make a case for the use of restorative justice in cases of acquaintance sexual assault alongside an approach to sex informed by a 'pleasure and care-centred ethic of embodied and relational sexual Otherness'. I maintain that adopting restorative justice serves survivors better, attends to the roots of gender-based violence, and is consistent with the objectives of #MeToo.

In subsequent chapters, all case studies are then examined through this lens vis-à-vis the models of sex relied upon or assumed (in relation to both court cases and/or the court of public (mediated) opinion); the possibility that adjacent models might work better than the criminal justice system (in service of social justice goals); and whether or not the model I propose (the 'pleasure and care-centred ethic of embodied and relational sexual Otherness'), when coupled with restorative justice, offers a superior way forward; specifically, one in which consciousness raising and acts of solidarity work together with a fulsome analysis of 'structural barriers – the way sexual harassment and violence shape women's lives at work and away from it, the way class [and race] hierarchies are brutally maintained – in a way that emphasizes the breadth and depth of the problems' (Jaffe 2018).

It is also useful to consider the contributions of socio-legal research to discussions around #MeToo, gender-based violence and justice. In socio-legal studies, the law is seen as a tool through which social order is enacted, maintained and justified. As such, socio-legal scholars study the co-producing role played by history, economics and politics, how the law operates in practice, the justification of decision-making practices, and how legal decisions impact those who experience their application (Banakar and Travers 2005; Creutzfeldt, Mason and McConnachie 2019).

Existing research on #MeToo by scholars using a socio-legal framework, particularly feminist ones, is critical of the way in which legal structures have been unable to deal equitably with gender-based violence and sexual harassment. The law, whether that is employment law, business law or discrimination law, is charged with being inadequate and 'rooted in the pervasive, daily, socio-cultural nature of misogyny and its patriarchal roots' as well as liberal conceptions of consent, persistent gender norms and power differentials (Jurasz and Barker 2019). Scholars have used the socio-legal framework to study the impact of #MeToo on policing behaviour (Ross 2018), the rights of the accused (Coleman 2019), the relationship between changes in rape law and media depictions (Spalding 2019), and the neglect of women's embodied experience in trials involving sexual violence (Henry and Powell 2015). In a way, the approach I have taken in this book is socio-legal in that it takes up many of these themes and places law in its historical context; however, it differs in my centring of the co-constitution of sex and justice specifically.

While a distinction is often made between restorative and transformative justice, wherein the latter is more in line with work done by racialised communities and the project of dismantling all structures of oppression, I use the two terms interchangeably. As such, a restorative project is one that is transformative, encompasses the state and non-state actors, is both structured and flexible, and operates in line with the 'leadership and interests of marginalized communities' (Kim 2018: 226).

RESTORATIVE JUSTICE

Restorative justice is a bit of an umbrella term meant to cover a host of alternatives to traditional, state-led forms of justice that involve the police, courts, judges, juries and, potentially, the incarcerated (Van Ness and Strong 2014; Strang and Braithwaite 2017; Daly 2016; Zinsstag and Keenan 2017). There are several definitions of restorative justice that have emerged out of academia, activist groups, NGOs, civil society and state actors. In the academic context, Van Ness and Strong define restorative justice as a non-retributive system of justice that

> does as much as possible to restore the situation. The community offers aid to the victim; the offender is held accountable and required to make reparation. Attention would be given not only to the outcome, but also to evolving a process that respected the feelings and humanity of both the victim and the offender. (Van Ness and Strong 2014: 138)

The US-based feminist activist group INCITE! defines restorative justice as an

> attempt to address crime from a restorative and reconciliatory rather than a punitive framework. That is, as opposed to the US criminal justice system that focuses solely on punishing the perpetrator and removing him from society through incarceration, restorative justice attempts to involve all parties (perpetrators,

> victims and community members) in determining the appropriate response to a crime in an effort to restore the community back to wholeness. (INCITE! 2020)

Similarly, states like California characterise restorative justice practices as seeking to

> repair the harm done to all parties affected by crime – the victim, the community, and the offender; to hold offenders accountable; and to improve community safety, while increasing the ability of the youth who comes into contact with the juvenile justice system to contribute to his or her family and society. (George 2006: 1)

The throughline in each of these definitions is that of (1) *repair*, inclusive of the relations between the survivor, perpetrator (particularly if the accused is a family member or part of the victim's life) and community; (2) *accountability* as it relates to the accused, who must confess to the crime, offer an apology, and work to make amends (where the amends are determined by the survivor and can include education, community work, reparations, etc.); and (3) *reintegration*, wherein the offender is offered a supported way through which to become part of the community again (Marshal 1998; Hermann 2017). Restorative practices are also mean to be non-adversarial, voluntary and non-retributive.

There are a number of models of restorative justice in use around the world with generally positive outcomes relating to survivor satisfaction and recidivism (Van Camp and Wemmers 2013; Bidois 2016; Scorcia-Popescu 2017). These processes can be *sui generis* community initiatives, offered as an alternative to the criminal justice system (but sanctioned by it), or part of criminal proceedings (hybrid). Restorative justice is increasingly being seen as a viable path towards doing justice in an unequal society, with the victim's personal experience and affective concerns taking centre stage.

Many if not all uses of restorative justice borrow from established Indigenous frameworks that serve as a practical and ethical counter to Western models. There are, however, a set of critical arguments against the de-contextualised use of Indigenous practices in non-Indigenous settings from the perspective of cultural appropriation and homogenisation. Specifically, the argument is that Western applications of restorative justice risk enacting a form of symbolic violence by taking a situated and localised cultural practice, changing it as needed, and using it for one's own purposes – possibly in ways in which it was not intended to be used and without a wider understanding of the culture from which it is taken (Daly and Stubbs 2006). Juan Tauri makes the case that the seemingly altruistic use of restorative justice sits uneasily with the violence of Indigenous policing by colonial authorities, the over-representation of Indigenous communities in jails, and the silencing of Indigenous voices on these subjects. He argues against the use of restorative justice approaches that do violence to their original intention, are 'exaggerated and inappropriate [in their] use of elements of indigenous lifeworlds', and interfere with the ability of Indigenous people to 'resurrect our traditional justice processes and/or achieve some measure of jurisdictional autonomy' (Tauri 2014: 35). LaRocque takes this one step further, arguing that the 'traditions' upon which restorative practices are based are themselves a chimera:

> no one considered those Aboriginal traditions that punished sexual offenders with severity. If programs are claiming to apply traditional measures, then they should. But traditional justice is unrecognizable here, as in most other mediation and circle healing programs. (LaRocque 1997: 84–5)

These claims and critiques are critical in coming to terms not only with how material and symbolic exploitation continues today (Proulx 1998).

Despite these concerns, as well as the possibility that restorative practices might be used to paper over larger structures of oppression, I argue that restorative justice, when carefully applied, offers a number of possibilities for non-carceral forms of repair relevant to #MeToo that should be explored. In what follows, I outline several frameworks – not all of which are applicable to the kinds of sexual offences taken up by #MeToo but which are important since they speak to its ethos and objectives. Each model forms part of a wider network or assemblage of restorative practices that see crime not as occurring against the state, but 'as a violation of people and relationships, causing harm for which offenders and communities are accountable and have an obligation to repair' (Koss and Achilles 2008: 1).

MODELS OF RESTORATIVE JUSTICE

First is the restorative justice framework known as victim-offender mediation in which both parties meet (with a mediator) for a structured dialogue where guilt is admitted and a survivor-led plan is produced to make amends. This approach may be the least desirable in the case of gender-based violence in that it can be far too intimate for the victim but it has been used successfully in cases of intimate partner violence (Umbreit, Coates and Kalanj 1994; Tamarit and Luque 2016). Another approach is community reparative boards which are traditionally used for juvenile offenders; this involves a board, community members, representatives of the state, and the offended party working together to produce a plan of action and sanction with strong follow-up to ensure offender compliance (Jordan Grant 2020; Karp and Walther 2001). Citizen ownership is a central plank of these boards and their purpose, uniquely, is interventionist so that offenders are diverted from future criminal activities. However, like victim-offender mediation, community reparative boards may not be the best option for sexual assault cases since they can be offender-centred and are often state-led.

Family group conferencing is a restorative approach used in several countries including Canada, New Zealand, Australia, Sweden and Guatemala. The Wagga Wagga model, used in New Zealand, is explicitly community-centred and involves the victim, offender, family and friends working with a facilitator to address harms and produce a plan for repair (Crnkovich 1996; Bernal 2019). Family group conferencing tends to be used in the context of youth offenders and child welfare cases (including child abuse) and works best where there is a strong community infrastructure in place (Van Wormer 2009). The themes or objectives of such circles include '"Widening the circle" (involving extended family), "Taking/sharing responsibility for solutions", "Culturally competent practice", "Family leadership and empowerment", non-adversarialism and the use of "Private family time" for decision-making' (Barnsdale and Walker 2007: 2). Because of its rootedness in familial repair and strong community ties, family group conferencing might be less than ideal for the kinds of acquaintance assaults taken up by #MeToo.

Healing circles, however, represent a form of restorative justice that has been and continues to be used to address sexual assault specifically. Circles that hew closely to Indigenous traditions often use a 'talking piece' to provide structure and prioritise dialogic communication and consensus-based decision-making (Pranis 2005). In these circles, the survivor is provided with ample room to relay their experience, articulate harms, ask questions, and communicate what it will take to repair relations. The offender must admit guilt and is given space to ask for forgiveness and make amends. A strong sense of community support is built into this approach. As such, restorative circles can go on for a few weeks to months, often meeting on a regular basis to ensure accountability (note that the survivor may or may not attend all these meetings). In Canada, healing circles have been used post-sentencing (as part of reintegration), while in other jurisdictions, such as the US (Arizona specifically), they have been used to address intimate partner violence (Mill, Barocas and Ariel 2013). Healing circles have also been utilised in the context of universities. The University of Michigan, for example, gives survivors of sexual assault an option of a no-contact circle of accountability that invites 'multiple members of the community to explore individual and community impact, harm, obligations, and opportunity for repairing them' (University of Michigan 2019). Scholars argue that these circles can be useful in addressing sexual violence because they are flexible, sensitive to the role of asymmetrical power relations, and firmly attuned to the needs of survivors (Backhouse 2012; Randall 2013). It is important, however, to consider how these frameworks operate in practice.

RESTORATIVE JUSTICE IN PRACTICE

Each of the restorative frameworks delineated above is consensus-based, victim-focused, includes multiple stakeholders, and is robust in follow-up. Hybrid schemes that rely on restorative principles are also available and have been used by Indigenous communities. A salient example is the Hollow Water Community Holistic Healing Circle (CHHC) project in Manitoba, Canada, which was a programme used by the Ojibwa Nation to provide a restorative justice alternative supported by fully funded community counselling and assistance for survivors (Proulx 1998). It was a pilot programme that posthumous studies judged was generally successful with respect to recidivism, rates of domestic violence, youth incarceration and quality of life (Edwards and Sharpe 2004). Similarly, New Zealand's Maori-focused Family Group Conferencing (FGC) programme, another hybrid, focused on child welfare and youth justice and offered 'Maori a culturally appropriate and empowering justice process' (Moyle and Tauri 2016: 88). Evaluation of this programme's effectiveness is largely positive (it is ongoing) and registers high with respect to community satisfaction (Triggs 2005; Maxwell and Hayes 2006). More recent, and even more removed from state-led processes, are projects like Philly Stands Up, a Philadelphia-based community accountability group, and Creative Interventions, which works out of San Francisco to support 'community based interventions to domestic and sexual violence' (Kim 2018).

Significantly, the majority of empirical and qualitative evaluations of restorative programmes report either positive or marginal impact. While the focus of this chapter and the book is not to assess restorative justice practices, it is important to point out a growing consensus that restorative justice can function as an alternative to criminal justice and does particularly well when measured against survivor satisfaction, recidivism, offender reintegration and community safety (Latimer, Dowden and Muise 2005; Bouffard, Cooper and Bergseth 2017; Kennedy et al. 2019; Boutilier and Wells 2018).

Despite this, examples of the sustained use of the restorative alternatives in relation to acquaintance sexual assault are few and far between. One of note is RESTORE (Responsibility and Equity for Sexual Transgressions Offering a Restorative Experience), a programme developed and used in Arizona between 2003 and 2007 which instituted a restorative conferencing option for first-time-misdemeanour sex offenders and which centred on/around accountability, validation, safety and justice. As McGlynn puts it, RESTORE aims to 'facilitate a victim-centred, community-driven resolution of selected individual sex crimes that creates and carries out a plan for accountability, healing and public safety' (McGlynn 2011: 832; Koss 2014). Notably, RESTORE was supported by the Centers for Disease Control (CDC), with some involvement of the police and social services case managers for follow-up. The programme only took on cases that involved non-penetrative first-time sexual offences where the perpetrator used minimal force. Its objectives included: (1) being able to offer 'victims [a] choice about how their violation is addressed and . . . [empower] . . . them in the context of a nonadversarial process'; (2) maximising 'the effectiveness of community-based sexual offender treatment by ordering and monitoring participation starting at the first offense'; and (3) improving 'recovery outcomes and [reducing] revictimization by providing victims with social validations and increasing access to services' (Koss, Bachar and Hopkins 2003: 392).

Primary post-project quantitative studies of the RESTORE programme found the results to be largely promising. For example, researchers found 'results [that] support cautious optimism regarding feasibility, safety, and satisfactory outcomes' including a decrease in survivor PTSD, overall satisfaction (especially with respect to having a say in the process), and general agreement that the conference was successful (Koss 2014: 1,623). RESTORE was subsequently replicated in New Zealand as Project Restore (Jülich et al. 2010).

Similar models using conferencing and reintegration have been used in Denmark (the Copenhagen Rape Crisis Centre) and South Africa (the Phaphamani Rape Crisis Counselling Centre) (Koss 2010). Both the Copenhagen programme and the Phaphamani Centre's projects found success using mediated victim and offender dialogues (Madsen 2004; Skelton and Batley 2006). Finally, the AIM project in Manchester focuses on young sexual offenders via referral orders, with a concentration on providing training and guidance to courts in the UK (Calder 2007). There are a plethora of other ad hoc and more formalised programmes throughout the world yet, as stated, a large proportion focus on youth offenders and/or intimate partner violence. There is one paradigmatic case worth noting of a widely reported restorative justice process involving an acquaintance assault on an Indigenous woman in Canada whose experience does fit the #MeToo frame. In an article for CTV News, 'Liss' provides an account of her rape and the Indigenous-led restorative process that followed – which she describes as healing. Remarkably, her request for a mediation circle came after a traumatic criminal trial. According to Liss, her objective was to be heard, to be assured the offender will not reoffend, and to mend:

> 'We need to let survivors take the front seat. The restorative justice process offers such deep healing and lasting transformation for all parties involved and for our culture beyond individuals,' she said. 'It's not just about making sure this person doesn't do this again; we can go beyond that. We can go beyond fixing it and we can use this story to help make change.' (Neustaeter 2019)

While this bit of anecdotal evidence may not be generalisable, it does provide a basis from which to think about what is possible. A programme that allows #MeToo survivors to demand accountability and have the harm they experienced acknowledged from a position of safety and empowerment is consistent with the #MeToo movement and the social justice objectives of contemporary feminism. This approach is also firmly embedded in the transformative principles of care, repair and healing (as opposed to carceral violence), as discussed by advocates like Ruth Wilson Gilmore (2007).

RESTORATIVE JUSTICE AND SEXUAL VIOLENCE

As stated, some restorative justice models are more appropriate than others for dealing with acquaintance-based sexual violence. This is because cases vary tremendously in terms of offence, legal particularities and age (remember that restorative approaches are often seen as a desirable way to deal with juvenile offenders). It is also important to point out and probe why applying restorative justice processes to address sexual assault and rape is often seen as anathema. Gender-based violence is in fact the least likely offence to be part of a restorative process largely because of the perceived severity of the offence. This understanding of sexual violence as exceptional is rooted in historical and patriarchal conceptions of female purity whose violation results in personal annihilation and moral ruin – what Jed Rubenfeld refers to as 'innocence robbed' (Rubenfeld 2013). Laws related to sexual assault are historically and ontologically proximate to that of enslavement and torture due to their shared conception of the shattering criminal violation of the bodily self-possession.

In my discussion of sexual violence in Chapter 1, I reviewed the scholarly and empirical work on rape as an act of affective destruction that damages the victim by denying them bodily autonomy and sexual integrity. As stated, the patriarchal construction of virginity as valuable and women as property also informs this sense of damage (Cahill 2001; Weitz and Weitz 2016). As a result, anything short of punitive retribution is considered unacceptable. Survivors themselves, however, are not well served by the options given to them by the criminal justice system. As I discuss below, empirical and qualitative studies of sexual assault in terms of reporting, criminal charges, (adversarial) trials and sentencing show high levels of survivor dissatisfaction (Berkseth, Meany and Zisa 2017; Department of Justice 2014). A lack of psychosocial support and clear information, the inability to exert choice and agency, and an overall unhappiness with the outcome of the process leaves much to be desired (Henninger et al. 2020).

One of the most salient criticisms of how gender-based violence is handled by the police and courts is that it alienates women from the proceedings and revictimises them because of the way in which it is structured. Women are forced to deal with an adversarial system that requires they recount the event, prove their credibility, and do so under the stress of cross-examination (if it gets to that). Moreover, the clear-up rates of sexual assaults are abysmal. The most recent statistics in the US show that three out of four women assaulted do not go to the police; 995 perpetrators out of every 1,000 assailants go free; and of the 50.8% who are arrested for rape, only 6% serve a night in jail. The end result is that fifteen out of sixteen men accused of rape never see jail time at all (RAINN 2020a; Central MN Sexual Assault Center 2020; Searles 2018).

Troublingly, those cases that do go forward do so under conditions that are less than ideal. For example, they tend to perpetuate cultural stereotypes about 'real rape' defined as assaults that are perpetrated by a stranger (ideally with a weapon), resulting in real physical harm, having occurred very recently, and involving some degree of incapacitation (Lonsway and Archambault 2012). Additionally, the rates at which white women have their cases go forward far outstrip those of women of colour, which, according to Reema Sood, reflects 'centuries-old racist biases stemming from the institution of slavery' (Sood 2018: 427). This has meant that 'Crimes against Black women are poorly investigated and sometimes ignored altogether' (Sood

2018: 407; Slatton and Richard 2020). Convictions of perpetrators of sex crimes against Indigenous women are similarly dismal despite the fact that they are two and a half times as likely to be assaulted (Young 2019).

The normative social construction of the ideal victim is important since it is the case that for victims of assault and rape to have their experience taken seriously, they often have to fit within a narrow set of gendered, raced and classed expectations. The ideal victim is generally held to be white, middle class, female and cis. The assault itself must have been committed by a complete stranger, an official complaint needs to have been filed immediately, and tangible evidence of violence should exist – ideally, inscribed on the victim's body. Also expected is that the victim's sexual past and general appearance are uncontroversial, the conditions under which the assault occurred innocuous (e.g. not in a part of town deemed morally suspect), and alcohol or other substances ought not to be a factor (Christie 1986; Duggan 2018). Dignan distils the ideal victim archetype into six characteristics:

1. Weak in relation to the perpetrator; meaning physically weak, vulnerable and/or most likely a female.
2. Going about their normal, everyday business; provided it is legitimate.
3. Blameless because they were in a decent place, at a decent hour.
4. Unrelated to and unknown by the perpetrator.
5. Victimized by a comparatively big and 'evil' perpetrator.
6. Strong and powerful enough to make a case for herself and claim status as the ideal victim. (Dignan 2004: 17)

These frames saturate media, popular culture and institutionalised justice. In an adversarial trial, defence attorneys often use a victim's inability to comply with these standards to discredit their testimony. Moreover, 'Racialized and marginalized women', as Randall argues, 'who are less valued and less credible in a society characterized by racism are, by definition, less readily identified as "ideal victims" and more easily stigmatized as "bad" or "undeserving" (if their victim claims are heard at all)' (Randall 2010: 410).

Yet, even women who meet these stringent criteria are often not afforded the epistemic privilege given to men as it relates to truth claims and moral probity. We only have to look at the #MeToo-related case of Christine Blasey Ford, whose testimony alleging an assault by the soon-to-be Supreme Court Justice Brett Kavanaugh met most if not all of these criteria but was still considered inadequate. Compare this to the way in which Anita Hill, a Black woman, was treated while testifying about harassment at the hands of Supreme Court Justice Clarence Thomas in 1991. According to McGinley, it was 'Blasey Ford's race and her more submissive demeanor' that 'made her testimony more acceptable and credible to onlookers' (McGinley 2019: 68; Bratskeir 2018).

For advocates of #MeToo, it is important to consider how firmly entrenched ideal victim discourse is and how it has been weaponised in criminal justice settings in ways that perpetuate and normalise sexual violence. There are moves under way to challenge many of these assumptions, including those of timely reporting and contact with the offender post-assault, and dismantle dominant assumptions regarding what constitutes the right kind of victimhood. #MeToo as a movement has challenged some of these tropes within the context of the hashtag campaign by enabling broad and inclusive participation through 'viral visibility'. Yet, it remains the case, as Clark-Parsons contends, that restricted 'access to mainstream media representation continues to be structured by race, sexuality, and class' (Clark-Parsons 2019: 12).

Some of the reasons women give about why they do not report their assaults at all or in a 'timely manner' have to do with trauma, shame, distrust of the system (i.e. that they will not be believed or the system will not work for them), fear of being revictimised by being put on trial, fear of social censure, and the existence of a pre-existing relationship with the perpetrator (Jülich and Thorburn 2017; Spencer et al. 2017; Engel 2017). There is also the issue of survivor stigma as it relates to labelling and categorisation. Research has shown that women who have been assaulted or raped are often reticent to take on that label due to its negative connotations and the emotional baggage it carries. In a recent meta-analysis conducted by Wilson and Miller, they determined that a large proportion of women who have been definitionally raped (up to 60%) reject the label due to denial, post-traumatic stress, the internalisation of rape myths, and not wanting to be seen as a victim (Wilson and Miller 2016; see also Bondurant 2001). The desire to avoid legal authorities, not wanting to label the male assailant 'a rapist, not feeling as though the incident was violent or forceful enough to be considered rape, or feeling as if their own behaviour made them partially responsible' are other oft-cited reasons for disidentifying with the rape label (LeMaire, Oswald and Russell 2016: 332). It is important to think critically about the reasons for this rejection – specifically why legal definitions and norms are so misaligned with women's felt experiences (Johnstone 2013). I would also point out the danger in researchers categorising sexual assaults as rape despite interviewees rejecting the label without a deeper interrogation of motivations, intent and agency.

On the other hand, recent research around #MeToo and other forms of self-reporting via social media shows that these platforms may be encouraging ownership of the rape and assault label. The Twitter-centric nature of the movement, at least in its initial stage, provided a largely anonymous, collective and supportive environment within which the stigma associated with rape and victim identities is mitigated. In this sense, as I stated earlier, Twitter confessions function as cathartic technology through which

> Victims are able to voice their thoughts and frustrations on a platform and in a movement where they feel heard . . . this led to a higher appearance of victims sharing that they did not report because of a belief, fear or evidence that nothing will be done if they did come forward. Twitter provides a voice to people who feel voiceless. (Garrett 2019: 36)

Restorative justice opens up further avenues to (re)gain agency and control within a supportive setting wherein women drive the process. Another complaint about the traditional justice system made by survivors is that they are rarely kept apprised of legal proceedings and feel steamrolled by the prosecution whose desire for a conviction is paramount. There are some troubling cases of women who want to drop charges and are subsequently forced to continue under penalty of arrest. These 'no-drop' policies criminalise the victim, 'undercut efforts at victim empowerment' and cause other 'unwanted side effects such as an increase in the risks of retaliation and discouraging victim reporting' (Corsilles 1994: 857). Restorative justice, through its centring of victim needs, rehabilitation and repair, offers an alternative to this while also challenging the logic of a racist system in which certain groups are seen as inherently suspect.

With respect to gender-based violence and #MeToo, it bears repeating that sexual assaults committed by an acquaintance (as these tend to dominate the #MeToo movement) have not been the subject of most restorative justice programmes. There is, however, a growing body of work on restorative justice in the context of marital and partner abuse that can be used as a starting point for #MeToo cases (Armatta 2018; Westmarland, McGlynn and Humphreys 2018). Overall, using these frameworks offers a more reparative way forward by attending to the survivor's desire to assert agency, be heard, reclaim autonomy, and be a part of the process of restitution and reintegration. On the offender's side, restorative justice allows for the opportunity to take responsibility as well as restore and repair relations. Programmes that offer therapy and counselling after the fact can also help stop cycles of violence and pinpoint avenues for behavioural change. It then becomes society's responsibility to treat and monitor so that reoffence is less likely.

CRIMINAL JUSTICE, RESTORATIVE JUSTICE AND SOCIAL JUSTICE

Overall, criminal justice norms and laws have not produced desired levels of accountability, safety and rehabilitation. In addition to the reasons given above, this is also because our current legal system exercises a form of sexual regulation and control that is heteronormative and in which particular kinds of sexual practice are seen as anathema (Dwyer 2011; Howarth 2004). Additionally, many criminogenic approaches become overly broad as in the case of sex offender registries which have been extended to include relatively minor infractions (like public urination and teenage sex), and the mere possibility of reoffence can result in indefinite civil commitment. These rules, according to Halperin and Hoppe, subject an entire group of people to a 'social death' wherein holding a job, getting housing, and living in a community are all but impossible (Halperin and Hoppe 2017; Megale 2011). Notably, the Adam Walsh Act and Megan's Law, which brought in many of these provisions, were supported by prominent feminists (Meiners 2009).

Roger Lancaster points out that Black and minority men have been disproportionately represented on sex offender registries, while Aya Gruber, in her book *The Feminist War on Crime*, illustrates how legislation like the Violence Against Women Act (VAWA), coupled with stricter rape law enforcement, has led to a situation wherein the 'remedy to social harm obscures the reality that criminal law is also a primary driver of social harm' (Gruber 2020: 192). The punitive criminal framework also, as Halley contends, reinscribes many of the assumptions around gender and sexual relations associated with the consent model that I described and critiqued in Chapter 1. Remember that this model sees 'Men as active and women as passive in sex; women as subjective and men as objective; women with feelings and men with reason; women with no role in shaping events in the world and men with all responsibility for them' (Halley 2016: 276). Despite this, there remains significant moral and societal difficulty in reconciling a programme of transformation and restitution over incarceration for behaviours that are so intimate. However, given current circumstances and the failure of past approaches, I argue that it is worth considering.

Many scholars, including myself, argue that restorative justice is also desirable as it relates to conceptions of social justice in light of important work reflected in critical race theory, decarceration, state/police violence and prison abolition (Bell 2018; Spade 2013; Cacho 2012). Connections between prison and police abolition, reparations and the classroom-to-prison pipeline by scholars like Patrisse Cullors (a co-founder of BLM) are of particular importance, as is other activist work coming out of the BLM movement (Cullors 2018; Davis 2019; González and Buth 2019). In a speech at the University of Notre Dame Opal Tometi, another BLM co-founder, argued specifically for a mode of 'unapologetic activism' that includes restorative justice as a way to 'chip away at a criminal justice system that's really not working for us' (Tometi as cited by Berardino 2019).

Restorative justice thus fits with the principles of #MeToo vis-à-vis its focus on collective healing, community and solidarity. Like #MeToo, restorative justice is feminist, anti-racist and anti-colonial. It also pushes up against patriarchal and entrenched models of justice that rely on a victim-perpetrator binary to reinforce inequalities of power. It should also be noted that despite only a slight turn in public opinion, as evidenced by media coverage, many feminists like Tarana Burke, Kimberlé Crenshaw and Mariame Kaba (all supporters of #MeToo) are keen to point out the need for a more restorative approach. Kaba, in an interview with *The Bleader*, refers to #MeToo as ushering in a public 'reckoning', but one that 'needs to find a way of thinking about sexual violence and ending it that doesn't rely on the death-making institutions of police and prisons and surveillance, which we've been using to supposedly eradicate rape' (Kaba as cited by Dukmasova 2017).

Burke, whose work around #MeToo from its very inception has been supportive of the restorative model, speaks from a perspective that is distinct from mainstream manifestations of #MeToo by insisting on radical social change. This is reflected in her and her organisations' (Just Be Inc. and metoomvmt.org) work on anti-racism, decolonisation, LGBTQ+ justice, disability justice, prison abolition and radical democratisation. In a 2017 interview with *Elle Magazine* (Murray 2017), Burke highlights the need for perpetrator accountability and transparency as part of a project of mass healing. In another interview, she argues that a move towards restorative justice is necessary since

> many perpetrators are themselves survivors of sexual violence, particularly child sexual abuse. And that complicates a lot of things. We've got to get a clearer understanding of what justice is and what people need to feel whole. And if we're ever going to heal in our community, we have to heal the perpetrators and heal the survivors, or else it's just a continuous cycle. (Adetiba 2017)

Mainstream discussion of restorative justice outside the activist community, in what we might call legacy media as well as popular digital publications and social media, has also increased and begun to question #MeToo's carceral logic. *The New York Times*, for example, recently published an article by two law professors titled '#MeToo doesn't always have to mean prison' in which they lay out a holistic programme of restorative justice, while *Vox* ran a popular piece on the potential of restorative practices in colleges (Bazelon and Gruber 2020; North 2019b). NPR ran a compelling story in 2019 about Charlie Hallowell, a prominent California chef and restaurant owner who underwent a mediation process with one of his victims (Tovia Smith 2019), and *The Guardian* reported on restorative justice in several articles – most recently in a moving opinion essay by a survivor of sexual violence who, while expressing their visceral anger and fear, calls for a solution that 'doesn't preclude the possibility of rehabilitation and restorative justice' (Anonymous 2020). A re-examination of #MeToo's carceral leanings has also been called for by journalists and activists through pieces like '#MeToo must avoid "carceral feminism"' (Press 2018), 'Restorative justice lets sexual-assault survivors take back their power' (Comeau 2019) and 'Enough with naming and shaming: It's time for restorative justice in Hollywood' (Hornaday 2018).

The majority of these articles follow a similar format beginning with a delineation of the failures of the criminal justice system as it relates to sexual violence (and in light of #MeToo). Restorative justice is then introduced as an alternative with outlets as mainstream as *The New Republic* running stories like 'No justice for Harvey Weinstein's victims', which makes the case for a system that offers 'accountability practice[s] dependent on mutual consent and existing relationships' and which plays 'out on a community level' (Melissa Gira Grant 2020).

It is important to point out, however, that the move to prison and police abolition is not a new concept within the social justice community. Noted prison abolitionist and feminist Angela Davis has been arguing since the 1960s for abolitionist alternatives like

> demilitarization of schools, revitalization of education at all levels, a health system that provides free physical and mental care to all, and a justice system based on reparation and reconciliation rather than retribution and vengeance. (Davis 2011: 107)

Taken together, this refocusing on harm over crime, the clear articulation of critiques of the prison industrial complex, and the exploration of the possibilities offered by abolitionisms rooted in the historical struggle against colonisation, imperialism and slavery work as important precursors to full restorative justice. Its principles are also present in liberation theology, Marxist and materialist critiques, post-Enlightenment theory, racial justice movements (e.g. the Black Panthers), intersectionality and critiques of settler colonialism (Brown and Schept 2017; Hulsman 1991; Scott 2013; Russell and Carlton 2013).

A direct throughline can be traced between slavery and prison to police impunity (e.g. racialised social control, slave patrols, sundown cities) and the institutional dehumanisation of the marginalised. As such, the historically informed carceral logic of #MeToo, despite cracks along the edges, remains tied to prison, trials and prosecutions. The jubilation that accompanied the sentencing of Harvey Weinstein, Bill Cosby and Larry Nassar are just three examples of cases wherein public reaction, while understandable given the magnitude of the offences, only meets #MeToo's objectives of consciousness raising and legal enforcement. It does not, however, adequately address the objectives of long-term survivor care and repair or cultural transformation. As Deborah Rhode writes,

> In the era of #MeToo, after major publications such as *Forbes* declared that we were seeing 'the end of patriarchy,' feminist commentator Susan Faludi responded dryly: 'Look around.' The structures of patriarchy, she noted, were doing fine. And as others have pointed out, the self-confessed 'pussy grabber' now serving as commander in chief has hardly been hobbled by accusations of sexual misconduct by at least nineteen women. (Rhode 2019: 380)

RESTORATIVE JUSTICE UNDER THE MICROSCOPE

There are, however, a number of potential drawbacks associated with restorative justice that need to be addressed in light of #MeToo and with respect to gender-based violence. First is the possibility that decision-making based on consensus might undermine the interests of the survivor whose voice is drowned out or who may find it difficult to object to the trajectory of the process itself. A closely related concern is that survivors might be pressured by their communities to forgive the accused. While this might not be applicable to the majority of acquaintance assaults, since the communities are not always shared, this pressure can be harmful and counterproductive coming from either side. Evidence has shown that these twin worries of individual agency and community pressure can be mitigated by a trained and experienced mediator who is able to ensure that the voice and experience of the survivor is supported throughout the process (Dhami and Joy 2007).

On a structural level, as Ptacek suggests, there is also the worry that panels and circles might play into and perpetuate silences and inequities. Thus, specific to acquaintance assaults, restorative circles or panels should not be permitted to rely on the 'mistaken assumption that all parties are equally empowered to express their needs' (Ptacek 2010: 263; Stubbs 2007).

Race, age, socio-economic status, education and of course gender work in intersecting ways to render the voices of the marginalised less 'reasonable', accountable, legible and legitimate. Structuring restorative practices in a manner that mitigates these factors by addressing them head-on is essential.

Another oft-cited criticism of restorative justice is that assailants can be adept at manipulation by performing contrition and a willingness to change. As such, the victim is more likely to forgive and agree to less strenuous conditions, allowing for the offender to return to previous habits and behaviours. While this may be the case in terms of intimate partner violence, wherein the dynamics of power and control are well-established and factors other than violence are taken into account (i.e. children, financial dependency, family cohesion), for acquaintance crimes these dynamics are less entrenched and subject to challenge by the facilitator, victim and community. Relatedly, on the perpetrator's side, the process has the potential to result in what von Hirsch calls 'compulsory attitudinising' wherein 'any contrition or self-criticism expressed by the actor must – if his moral agency is to be respected – reflect his own views. If those views are inconsistent with the attitudes he is required to for restorative approaches express, then his agency is not respected' (von Hirsch 1993: 83–4; Bennett 2006). It is the case that the success of restorative justice relies on the commitment of participants to act in good faith within an environment that is not coercive or pressurising for either party. Structuring circles to guard against compulsion and ensure the offender sincerely abides by the acts of restitution and reform required of them is the task of the conveners and facilitators who act as a buffer to insincerity and a guarantor of non-coercion.

Additional sources of disquiet include the potential that restorative justice reprivatises violence – i.e. that it moves it away from a view of crime as a social violation against society best dealt with through public channels. The push to make sexual assault a crime that the state and its representatives take seriously has been a feminist objective for decades, with second wave feminists in particular objecting to the 'withdrawal of the law from the so-called domestic sphere on the basis that the withdrawal left women unprotected from abuse and gave the ideological message that domestic life was less important than commercial life or other aspects of society governed by law' (Olsen 1993: 323). As such, restorative practices might appear to reinforce this tendency were it not for the involvement of friends, family and community in the process. It is also the case that a restorative approach would not be solely an option for cases of assault, but would be part of a larger project of judicial and criminal-legal transformation.

The belief that restorative justice is just too easy – that is, that it lets offenders 'off the hook' – is a common one and is far from trivial (Daly and Stubbs 2006; Fauble III 2018). The telos of the criminal justice system as punitive is not capricious but the product of centuries of socio-cultural choices. Offenders are intentionally constructed as dangerous and disgraced actors for whom incarceration represents the paying-off of a public debt. As such, a binary has been framed as dangerous rendering anything outside of the total appropriation of one's freedom as 'too easy'. Yet, the demands for increased public safety, low recidivism, rehabilitation, healing and justice have not been met by the carceral approach. Moreover, as Judy Hostetler Mullet argues,

> no reconciliation process is simple; restorative justice is hard work and thrives on the principles of obligation, empathy, dignity, and making things right. Wrongdoers do not 'get away' with anything. They recognize their obligations and commit to restore, reconcile, and make restitution, which are real consequences of their actions. (Mullet 2014: 161)

Finally, there is the issue of fear, both of the process, which can be anxiety-inducing if held face to face, and of retribution or revictimisation. The former can be and has been addressed through the use of proxies, video and read letters so that the victim does not have to see the offender if they do not wish to, in addition to the expectation of community enforcement and support which, in the case of assault and rape, can mitigate the danger of revictimisation. Most of the #MeToo cases which have garnered media attention are ones in which the parties do not have a strong pre-existing relationship. Restorative justice practices that focus on intimate partner violence, however, must address these dynamics in more detail.

All of these concerns are reflected in the #MeToo cases discussed in the chapters that follow. Also explored is my contention that the model of sexual relations I propose, namely that of the 'pleasure and care-centred ethic of embodied and relational sexual Otherness', is most compatible with the circle sentencing approach delineated above. Acquaintance and workplace assaults (inclusive of rape) and harassment that takes place in professional contexts or on a date have been addressed either by corporate bureaucracies motivated to sweep things under the rug or by a criminal justice system ill-equipped or unwilling to deal with gender-based violence in ways that are victim-centred. This is not helped by institutions like human resources, the police and the courts who are fixated on individual acts rather than the structures of patriarchy, racism and misogyny that give rise to violence in the first place.

RESTORATIVE JUSTICE AND #METOO GOING FORWARD

Taken together, if the objective of #MeToo is to end gender-based violence through the enactment of social change, restorative justice needs to be made a viable and supported option. Creating a system that is based on an acknowledgement of harm, the obligation to put things right, the engagement of community, and the experience and needs of the survivor is not unachievable. Nor is the layering on top of this framework a reconceptualisation of sex as, in its idealised form, as reflective of the needs of the Other, of care, and felt affective pleasure. Without the pressure of proving the assault took place under conditions that incentivise the accused to maintain their innocence, a more productive conversation can take place about power, exploitation, care and violation – which moves us closer to the conditions of equality we desire. Further movement can only occur by addressing structural oppression and operationalising and funnelling the energy of #MeToo (understood as acting as its own 'kind of spontaneous truth and reconciliation commission') into community-driven and victim-focused sites of learning and repair (Levine 2017).

In the chapters that follow I explore this possibility in light of the five #MeToo cases identified early on – namely, Harvey Weinstein, Louis C.K., Jian Ghomeshi, Avital Ronell and Aziz Ansari. Methodologically, I examine these as case studies by describing and contextualising them and studying how they have unfolded via media reports and academic texts, as well as police and legal records where available. I then assess each case through the lens of the multiple models of sexual relations articulated in Chapter 1, my own model, and the potentials and opportunities offered by restorative justice to meet #MeToo's objectives of social justice and repair.

5. Case Studies, Methodology and Harvey Weinstein

The primary method of analysis used in these chapters is case studies along with an adapted form of interpretive or discourse analysis (Bell 2011; Gerring 2008). Case studies are helpful in research like this because they ground and limit shifting discourses and multiple examples to a handful of exemplar cases and do so with an eye to detail, historical context and socio-cultural nuance. As Zainal argues, case studies allow for analysis rooted in a particular context and environment over time, the possibility of quantitative *and* qualitative insights, and the production of thick, in depth-descriptions of real-life phenomena (Zainal 2007). In what follows, I draw on the Bill Cosby case to illustrate how I have operationalised this methodology and to give the reader a sense of what is to follow.

Overall, my approach to the study of these cases is descriptive, in that I provide a narrative account of the case; explanatory, wherein I examine details, facts and nuances often left behind in empirical and quantitative work; and interpretive/discursive through via a focus on meaning, language and power (Feagin, Orum and Sjoberg 1991; Van Dijk 2001). My method of analysing discourse draws on an adapted form of discourse analysis that involves deploying a critical lens to texts in order to unearth and unpack values, connotations and taken-for-granted assumptions about, in this case, sexual relationality, (in)justice and gender norms. Taking the case of Bill Cosby as an exemplar, this would involve compiling not only the history of media coverage of the numerous allegations against him (both historical and contemporary, media and law), but also the trial itself, the testimony of his victims, legal arguments, as well as the singular role Cosby played in popular culture. This data would then need to be examined using discourse analytic tools that include specifying dominant ideas around sex, consent and justice (*description*), language use (i.e. terms, assumptions, framings) (*interpretation*), and cultural structures (*explanation*). These texts would then be used to provide evidence for the claims made by the discourse analytic work (Wang 2006).

The role of race, power, celebrity, class and Black fatherhood would also have to be examined – particularly as it relates to the wider culture of gender injustice and power asymmetry in which these assaults took place. It is notable, for example, that coverage of the Cosby case just prior to 2015 tended to stick to straightforward reporting in a manner consistent with 'journalistic objectivity' (Hibberd 2014; Rogers 2015). Just a year later, these same media outlets took on a more activist role by highlighting the testimony of his accusers, as in the case of Andrea Constand, whose quote 'Bill Cosby took my spirit and crushed it' was widely reported – as was the harrowing testimony of his sixty-odd accusers (Associated Press 2018; Mallenbaum, Ryan and Puente 2018). This indicator not only marks a significant change in public rhetoric surrounding this particular case, but also serves as an indication of the shifts in the discourse around sexuality, consent and justice that are to come.

Each case required the assembling of academic and media-related texts using academic databases, Nexis, googlescholar, googlenews and social media analytics, beginning in 2016 and intensifying during weeks where further media attention was drawn to one case or another (e.g. if an apology or another allegation was made). Legacy media, defined as those outlets that were established before the digital age, including *The New York Times*, *The Washington Post*, *Los Angeles Times*, *The Globe and Mail*, *Toronto Star* and *USA Today* as well as magazines like *The New Yorker*, *Time*, *Newsweek*, *Maclean's*, *Rolling Stone*, *Vanity Fair*, *Teen Vogue* and *Elle*, were focused on specifically. I also analysed commentary and insight from digital outlets that have become widely read like *Slate*, *Vox*, *Huffpost*, *Jezebel*, *Salon.com* and *BuzzFeed*. Decisions had to be made with respect to which articles were considered to have informed public debate – particularly in light of the quantity of content that exists. The amount of commentary, reportage and academic analysis on the Cosby legal action, for example, is enormous, with Nexis returning over 10,000 hits and googlescholar returning well over 5,000. Popularity, presence on social media (shares and retweets), saliency, recency, sources used and typology (opinion vs reportage) constitute the criteria used to narrow down the pool of sources in each case.

Twitter was the primary social media platform relied upon due to its direct connection to #MeToo (where it started), and its role as a site of primary digital knowledge production (Johnston, Coulling and Kilty 2020). Particular attention is paid to the content/text as well as the progenitors of high-profile (i.e. retweeted) tweets unearthed using general keyword and hashtag searches aided by ScraperWiki. Also examined are tweets that were subsequently republished on mainstream media (McCormick et al. 2017;

Marwick 2014). Twitter provided a snapshot of the public zeitgeist which, while not particularly inclusive in terms of participation, representation, identity positions and political leanings on the topic of #MeToo, 'offers us the opportunity for the first time to both observe human behaviour and interaction in real time and [as it moves to other countries] on a global scale' (Golder and Macy 2011: 1,879). For example, when applied to the Cosby case, what becomes clear is the extraordinary amount of Twitter engagement with the phrase 'Bill Cosby' itself. Debates circulating around #billcosby, which existed for several years prior to 2014, are symptomatic of the dialogue around race, celebrity and sexual norms that is to come. In this particular hashtag, there is a deep schism between participants tweeting in support of Cosby, likening his trial to a persecution led by a racist system, and others who reflect the ethos of #MeToo by vocalising their support for affirmative consent, justice and eradicating the culture of sexist misogyny in Hollywood and beyond.

The range of cases taken up in this book leaves room for replicating this kind of analysis in other instances of sexual assault and harassment (particularly those outside Hollywood). These case studies can be used as ideal types that reflect enough of everyday sexual offences as to be informative and relatable. However, while I maintain that these cases serve as a locus of larger social trends and concerns, I do not argue that they are generalisable in the traditional sense. Case studies are meant to capture the complexities of real life, offer in-depth critical insights, and build thick narratives that can, and do, inform further action (Harrison et al. 2017).

While I explained my decision to include these cases in the introduction, it bears repeating that they are all high profile enough to be widely known, representative of acquaintance assaults, and reflect an element of controversy or 'greyness' as to how they might be handled. The amount of discussion and media coverage each case has generated over an extended period of time speaks to the important social ambiguities and tensions they reveal.

Step one: Narrative and interpretive analysis

For each case, I begin with an introduction and discussion of the case in narrative form, detailing relevant events chronologically and qualitatively, drawing on surrounding academic research as well as social and traditional media accounts and responses. In most cases, the events can only be reconstructed from media and legal/police documents, survivor accounts and the refutations or apologies of the accused. This act of reconstruction is discursive, done from my standpoint, and thus stands as an interpretive intervention into each case (as I demonstrated above using the case of Bill Cosby). The intersections of power, gender, race, class, dis/ability and sexuality are focused on in detail with particular attention paid to how overlapping structures of power and experiences of oppression work to construct subject positions that are complex, shifting and situated. This intersectional approach calls attention to the 'social processes of categorization and the workings of exclusion and hierarchy that mark boundary-drawing and boundary maintenance' as well as re- and de-constructing how the overlapping nature of these sites of marginality constructs subject positions that are traditionally ignored (Nash 2008: 5; Crenshaw 1991; Collins and Bilge 2020). As stated, doing this for the Cosby case would assess all of the socio-legal and digital/legacy media materials as well as provide an overview of how this case evolved culturally and rhetorically vis-à-vis the important categories of sexuality, justice and power.

Step two: Critical discourse analysis

After the overview, I draw on the tools of critical discourse analysis to examine how sexual relationality is expressed through the various permutations of consent, sexual autonomy and sexual integrity as they are reflected in the cases themselves as well as in media and public discourse (with a focus on the #MeToo campaign). My discussion of traditional media coverage tends to focus on how different media, particularly newspapers and news magazines, contribute to and shape public perceptions of each case using existing research. This is so I can focus on the production and examination of primary sources related to #MeToo specifically.

Step three: Possibilities of a 'pleasure and care-centred ethic of embodied and relational sexual Otherness'

Following this, I explore the possibilities of the 'pleasure and care-centred ethic of embodied and relational sexual Otherness' model as an alternative sexual ideal. While none of the cases meet this bar, it is important to understand why, what precisely is missing, and what needs to change for more sexual interactions to meet this bar. Remember that this framework is an ideal type, representative of what can be but what is not yet. It is reminiscent of what Jacques Derrida refers to as a regulative ideal in that it can orient us towards a future state that cannot be guaranteed (Bennington and Derrida 1993; Derrida 2001). As such, the 'pleasure and care-centred ethic of embodied and relational sexual Otherness' framework is flexible and must, as stated in Chapter 1, be open to contradiction, limit cases and change – particularly as it relates to transactional sex/sex work, mundane sex and transgressive sexual practice. In brief, again drawing on the Bill Cosby case as an example, this would entail a deep engagement with how understandings of consent, sexual autonomy, sexual integrity and sexual freedom are reflected in the case by asking how they were taken up in mainstream and social media specifically. This would include any significant changes to norms around sexuality, salient controversies and formative events (i.e. the rise of #MeToo). I would maintain that all permutations of consent, sexual autonomy and sexual integrity were violated by Cosby, leaving little grey area to debate over (putting aside outright deniers), and even the more capacious framework of sexual relationality I have articulated leaves little room for (re)interpretation. That is, each described interaction/assault reflects a total violation of every principle of sexual relationality consistent with a 'pleasure and care-centred ethic of embodied and relational sexual Otherness'.

Step four: Restorative justice

Finally, I explore the possibilities of restorative justice as a viable alternative with respect to what we know (through media – both traditional and social), the formal legal complaints and processes that have been brought to the fore, the standpoints of both the accuser(s) and the accused (i.e. in the form of public apologies and statements), and what this means for the future prospects for movements like #MeToo. Taken together, these four steps (interpretive and narrative, discourse analytic, pleasure and care-centred, and restorative) provide a robust framework for exploring the possibilities for transformative change going forward. Inevitably, as in most research, there will be aspects left out and insights overlooked. What I have tried to do in these case studies is to offer a novel way to think about sex and gender (and also race and class) using concrete, publicised events (that everyone seems to have an opinion on), a global social movement (#MeToo) and a social justice framework (restorative justice) in order to better understand the moment we are in and to map a pro-social way forward. As in the Harvey Weinstein case that follows, the Bill Cosby saga is particularly difficult to assess with respect to restorative justice in that, due to his blanket public denials, there is very little indication Cosby would be interested in participating in such a process, or indeed that his victims would (Selter 2014; Levenson and Cooper 2018). As such, this case represents a bit of a paradox for restorative justice proponents but one which is important in light of its possibilities. This is particularly true given the repeated failure of the traditional justice system and the options for healing restorative justice might have made available for these women had it been a possibility for them decades ago.

HARVEY WEINSTEIN

The saga of Academy award-winning and highly influential Hollywood producer Harvey Weinstein symbolises the penultimate #MeToo case for which a clear-cut argument for restorative justice and the norm of a 'pleasure and care-centred ethic of embodied and relational sexual Otherness' is incredibly difficult. As in the case of Avital Ronell, it was *The New York Times* which first published a feature piece in 2017 detailing all of the allegations of sexual assault, harassment and rape against Harvey Weinstein made by high-profile women like Ashley Judd, Rose McGowan and Cate Blanchett. The article, by Jodi Kantor and Megan Twohey (2017), chronicles, in startling detail, a several-decades-long series of sexual assaults, often facilitated and/or covered up by assistants and co-workers, in which Weinstein would invite women to his hotel room, ostensibly for work purposes, and then proceed to solicit or demand sexual favours. Many of the women who complained or wanted to go public were given monetary settlements in exchange for their silence. These women were required to sign non-disclosure agreements (NDAs) as part of the settlements (*The New Yorker* 2017). Weinstein's behaviour was not a secret and formed an important part of the Hollywood whisper network. It also gave rise to the 'shitty media men' list that followed soon thereafter.

After the *New York Times* allegations were made public, Weinstein issued an apology, also through the newspaper, in which he acknowledged the pain he had caused (without specifying any acts, actions or persons) and promised to change:

> Though I'm trying to do better, I know I have a long way to go. That is my commitment. My journey now will be to learn about myself and conquer my demons. Over the last year, I've asked Lisa Bloom [his high-profile lawyer] to tutor me, and she's put together a team of people. I've brought on therapists, and I plan to take a leave of absence from my company and to deal with this issue head on. I so respect all women, and regret what happened. (Weinstein 2017)

In the months that followed, upwards of a dozen more women accused Weinstein of assault and/or rape, with high-profile actresses like Gwyneth Paltrow, Angelina Jolie, Asia Argento (who later had to face her own #MeToo allegations), Mira Sorvino and Lucia Stoller going public (Farrow 2017). After the publication of his response, Weinstein, through his spokesperson, denied all allegations of sexual assault even as other women, like Annabella Sciorra, Natassia Malthe, Uma Thurman and Lupita Nyong'o, made further accusations. In May 2018, Weinstein was charged with rape and sexual abuse in New York and, a few weeks later, was indicted. Other charges, accusations and lawsuits followed, during which time the trial commenced with Weinstein insisting that all relations were consensual. As the trial went on, revelations of further payouts and the use of an Israeli company called Black Cube to investigate the women making allegations and stop *The New York Times* from publishing another damaging article were made public. Also made public were further media statements and interviews by Weinstein, often accompanied by his lawyer, asserting his innocence (Pilkington 2020a). In an interview with the *New York Post*, Weinstein decries (the article says 'whines') that his important work and the fact that he gave opportunities to women were being forgotten: 'I feel like the forgotten man . . . I made more movies directed by women and about women than any filmmaker, and I'm talking about 30 years ago. I'm not talking about now when it's vogue. I did it first! I pioneered it! . . . It all got eviscerated because of what happened . . . My work has been forgotten' (Rosenberg 2019). Reaction to the interview was swift, with Rose McGowan calling him a 'prolific rapist' whom *she* has not forgotten (Jennifer Smith 2019). In a joint statement with twenty-two other women, McGowan asserted the following:

> 'Harvey Weinstein is trying to gaslight society again. He says in a new interview he doesn't want to be forgotten. Well, he won't be. He will be remembered as a sexual predator and an unrepentant abuser who took everything and deserves nothing,' the group, The Silence Breakers, stated. 'He will be remembered by the collective will of countless women who stood up and said enough. We refuse to let this predator rewrite his legacy of abuse. (Haas 2019)

In the end, Weinstein was found guilty of a criminal sex act in the first degree against Mimi Haley, a former production assistant, and rape in the third degree which took place in 2013. He was acquitted of the three other charges.

From this case, a number of #MeToo- and justice-oriented undercurrents are brought to the fore. The first is that the tweet that started the most recent iteration of the #MeToo movement (remember, it originated with Tarana Burke in 2007) was posted by Alyssa Milano in October 2017 in reaction to the Weinstein case. This marked the beginning of woman after woman coming forward with her own experiences – likely encouraged by the sheer number of complainants and the lower-risk solidarity it facilitated. The deluge of women posting their own #MeToo stories added to this environment of support. While the synergistic effects of #MeToo apropos the Weinstein case are laudable, there is a concern it does not go far enough in creating the conditions for structural change. The worry that the social media solidarity surrounding the Weinstein case is simply the latest iteration of hashtag feminism is not unfounded. While effective at consciousness raising, movements of this sort are less successful in attending to the causes of patriarchy, sexual exploitation and gender bias that have to do with asymmetries of power, resource allocation, access to capital (economic, cultural, symbolic), racism and misogyny (Khoja-Moolji 2015; Small 2020; Sebring 2019).

For instance, there is a robust critique of mainstream media coverage and public discourse (often filtered through #MeToo) that challenges how the Weinstein case has been covered and how he was portrayed wherein Weinstein, discussed as *the* singular monstrous figure of the #MeToo movement, becomes the centre of media focus. Again, this makes having conversations about the root causes of gender-based violence easy to gloss over, not only because the former stories are compelling, but also because the latter is really hard work. Suzanne Moore, in an article for *The Guardian*, makes the case for a shift in culture by drawing attention to the fact that the use of the monster narrative makes publicised instances of assault and rape seem like a one-off:

> So the tabloids are calling him a beast or a monster, usually alongside a picture of young, half-naked women. God forbid any link should be made between his behaviour and the way women are represented. God forbid any link should be made between him and the way other men behave. Contain him in his repulsiveness, and the more extreme he appears to be, the less like other men. (Moore 2017)

Catharine MacKinnon, in a piece in *The Atlantic*, argues that the Weinstein case represents a turning point – serving as a 'match [being thrown] into this tinderbox' which 'revealed that perpetrators of sexual abuse were not just those [monstrous] men over there but our men right here'. She concludes with a call for de facto and de jure equality, in the form of the Equal Rights Amendment (ERA), stricter laws against prostitution, and cultural and linguistic changes that get to the roots of rape culture. Notably, even MacKinnon, who remains a supporter of the criminal justice system, ends with a call for 'rehabilitation . . . [albeit] with, not without, reckoning' (MacKinnon 2019).

This use of the monster frame is important on two levels. The first is with respect to media agenda setting and the cultivation of public conversations wherein, if we focus solely on individual, high-profile cases, the 'how' and the 'why' of the abuse is left unaddressed. Specifically, it facilitates what Hillstrom calls the systemic neglect of the underlying 'gender based power structure' that produces a distorted model of sexual permissibility and is then 'combined with ingrained attitudes of entitlement and privilege among men' (Hillstrom 2018: 2). Salma Hayek's *New York Times* op-ed, titled 'Harvey Weinstein is my monster too' (Hayek 2017), *The Hollywood Reporter*'s article 'Young Harvey Weinstein: The making of a monster' (Johnson and Galloway 2017) and the *Financial Times*'s 'Harvey Weinstein is Hollywood's monster' (Gapper 2017) are emblematic of the monstrous man framing. While comforting in that it reinscribes faith that 'success' in this one case represents change, what it also reveals is that real structural change requires much more.

Second is the introduction of a neoliberal framing under which, beginning in the 1980s, crime and criminal behaviour began to be seen as a product of individual pathology. Socio-culturally, this neoliberal emphasis on personal responsibility and choice is co-constructed with and by larger changes including economic privatisation, the gutting of social programmes, and the introduction of market logic into all domains of life (Harvey 2007; Saad-Filho and Johnston 2005; Cahill and Konings 2017). Neoliberalism, as Wacquant argues, also gives rise to a kind of civic morality in which the public is encouraged by elites to funnel their anger from a system that does not serve them to the reconstructed deviant criminal, thug or predator whose actions occur in a vacuum (Wacquant 2009). The media tends to perpetuate this framing from both ends such that the complainant's behaviour is placed under scrutiny for their individual actions and the accused's for theirs, thereby obviating demands or more substantive transformations to education, employment, housing and community support.

However, there are also important aspects of the Weinstein case that deserve discussion as they relate to progressive social change. First, since Weinstein himself is a powerful white man, his comeuppance, if we can call it that, serves to flip the traditional narrative of cases featuring the dangerous racialised man, thereby laying bare what Shelley Cobb and Tanya

Horeck refer to as the much longer history 'of the systematic abuses of white patriarchy that are now being so vocally discussed as part of the "Weinstein effect"' (Cobb and Horeck 2018). Additionally, it should be recognised that if we believe the Twitter-supported community that this hashtag produced was pivotal in creating conditions under which women feel comfortable coming forward with their allegations (against Weinstein and others), I suppose it functioned as intended. This result, as Dixon puts it, would probably not have occurred without the creation of this agential 'virtual space where victims of inequality can coexist together in a space that acknowledges their pain, narrative, and isolation' – something the criminal justice system has not been able to do (Dixon 2014: 34). The fact that it resulted in a public trial is also significant.

Before turning to a discussion of consent, sexual autonomy and justice, it is important to point out and speak to the aspects of workplace harassment and an enabling culture that this case reveals. It is noteworthy that many of the allegations made against Weinstein involved inviting women to a meeting with him, often in a hotel room, under the guise of a professional opportunity. This opens up issues of industry norms, workplace ethics and codes of conduct. It also draws attention to the fact that women often 'lack . . . power in the workplace' and, in this case, were made to feel that these interactions were normal, or at least ones they could not afford to question (Reese and Coontz 2018: 40). Hollywood, notorious for its 'casting couch' lore, is an industry in which sex, celebrity and power are inextricably linked. As such, these sexualised myths and scripts have been used to play up the assumption that 'sex is the down-payment demanded by powerful men from powerless women (and in some cases men) in exchange for the potential pay-off of celebrity status' (Kavka 2020: 10–11). This narrative is also supported by the media's focus on the celebrity victims of Weinstein while disregarding the experiences of women who worked for him, including his assistant who reported sustained emotional and psychological abuse, as well as others who reported being cursed at, yelled at and subjected to sexist and homophobic slurs without a safe means of recourse (Hudson 2018). The fear of ramifications related to one's career is palpable in all of these cases. Moreover, they are not limited to Hollywood, with complaints being either ignored, settled (via payment) or rendered moot by accusers withdrawing them.

A final important part of the Weinstein saga is the role of enablers including assistants who set up the 'business meetings', lawyers who drew up NDAs, and private investigators who dug up dirt on the accused. In an article for *The Guardian*, Ed Pilkington chronicles how, 'At trial, the jury heard of several [female assistants] who were used to arrange "appointments" with his potential victims, luring them with offers of auditions or production jobs, then making them disappear when all was done' (Pilkington 2020b). I mention this because it widens the discussion beyond Weinstein by drawing attention to the pervasiveness of the asymmetrical power relations that produce environments of intimidation, entitlement and hierarchy – all of which require attending to.

The fact that this case went through the legal system publicly is notable and important in that it adds a layer of further discursive work by the media, legal experts, academics and #MeToo supporters. Moreover, it also serves as a concrete example of gendered violence that can be evaluated from the perspective of justice and accountability by those immediately affected. Before discussing these factors it is important to point out that although Weinstein claims all relations between himself and his accusers were consensual, the stories of each of the women render his defence improbable. The sheer number of women and the consistency of their stories made any defence, outside of one that sought to undermine his accusers, supremely difficult:

> Throughout the trial, Weinstein's defense attorneys sought to undermine the veracity of each woman's narratives. Rotunno and Damon Cheronis highlighted some accusers' inability to recall exact dates and times of the alleged assaults, or confronted them with e-mails and other evidence that they stayed in contact with the mogul after the alleged violent rapes they described. And the defense insisted that the women were not victims, but opportunists seeking connections and acting roles. (Newberry and Queally 2020)

Much of the trial came down to the adjudication of the 'he said, she said' binary because of a lack of any physical evidence or witnesses that could corroborate events. In the end, the jurors believed former production assistant Mimi Haley and former actress Jessica Mann over Weinstein – this despite the fact that some of the encounters, Mann's in particular, were described as consensual and ongoing. Added to this is the ever present 'why didn't you just leave?' question which pops up again here and which assumes a kind of subjectivity, agency, power and 'clarity of selfhood' that exists outside of gender, culture, psychology and socio-economics (Goldner 2020: 243). This is an important point since Mann's credibility persisted despite the typical assumptions around appropriate victim behaviour when it comes to rape and assault. Remember that it is often the case that acquaintance assaults, despite being the most common, result in the accuser continuing to maintain some kind of contact or relationship with the accused.

The fact that this was not held against Mann might indicate a degree of positive cultural change or at least a shift in expectations around victim behaviour. Holding simultaneously that someone could consent to sex on one occasion and not on another has been a difficult reality for juries to contend with and speaks to the complexities inherent in hinging culpability on the binary 'yes means yes', 'no means no' options offered by the consent framework. This is applicable to all of its permutations, including affirmative/enthusiastic or communicative consent, since the central question remains that of its presence or absence – which, again, often rests on who the jury believes is more reliable. Gendered norms and sexual scripts, unfortunately, make it even less likely that the reliable party will be the female-identifying accuser (Gruber 2020; Cowan 2019). Additionally, the 'beyond a reasonable doubt' standard, together with the subjective assessment of whether the accused sought a basic or affirmative 'yes' using a robust communicative framework (and whether this entire scenario is reasonable), will either place the bar too high, since sex can be instrumental or reluctantly entered into but still non-coercive, or too low, wherein silence is understood as permission. At one point, during deliberations, the jurors asked the judge for a legal definition of 'consent' and 'forcible compulsion', which, while not especially unusual, speaks to how complex and multifaceted these cases can become (Barr 2020).

Moreover, the continued expectation of there being some kind of physical force resulting from the anticipation of resistance, even if juries are directed to ignore this bar, takes us further away from the more capacious models of consent and sexual autonomy #MeToo has put forth. This, as Edwards argues, 'serves to perpetuate the myth that rape is accomplished by physical violence beyond unwanted penetration' (Edwards 1996: 241). It is also important to think about how sex actually happens and whether consent and sexual autonomy need to be rethought in a manner similar to the 'pleasure and care-centred ethic of embodied and relational sexual Otherness' approach I put forth in which they are seen as regulative ideals, not as juridical standards. I return to this below.

Despite these caveats, it is commonly accepted that, in this case, the jury got it right. Even if just narrowly, the jury was able to determine guilt while also overlooking the issue of physical force, applying a consent standard and determining it had not been met, and holding that victim experiences and actions are rarely consistent with normative expectations (and that this is okay). This optimistic outcome, however, is somewhat mitigated by the defendant himself since Weinstein fits easily into the sexual predator frame. It is also lessened by the defence's strategy which was to allege that the relationship was one of exchange – fame and career advancement for sexual gratification. To say that the women were incapable of entering into such a relationship risks denying them agency and reinscribing the 'woman as sexually naïve' trope. Weinstein's defence attorney made this assertion when she challenged the accuser to account for her inconsistent behaviour and motives, stating, 'You made a choice to have sexual encounters with Harvey Weinstein when you weren't sexually attracted to him . . . You liked the parties and you liked the power' and casting her as the guilty party: 'You manipulated Mr. Weinstein every single time, isn't that correct?' (Associated Press 2020).

Suffice to say, none of the women who testified had an easy time of it. Actress Annabella Sciorra and two other women testified despite the fact that their charges could not be prosecuted on their own. Sciorra's alleged rape had taken place in the early 1990s (Newberry and Queally 2020; Dwyer and Romo 2020; *Financial Times* 2020). Unlike Mann and Haley, Sciorra's testimony was not taken as credible, with the defence attorney pointing out inconsistencies in dates, circumstances and details, probing her behaviour after one of the alleged assaults, and asserting that she was just an actor acting. At one point, Rotunno (the defence attorney) brought up Sciorra's drinking during the night of the incident and the fact that she was being sued by her landlords. She also played a video from an episode of David Letterman in which Sciorra claimed she liked to make up stories for the press (O'Connor 2020; Johnson 2020). Overall, the adversarial structure of the trial facilitated interactions in which the women broke down a number of times and were challenged to defend not only their allegations but also themselves.

Sciorra, after the verdict, emphasised her belief in justice and the impact of testimony in 'speaking truth to power' in order to 'pave the way for a more just culture, free of the scourge of violence against women' (López-Fernández 2020). Haley and Mann expressed relief, with Mann asserting: 'I have found my voice and hope for a future where monsters no longer hide in our closet' (Evans 2020). The celebration of the guilty verdict amongst the myriad Weinstein accusers revealed similar sentiments while also doubling down on the need for carceral forms of justice. Ashley Judd, for example, tweeted: 'For the women who testified in this case, and walked through traumatic hell, you did a public service to girls and women everywhere, thank you. #ConvictWeinstein #Guilty' (Judd 2020). Journalist Gretchen Carlson, also on Twitter, stated, 'I hope the handcuffs are tight . . . #metoo #weinsteintrial' (Carlson 2020). Finally, Rose McGowan spoke to the media following the verdict, stating, 'For once he won't be sitting comfortably. For once he will know what it's like to have power wrapped around his neck . . . Today is a powerful day and a huge step forward in collective healing' (McGowan as cited by Gillespie 2020). Significantly, Weinstein still faces charges of rape and sexual assault in Los Angeles, a host of civil lawsuits, and an appeals process.

Despite these expressions of relief, satisfaction and justice, all of which should be taken as genuine, there remain a number of possibilities in this assemblage that need to be accounted for. With respect to consent and sexual autonomy, it is clear that Weinstein was disinclined and unwilling to consider the women he assaulted as desiring counterparts deserving of either. The basics of affirmative and enthusiastic consent, including 'positive cooperation', 'affirmative manifestations' and 'free agreement' (Tuerkheimer 2015: 450–1) were not present – although what might be called 'reluctant consent' was on a few occasions. A basic level of communicative consent wherein consent is expressed repeatedly through actions and words, and where the onus is on the initiator to secure said consent, is definitely absent. Communicative consent, as Burgin argues, means that 'Submitting to an act, or lack of active agreement, is not enough to assume consent' (Burgin 2018). Understood in this way, even sex entered into reluctantly by these women would be suspect.

Moreover, sexual autonomy is lacking, with the women consistently testifying to the fear they felt. Remember that sexual autonomy requires free choice, as well as what Kiefer and Sanchez call 'authentic expressions of the self' (Kiefer and Sanchez 2007). Thick notions of autonomy demand conditions that encourage the intersubjective co-creation of meaning and sexual capabilities (Nedelsky 1989). As I have argued, it is difficult to find conditions under which vigorous equality of this sort is present in light of the endemic asymmetries of gender, race, class, culture, sexuality and dis/ability. The power differentials between Weinstein and the women making allegations against him are palpable. However, it is also true that such distinctions exist, to some extent, in all sexual interactions.

On the surface, my proposed model of a 'pleasure and care-centred ethic of embodied and relational sexual Otherness' is also absent at all stages. A solidaristic ethic of relationality, care and embodiment is missing, not only on the part of Weinstein, whose instrumental and violent approach to sex has been established, but also from the larger assemblage inclusive of the media, courts and police. Which is to say that the conditions that might allow for such a robust conception of sexual relationality to take hold, or to at least be held as possible, were reduced by all parties to competing accounts of whether the sexual activity that took place was consented to.

What the sexual framework I propose does allow us to (re)consider are the limits of permissibility and consent. Remember that sex, as an activity, is rarely logical and discrete. Rather, it can be simultaneously desired and rejected, risky and pleasurable, dangerous and loving. The accounts of consented-to and not-consented-to sex throughout this book speak to this reality. Thus, whether a sexual interaction culminates in a transparently wanted encounter cannot be adequately adjudicated by a juridical process in which consent and an adversarial trial are the ultimate arbiters of harm. The ideal that I put forth is meant to facilitate reflection on an ethic of self-care, non-normativity, pleasure, communication and Otherness, while also allowing for sex that is transactional (i.e. sex work), gift-oriented (i.e. for the Other – as in a committed relationship), creative, and attendant to the context within which sex takes place.

To begin with, the sexual assemblage in which each of these encounters took place was constituted by unequal power relations, given Weinstein's power and clout, and premised on the promise of career enhancement (under the guise of business meetings). Ashley Judd, who met Weinstein in his room for a 'business meeting' and refused his advances, suffered in her career and later, unsuccessfully, sued Weinstein for damages. Director Peter Jackson, of *The Lord of the Rings* fame, has since come forward to confirm that he removed Judd's name from a casting list due to 'information' about her from Weinstein's camp (BBC News 2019). The asymmetries that constituted these encounters were also gendered, with expectations around resistance and agency coming up against masculine pressure and overt control. This came in the form of threats, such as telling actress Salma Hayek, after she refused his advances, that 'I will kill you, don't think I can't' (Desta 2017). It was also present in Weinstein's persistent badgering and coercive behaviour, as evidenced in a harrowing piece of audio from a police sting in which model Ambra Battilana Gutierrez can be heard being pressured by Weinstein to come to his room, where he admits to fondling her breast on an earlier occasion; he exhorts her to play along, to comply, to 'sit there', promising he 'won't do a thing', begging her 'not to embarrass him' because he is a 'famous guy' (BBC News 2019; Farrow 2017; ABC News 2017). That so many women complied says less about Weinstein's desirability and more about how patriarchy, misogynistic tactics, economic pressures and gender scripts conspired to produce a situation in which a 'pleasure and care-centred ethic of embodied and relational sexual Otherness' became all but impossible.

Pleasure in all its iterations, from the normative to the transgressive and the mundane to the overwhelming, is one-sided, with Weinstein's sexual gratification taking precedence. The positive possibilities of pleasure-driven sexuality, inclusive of 'explorations of the body, curiosity, intimacy, sensuality, adventure, excitement, human connection, basking in the infantile and non-rational', are not extended to the women at all (Vance 1984). As such, care for the Other, whether that is in the form of simple concern for a counterpart's welfare and well-being or the more robust epistemic obligation of non-instrumental mutual gift-giving, has been severed entirely. Care for the self is exercised solipsistically by Weinstein with no thought to the mutual generosity that should extend from that. Care for the self is also interdicted so that the women themselves are prevented from engaging in the self-crafting and exploration – what Foucault calls the 'reflective mode of relation to oneself, to one's body' – necessary for good or even mediocre sexual relations (Foucault 1987: 3; Bell 2005).

The principles of embodied communication have also been severed from these sexually coercive encounters, with the women verbally and through clear body language conveying their reticence and, in the case of Ambra Battilana Gutierrez, her outright refusal. Recollect that embodied communication is a capacity generated from lived experience which, in the context of sex, should work to cultivate an emergent intimacy between partners (Shusterman 1999; Gomez 2017). It also, helpfully, complexifies the 'yes means yes' and 'no means no' dichotomy which, as this case demonstrates, often does not reflect real-life experience. Embodied communication also undermines the mind/body binary, which tends to privilege rational thought by bifurcating the mind from the body (instead of viewing them as co-constituted) and challenges the 'woman as gatekeeper' model of sex. It also operates on the very clear assumption that all parties are generally capable of reading and understanding bodily cues, giving lie to the 'miscommunication' defence (Kitzinger and Frith 1999). As O'Byrne, Hansen and Rapley argue, 'conversation analytic findings on the normative interactional structure of refusals' show that 'men have a sophisticated understanding of these conversational "rules", and therefore deduce that male claims not to have "understood" refusals can only be heard as "self-interested justifications for coercive sexual behaviour"' (O'Byrne, Hansen and Rapley 2008: 173). From this, we can conclude that Weinstein simultaneously negated embodied communication and ignored how it was manifest by persisting in his requests for massages and sexual favours.

Cumulatively, in this case it is clear that the norms that constitute the sexual ethic of the 'pleasure and care-centred ethic of embodied and relational sexual Otherness' were violated by Weinstein inclusive of the incidents themselves and the coercive contexts in which they took place. Remember, however, that power differentials do not necessarily bar agential participation in all circumstances and can actually be desired. Considering the specificities of this case over the decades and the unfolding of the trial, however, leads me to maintain that relying on the courts, even in this case, is not the best way forward.

Instead, we can envision how this trial might have unfolded were it to have taken place under principles of restorative justice and the guiding regulative norm of a 'pleasure and care-centred ethic of embodied and relational sexual Otherness'. Under the best circumstances, this option might have produced the kind of permission structure that would allow for some of the earliest women who faced Weinstein's pressures and actions to confront him under conditions that were supportive, survivor-led and non-adversarial. Having a venue in which women can tell their stories and experiences without the trauma of cross-examination is critical to restorative justice in that it centres survivor voices instead of becoming mired in the adjudication of whether an explicit 'yes' was voiced during an interaction (Deer and Barefoot 2018; Marsh and Wager 2015). It also calls on the offender to 'acknowledge the harm and the negative consequences the crime caused a victim, for the offender to apologize, and for the offender to make up for what she or he did ("repair the harm") by penalties agreed to' (Curtis-Fawley and Daly 2005: 606).

As I discussed, Weinstein did offer an apology for his actions – albeit before the more serious allegations became public. In it, he expressed regret and contrition while also committing to deep self-reflection and monetary support for women's scholarships. Of course, this apology was short-lived since what followed was a flood of allegations by dozens of women followed by denials. Ultimately, we do not know whether Weinstein would agree to submit to a restorative process which would require that he admit culpability. Under the most optimistic circumstances, a restorative process might have (1) led to a better outcome by opening the door for an earlier reckoning; (2) facilitated a survivor-led framing of the proceedings; (3) required a fulsome apology that reflected the harm he caused; and (4) produced an agreement on how to make amends (inclusive of monetary reparations). A process like this attends to root causes. It also seeks to do more than restore things to the way they were but to 'change both the consequences of crime and the larger context of social inequality in which the crime occurred' (Ptacek 2010: 28; Backhouse 2012).

Yet despite these possibilities, added to my theoretical argument in support of transformative change over punitive state-driven logics, it remains the case that what Weinstein has done (and is alleged to have done) rises to a level of social transgression that many would say should bar him from participating in such a process. The Weinstein case poses the most difficult challenge to transformational processes of all the examples discussed in this book, not only in terms of the extent and level of gender-based violence, but also with regard to its role as the inciting incident of the 2017 #MeToo movement. However, the belief that such a process would be easy or exculpatory needs to be challenged since it ignores the very real difficulty of accepting one's behaviour in front of the person harmed (as well as the community they are part of), while also committing to a process of change that may take years. Weinstein, in court, did not take the stand and thus was not subject to the interrogation his victims were. A restorative circle or form of mediation would go beyond the issuing of a verdict and require that Weinstein hear a clear articulation of the harms he caused, issue a fulsome apology, and commit to make amends with the process being driven by the women he victimised. A trained restorative justice practitioner would ensure that guardrails are built in to guarantee that justice, repair and structural change are the guiding principles.

I submit that Weinstein's actions were permitted to go on for far too long largely because of the way in which the system is structured. For example, the legal proceedings, when they did take place, were gruelling and placed an evidentiary burden on the women. Moreover, with respect to the outcome, the court case did little in the way of addressing the root causes of sexual violence. It also failed to bring up and consider what a positive ethic of sexual relations might entail. Restorative justice attends to these deficits by requiring some form of education which would ideally include the 'pleasure and care-centred ethic of embodied and relational sexual Otherness' approach I have outlined. It at least would require that tough discussions about sex, gender and power take place. These requirements, at least publicly, are espoused by #MeToo proponents vis-à-vis consciousness raising and harm mitigation which requires 'uncovering the . . . scale . . . [and] confronting a climate of serial sexual predation – one in which women are belittled and undermined and abused and sometimes pushed out of their industries altogether' (Gilbert 2017).

What is more, while the Weinstein case ultimately went to trial and resulted in a guilty verdict, it does not mean that women who face similar situations will have their day in court due to asymmetries of power, money, celebrity and status. As such, an evaluation of carceral forms of #MeToo activism leads one to ask: 'what about women who lack the power or the opportunity to take on such giants? Moreover, what about the structures and systems that protected these men . . . ?' (Coleman 2018: 1). Restorative justice has the potential to function as a pedagogical and transformational process of healing that works in ways traditional criminal approaches have not. This is particularly true for women who face intersecting forms of oppression and doubly so if we embed within it the regulatory sexual ethic I have articulated (Crenshaw 1991). Concerns about continued predation can be addressed either by an appeal to public health models – what Caruso calls a public health quarantine model – or a myriad of *sui generis* accountability structures that would ensure that the objectives of survivor healing and structural change are met (Page and Arcy 2020; Caruso 2016; Pereboom 2014). The public health quarantine approach in particular has been used to justify separation only in extreme cases, wherein 'quarantine' must take place in a morally responsible way and be consistent with public health priorities, while community corrections have been used in Australia to change behaviour through education and treatment. A defence of alternatives is articulated eloquently in an article for *The New Republic* by Melissa Gira Grant, who argues that 'a carceral response to violence does not deliver justice' for any of the parties involved because it does not deliver 'accountability from those who have harmed them: to have them fully recognize and name the harm; apologize, privately or publicly; and take on the necessary and often long-lasting work of making amends' (Gira Grant 2020). Restorative justice and the 'pleasure and care-centred ethic of embodied and relational sexual Otherness', I contend, does.

In the following sections, I take up and examine other instances of publicised #MeToo cases using this framework with the objective of making a case for the model of sexual relationality I have put forth, coupled with restorative justice as more aligned to and consistent with the objectives of #MeToo as advocated by its earliest adherents.

6. The Case of Comedian Louis C.K.

Louis C.K. is a popular American comedian, writer and producer known for his biting social commentary, primarily in the form of standup (he has done several TV specials), but also through his hit television show *Louie* (2010) and several movie appearances. C.K. has also been a part of numerous film projects and television shows on the writing and production side. Much of his comedy is loosely based on his life and tends to poke fun at taken-for-granted social norms around gender, class, race and sexuality in ways that are personalised and self-effacing. For example, as part of a comedy routine, he once argued that since his 'body has no sexual meaning . . . if I can make people laugh with it, at least it's being used'. His comedy tends to be biting (verging on the offensive) and skirts right to the edge of what is acceptable. Jokes about September 11th and masturbation and the difference between men and women – he once stated that the core difference is that 'A man will rip off your arm and throw it into a river, but he will leave you as a human being intact. He won't mess with who you are. Women are non-violent but they will shit inside of your heart' – are emblematic of the kind of humour C.K. was known for (Ruppert 2013). He also had a reputation for being politically progressive, as someone who gave women comics opportunities in his projects, and who often incorporated a feminist perspective into his comedy. Examples include routines that involved comedically pointing out how men are the number one threat to women, the pervasiveness of gender-based violence – which he discussed in an interview on *The Daily Show* (but which he then followed up by stating that he can 'still enjoy a good rape joke') – and a set blaming men for not being able to satisfy women sexually while being easily satisfied themselves (Feldmen 2017). In 2020, Melanie Piper invited fans to examine the hypocrisy of this more progressive material, which she argued had been 'exposed . . . as a crafted front' (Piper 2020: 265).

On 9 November 2017, a few days before C.K. was to premier his new movie, *The New York Times* came out with a story chronicling the allegations of five women, four of which went on the record, about C.K.'s penchant for asking to masturbate in front of women he worked with going back to the 1990s. Incidents include: (1) asking to masturbate in front of two female comics he invited to his room after a set of theirs; (2) requesting the same of a fellow actor after the taping of a television pilot; (3) unpermitted masturbation while on the phone with one of the women; and (4) asking to masturbate in front of a woman working in production for a television show C.K. was writing on. The women characterised these incidents as 'unprofessional and inappropriate', asserting that it crossed a line, and that he 'abused his power' (Ryzik, Buckley and Kantor 2017). Some of the women were contacted by a contrite C.K. some time after these events – and after being warned by his staff against making anything public. None of the women felt there was any clear acknowledgement of wrongdoing or taking of responsibility during this communication.

The public outcry over the publication of the *Times* piece led to a tidal wave of articles, think pieces and hot takes. On Twitter, commentary at the time of the article fluctuated between surprise, anger at his hypocrisy, denial, fury at his accusers, and happiness that he had been publicly called to account (Sims 2017; Hayes and Chmielewski 2018). Many tweets that used the MeToo and Louis C.K. hashtags communicated overt anger at misogyny and rape culture in particular. It is important to point out that similar allegations had been swirling around C.K. since the early 2000s (see the section on whisper networks) with *Gawker*, in 2012, publishing a piece about a 'shameless funnyman' who likes to expose himself 'at the most inopportune moments, often at times when his female companions have expressed no interest in watching him go at it' (*Gawker* 2012; Framke 2017).

Following this, and not unlike Jian Ghomeshi and other accused celebrities, C.K. wrote a public letter admitting that these allegations were true, even naming the women cited in the *New York Times* story. In the letter, he describes what he did explicitly and identifies the power he had over these women as an object of admiration, a power which, he admits, was 'wielded' irresponsibly. C.K. writes,

> I also took advantage of the fact that I was widely admired in my and their community, which disabled them from sharing their story and brought hardship to them when they tried because people who look up to me didn't want to hear it. I didn't think that I was doing any of that because my position allowed me not to think about it. There is nothing about this that I forgive myself for.

After apologising to his colleagues and family, C.K. closes by promising to 'step back and take a long time to listen' (C.K. 2017). Reactions to the letter varied, with many criticising it as self-serving (note the number of times he talks about being looked up to), as insufficiently remorseful, and as failing to address the structural forces (misogyny, patriarchy) that gave rise to this kind of behaviour in the first place (Wadsworth 2017). Gabriel Bell, in *Salon*, writes,

> it seems Louis C.K. does not truly understand the problem at hand. He notes that one of the mitigating factors against his victims coming forward is that he 'was widely admired' in the comedy community. To be clear, this is not a question of talent or respect, but one of professional power. (Bell 2017)

Hanh Nguyen makes a similar argument for *IndieWire* in an article titled 'Louis C.K.'s statement follows in the footsteps of self-indulgent so-called apologies' (Nguyen 2017). As stated the apology serves as an important rhetorical act and tool in #MeToo discourse which, unfortunately, tends to operate less as a way to account for harms and make amends than as a means by which to manage one's image and professional reputation (Benoit 2014; Wetherbee 2019).

In 2018, C.K. launched one of several comedic 'comebacks' in a set at a comedy club in which he offended the audience and some fans by mocking the activism of Parkland shooting survivors and the transgender community's use of they/them pronouns (Holub 2018). The leaked set also expressed C.K.'s anger at the sensitivity of today's youth and so-called 'cancel culture', for which he used jokes that incorporated racial stereotypes and homophobic slurs. Reaction to this appearance was particularly harsh, with *GQ* describing it as 'cribbed from alt-right talking points' and stating that 'C.K. seems to have fully completed his transformation into an angry, unremarkable old man with a microphone' (Darby 2018). *Slate* went even further, calling the set 'positively sickening [and] . . . vile' (Dessem 2018). Condemnatory tweets from the family members of the victims of the Parkland shooting as well as ones from celebrities like Judd Apatow, Jason Alexander and Aparna Nancherla (all from the comedy community) led to another period of quiet, which ended a few months later with C.K. announcing a multi-country tour and special. In the special, made available on his website, C.K. addresses the allegations directly by underlining that in all cases consent was sought and given, but admits that more may have been needed. He then follows this with some fairly asinine jokes about accents, the use of the word 'retarded', and vegans (C.K. 2020; Logan 2020). In a recent surprise set at Dave Chappelle's 'socially distanced' comedy show (August 2020) C.K. was heckled by an audience member over the allegations in the *Times* piece.

Overall, the social media castigation of C.K. led by #MeToo activists and the women making the allegations can be seen as a kind of cathartic backlash that offers a semblance of accountability and justice within a social and occupational environment that has allowed this kind of behaviour to go on for too long. As I have argued, the support offered by acts of #MeToo confession in a mediated environment in which anonymity is possible, solidarity is widespread, and belief (by supporters) is unequivocal should not be dismissed. Neither should the satisfaction of angrily 'outing' perpetrators who have for decades been protected by workplaces, staff, colleagues and even the law. Orgad and Gill (2019), Traister (2018), Brittney Cooper (2018) and Chemaly (2018) have all written about the importance of feminist rage, particularly when it is used to 'creatively . . . undo . . . [the] structures and cultures that serve to legitimate the violation and subordination of women' (Savigny 2020: 14).

In the long run, however, I would suggest that this approach still does not adequately challenge the structures that give rise to sexual violence. This would require that we 'redefine in fundamental ways . . . accepted [sexual] historical categories and . . . make visible hidden structures of domination and exploitation' (Federici 2004: 13). Moreover, individualising C.K. as a 'harbinger . . . of fetishized evil' rather than as imbricated in these structures leads to little in the way of tangible social change (Pipyrou 2018).

In the end, the question becomes whether #MeToo, even with its consciousness raising and development of offshoot movements like #TimesUp, is capable of producing the strong counterhegemonies that are necessary (Dean 2005). With respect to Louis C.K., given his lack of accountability and personal development, as well as the heightened public scrutiny his accusers have been placed under, not much has changed. Rebecca Corry, in an article for *Vulture*, writes, 'Since speaking out, I've experienced vicious and swift backlash from women and men, in and out of the comedy community. I've received death threats, been berated, judged, ridiculed, dismissed, shamed, and attacked' (Corry 2018a). Given this unsatisfactory outcome, we can now move to address some of the stickier issues around consent, sexual desire, gender and structural asymmetries before moving on to an assessment of the possibilities offered by the approach I have put forward.

In turning to the assessment of the model and approach I propose, it is necessary to discuss how consent, in all its permutations, is understood, as well as the role played by other models including sexual autonomy and sexual citizenship. Overall, consent plays a particularly important role since in each of the interactions, specifically the allegations made by the women and Louis C.K.'s apology, C.K. does appear to have solicited consent or at least permission. This is important if we are operating on the assumption that the giving of consent (i.e. 'yes means yes'), as Hurd contends, is morally transformative in that its assertion renders an act that is otherwise morally objectionable, permissible (Hurd 1996). Never mind, however, whether that 'yes' is ongoing, desired or enthusiastic. It would appear, in some sectors of the court of mediated public opinion, that the simple indication of a yes, however reluctant it might have been, is sufficient.

Before continuing with the issue of consent, it is important to flag some significant contextual aspects of this case which differentiate it from the Ronell and Ghomeshi cases vis-à-vis who one might report to and the degree of perceived severity. For example, while some of the interactions were work adjacent, that is, an opportunity to make a connection, agreement was not explicitly connected to getting or losing a job – nor does there appear to be any overt threat of physical harm. In this way, these interactions could be thought of as unpleasant but consented to (Fischel 2019). Mark Breslin, who spearheaded C.K.'s first comeback by hosting him at his Toronto comedy club, made this case in an article for the *Canadian Jewish News*. Comedian Julia Wolov, one of the five complainants, wrote a piece in response, challenging Breslin's defence of C.K. by stating that 'Contrary to Breslin's accounting, what C.K. did was not done with consent. We never agreed nor asked him to take all his clothes off and masturbate to completion in front of us. But it didn't matter because the exciting part for him was the fear on our faces' (Wolov 2019; Breslin 2019). This speaks directly to the trouble with the basic consent model in which affirmative, enthusiastic and communicative norms are absent and yet agreement is assumed due to a lack of vocal opposition (I would hazard that C.K. was perfectly aware of the position he was putting these women in).

As such, consent would have to be understood in its thinnest and most basic sense for C.K.'s act to be justified. The bar of (1) communicative consent, in which mutual agreement, obligation and pleasure are centred; (2) affirmative and enthusiastic consent, wherein wantedness, as a mutually constituted form of desire, is explicitly solicited and manifestly conveyed; and/or (3) sexual autonomy, which requires the cultivation of the sexual self and the exercise of agency (whether autonomously or intersubjectively defined) has not been met in any of these interactions. Nor has a sense of sexual citizenship which would require that consent is expressed as part of a larger democratic morality. As I have argued, each of these models is insufficient in capturing the reality of #MeToo cases like this one – particularly as it relates to the impact of asymmetries of power, context, gender scripts;

the reality of how sexual acts are negotiated in practice; the ambivalence of 'consent' and desire; and the embodied way in which sexual communication occurs. None of these 'bars', in a juridical sense, attends to the specificities of each allegation. Moreover, a formal prosecution would probably result in the decentring of the complainant, it being a crime against the state, and include a robust cross-examination which, as I have argued, can be particularly traumatic for victims of sexual assault.

Conflicts around interpretation, permissibility and context would likely have been made even more complicated, had it been taken to trial, in light of statements like those made by comedian Sarah Silverman who, in a radio interview with Howard Stern, admitted that C.K. had asked to masturbate in front of her several times. She argues that her allowances, coupled with his unexpected celebrity, had distorted his decision-making:

> I've known Louis forever, I'm not making excuses for him, so please don't take this that way. We are peers. We are equals. When we were kids, and he asked if he could masturbate in front of me, sometimes I'd go, 'F— yeah I want to see that!' . . . It's not analogous to the other women that are talking about what he did to them. He could offer me nothing. We were only just friends.
>
> I'm not saying what he did was okay. I'm just saying at a certain point, when he became influential, not even famous, but influential in the world of comedy, it changes . . . He felt like he was the same person, but the dynamic was different and it was not okay. (Desta 2018)

Rebecca Corry (one of the complainants), in a response to Silverman, tweeted, 'To be real clear, C.K. had "nothing to offer me" as I too was his equal on the set the day he decided to sexually harass me. He took away a day I worked years for and still has no remorse. He's a predator who victimized women for decades and lied about it' (Corry 2018b). Silverman, who later apologised to Corry, spoke about feeling conflicted about C.K., stating that 'I am at once very angry for the women he wronged and the culture that enabled it – and also sad, because he's my friend' (Desta 2018). Her sister, Laura Silverman, tweeted that C.K. had done the same thing to her as well. She, however, had a similar view to her sister, stating: 'After that, it's Louis C.K., on a cross country trip before he was famous. About 20 times. Not criminal. But compulsive, rude & gross' (Nickolai 2018).

Scholarship critical of the thin consent model points to how it does not address the everyday undesired allowances that victims, primarily women, give, including agreement like that articulated by Sarah and Laura Silverman as well as ones in which 'she did not want to argue, she was tired and decided to get it over with, it all happened so fast, she felt embarrassed, or it was too late to leave' (Gruber 2020: 143; Loick 2020).

Addressing these engrained expectations and norms requires significantly more than what a punitive process has to offer. Of course, in this case, as opposed to the Weinstein and Ghomeshi ones, there is very little option for legal recourse or even for a workplace complaint to be lodged. It is also a difficult case to envision being litigated in a formal criminal trial given that it is less than airtight in an evidentiary sense. As I argued in Chapter 1, what cases like this represent is a particular fuzzy, often referred to as 'grey', area of the law. It might have been taken up as a civil matter (assuming we classify this as a form of harassment) or, in the case of misconduct, could be seen as criminal depending on the jurisdiction. For example, C.K. could be brought up on misdemeanour charges of indecent exposure or, in California, sexual misconduct. Formal charges, however, were never filed since this would require that the women lodge a police report, which none of them did, and for the statute of limitations to have not expired, which in most instances (depending on the specific charges) it has (Del Russo 2017).

A few further issues worth considering on the topic of sexual permissibility is the reliance on a thin notion of consent in media discussions and on social media. Additionally, sexual autonomy is barely mentioned in public discussions of this case yet it is an important alternative in the evolution of #MeToo and of sexual norms. Sexual autonomy, of the kind articulated by scholars like Drucilla Cornell (1998) and Jennifer Nedelsky (2011), sees bodily integrity, meaningful choice, relationality and personhood as existing a priori. Impairing one's sexual autonomy is thus a violation of one's very being. As such, it is quite clear that in each of these cases, sexual autonomy, even when defined solely through the lens of decision-making capacity, is attenuated when you consider C.K.'s celebrity status as well as the larger unequal social, occupational and cultural context that constituted these incidents. These constraining contextual factors are both overt and covert and involve disciplinary structures and assumptions about gender and sexuality that pervade women's lives (Bordo 1993; Foucault 1972). It is notable that, for many of the complainants, it was C.K.'s ability to help their careers which led them to the hotel rooms in which many of these interactions took place. Cumulatively, this renders the prospect of full autonomy not only unrealised but also potentially unrealisable given the fact that it is often presented as a formal rather than a regulative ideal. Finally, the more embodied iterations of autonomy, which thematise the non-rationalistic aspects of desire and pleasure, are definitely not present since they would require a level of non-instrumental mutuality that is simply not there.

We can now consider whether, for this case, the model of sexual relations I have described as that of a 'pleasure and care-centred ethic of embodied and relational sexual Otherness' within a restorative framework offers a more fruitful and just way forward. As a *regulative* ideal or guiding principle, this framework is capacious enough to consider permutations that suggest it is being strived for. First is the issue of the sexual assemblage of which each of these allegations forms a part and which, as I have argued, is revealed as unequal as it relates to gender and power. This asymmetry is revealed by the agential 'cut' I have made and exposes the underbelly of an industry and culture that permits unwanted sexual acts to take place.

Sufficient attention to pleasure and care for the Other is not present either given the instrumentality of the sexual act wherein C.K. has centred his own pleasure at the expense of the women he asked to watch him masturbate. These acts are inherently one-sided and therefore appropriative rather than shared. Remember that care for self and Other functions to cultivate a degree of legitimacy and trust that coheres with intersubjective desire. Sexual care for self, as Subotnik argues, sees sex as a site of liberty and transgression which, for the Other, should persist even under relations of difference (Subotnik 2006; Karaian 2013).

However, it is important to point out that this definition allows, in some instances, for care for the Other to be exercised asymmetrically and for sex to be instrumental if it is in pursuit of shared ends (e.g. pregnancy), to extend pleasure to a person one cares for (i.e. in committed relationships), or in pursuit of outcomes that are mutually agreed upon and for which power differentials are attended to (i.e. in the case of sex work or other forms of transactional sex). It also requires respect for the Otherness of sexual acts by barring the kinds of 'kink shaming' that have become a part of some iterations of #MeToo and risk undermining some of its more queer and transgressive goals. This interpretation of care-focused sexual relationality leaves room for a more sympathetic reading of Sarah Silverman's experience. Silverman appears to have had her own motivations for saying yes, namely, as a lark (she mentions at one point that 'she wanted to see it, it was amazing' (Nickolai 2018) or because C.K., her friend, asked her to and she acquiesced *for him*. It thus expands our definition of pleasure to include the associated, if difficult to understand, feelings it generated for Silverman. None of the other frameworks adequately makes room for this kind of dual experience.

Embodied communication, another key part of my 'pleasure and care-centred ethic of embodied and relational sexual Otherness' framework, focuses on the role of nonverbal and prediscursive bodily cues which, as articulated by feminist materialists, draws attention to how sex is both discursive and situated and where material bodies are seen to act in ways that may not be 'rational' but which are meaningful. Embodied communication is thus hermeneutic, self-making and requires an intimate understanding and respect for one's partner's feelings (Brady et al. 2018; Kukla 2018). In this way, each participant has to see the Other as subject rather than an object, something C.K. failed to do not only by instrumentalising the women he interacted with but also by refusing to consider the material and symbolic aspects of the body that are communicative. All of the women reported feeling disbelief, shame and paralysis in their encounters with him (Ryzik, Buckley and Kantor 2017). These feelings, I posit, were simultaneously felt and communicated by the women and ignored by C.K. Remember that embodied communication is linked to a Levinasian responsibility to the Other and a lived bodily ethos that is based on mutual respect, as an ideal, and which should play an important role in all sexual relations (Hunter and Cowan 2007). Moreover, the embodied self should be able to communicate willingness to sexual acts that are transgressive, inclusive of voyeurism and masturbation, and which can also include novelty, overwhelm and even the abject as long as there is an openness and ethic of communication that guides the experience (Saketopoulou 2019; Hurley 2018).

Suffice it to say that, from the complainant's perspective, all of the principles that form the regulative ideal of a 'pleasure and care-centred ethic of embodied and relational sexual Otherness' have been violated by C.K. This now brings us to the question of whether addressing his infractions within a process of restorative justice, in which the norms and values I have articulated are built into the evaluative and communicative process, could have led to a better outcome.

First, we require an account of the outcomes that did result. From the women's own testimonies and the initial reports of their experiences, none of them experienced a sense of justice or accountability. Dana Min Goodman and Julia Wolov reported on the backlash they experienced and their lost work opportunities, while Rebecca Corry faced death threats. Abby Schachner stated that 'the original interaction left her deeply dispirited . . . and was one of the things that discouraged her from pursuing comedy' (Ryzik, Buckley and Kantor 2017). For C.K., the Hollywood premiere of his 2017 movie *I Love You, Daddy* was cancelled and, in the immediate aftermath, he was slammed on Twitter, lost a deal with FX (a television network), was dropped by his manager, and received some quite negative press coverage. His former supporters and collaborators, like comics Tig Notaro and Kathy Griffin, as well as Marc Maron and Zoe Kazan, were publicly critical of him, with Stephen Colbert tweeting, in relation to C.K.'s apology, 'Louis C.K.'s apology leaves a lot to be desired. For example, I "desire" a time machine so I can go back and tell him not to masturbate in front of those women' (Colbert 2017; Puente 2019; Hohman 2018). For a while, C.K. was placed on a kind of time-out, one that was, at least partially, puportedly self-imposed in order to facilitate personal reflection and recompense (which is what public shaming is meant to do). #MeToo draws heavily on public shaming as a means by which to amplify the voices of the ignored and silenced, those who have no other recourse. As stated, it also promotes its own kind of social justice and solidarity which emerges through the sharing of stories (Pipyrou 2018). However, as I have argued, #MeToo-centric acts of social media catharsis are unable to address the structures of misogyny and patriarchy that permit this kind of behaviour in the first place.

Since the initial allegations were made public, C.K.'s career has recovered. He has, for example, been able to perform and tour – often to sold-out theatres. In an article for *The Washington Post*, journalist Elahe Izadi describes C.K.'s new audience and schtick, arguing that, with his jokes about 'Parkland shooting survivors, Asian men and gender identity', C.K. had taken an initial 'turn to right-wing comedy' in his set before returning to his regular fare: 'The meaninglessness of life, death, pedophilia, saying the r-word a bunch – it's not new terrain for him' (Izadi 2020). C.K. may now be less of a respected A-list celebrity, but he remains immensely popular, is making money, and has a platform and an audience.

Turning to the prospect that restorative justice might have offered a better option for all parties, it would have to have taken place early on, when C.K. first issued his apology, or even before that (when the events actually occurred), which would have been an ideal time to consider a restorative approach. This could have taken place in the form of a face-to-face circle in Rebecca Corry's case, since it occurred in a workplace setting, or using mediation. The fact that Corry complained to the then producers of the show she was a guest on (Courteney Cox and David Arquette) provides an institutional setting and formal impetus for such an approach. It also has a built-in community of accountability inclusive of the producers and executives of the show and the representatives of both sides. Remember, however, that restorative justice need not occur in a healing circle. Other options include dialogues or mediations, which are less formal processes and might have been an appropriate option for Dana Min Goodman and Julia Wolov, whose allegations in 2012 occurred in the context of a comedy festival. The Screen Actors Guild (SAG) is another body capable of setting up mediation or a circle, or there is the option of facilitating an ad hoc arrangement using not-for-profit programmes like Arizona's Circles of Peace programme or New York City's Restorative Center. What is important is that the victim is able to have a say in the direction and outcome of the process while also being able to confront the offender with their story and experience.

Being heard with the security of being believed at the outset, and not having to defend one's background, history or honesty, is important to complainants and this is only possible in a process that allows 'those who have been most affected by an incident to come together to share their feelings, describe how they were affected and develop a plan to repair the harm done or prevent a reoccurrence' (Wachtel 2003: 2; Gavrielides 2017). Avenues for prevention and repair in this case might include a public apology, monetary restitution, counselling, therapy, a public hiatus, investment in a programme selected by the women, and/or education. In the programme itself, whatever the format, I would suggest that the 'pleasure and care-centred ethic of embodied and relational sexual Otherness' framework I have devised should function as a signpost and guide to the process. Agreeing that sexual relations based on this regulative ideal are desirable can serve as a means by which to structure the telling of one's story through the articulation of specific harms using clear language about care, respect for the Other, embodied communication, mutual pleasure and reciprocity. Apologies and intention-setting can also benefit from this language and the identification of salient principles. Some education around this framework would also be ideal.

In terms of a willingness to agree to this, as in all cases, we will never truly know if C.K. would have been amenable to such an approach. On the one hand, his early apology is representative of at least some semblance of self-reflection, responsibility-taking and remorse. The fact that his apology extended to the cast and crew of the shows and movies he was on and that he acknowledged having harmed a larger community is an important part of restorative justice. However, C.K.'s earlier denials and evasiveness – for example telling *The New York Times* that 'I'm not going to answer to that stuff, because they're rumors . . . If you actually participate in a rumor, you make it bigger and you make it real' (Buckley 2017) – are telling. So are his later jokes about his sexual history: 'I like to jerk off, and I don't like being alone' (Lifshutz 2019), and his conflicting stance on consent in which he emphasises the 'need to check in often' but then follows it up with the assertion that 'women know how to seem okay when they're not okay' (Baldwin 2020). Either way, the option of a restorative process should ideally be offered to C.K. in order to give him the opportunity to learn, grow, make amends and restore relations with these women and his larger community. This might have been a more attractive and productive option than the media spectacle and attendant mutual harm that occurred in the period following the *New York Times* story.

For example, in a restorative process C.K. would have to be treated with respect. According to restorative principles, all parties would be made to move beyond what Theixos identifies as a strong tendency to sideline perpetrators' voices and perspectives entirely (Theixos 2018). This is because, in opposition to adversarial justice, emotions and labels like blame and guilt are replaced with accountability which the accused must actively take on. Additionally, if C.K. were to enter into a process of restorative justice with the women he harmed, he would have to clearly acknowledge that he made them uncomfortable, pressured, wronged and fearful of the repercussions on their careers, while also exploring his own feelings and history in a more fulsome way (Lynch 2017).

Taken together, the Louis C.K./#MeToo saga, I contend, would have had a much more favourable – as in just and mutually beneficial – outcome if all parties had been given the opportunity to engage in a restorative process in which a 'pleasure and care-centred ethic of embodied and relational sexual Otherness' acted as the guiding ideal. It is, of course, understandable, given the history of marginalisation women have been subject to, coupled with prevailing public narratives and dominant media framings, that even this process would not be entirely satisfactory. It would, however, offer a way for victims' 'voice[s] to be heard and for the impact and aftermath of the trauma to be more profoundly and widely considered'. It would also allow the offender to 'repay a moral debt, to contribute towards the healing of the victim and secondary victims, and for an apology and expression of sorrow' (Keenan 2018: 291).

Finally, I contend that this framework remains consistent with #MeToo's objectives on two levels. First is with respect to its goal of providing room for women to tell their stories in an environment in which they are not put on trial and where the accused admits culpability and commits to making amends (Gieseler 2019). This is in keeping with Tarana Burke's early intention that #MeToo form one part of a wider network of support for young women of colour who have experienced sexual violence. This approach also works to draw attention to harmful gender norms and stereotypes through a process that, if used widely with mass education, would do considerably more to address acts of misogyny and structural patriarchy than the traditional criminal justice system (Manne 2017).

Second, dealing with the Louis C.K. case using transformative practices can be seen as part of #MeToo's project of positive feminist world-building and transformative change. This speaks to its larger objective of public pedagogy. The integration of the 'pleasure and care-centred ethic of embodied and relational sexual Otherness' ideal type into a process of restoration, I contend, makes it even more consistent with the promotion of structural change. The act of bearing witness and cathartic storytelling made possible by #MeToo could continue, albeit in a different form, in which violence, whether interpersonal or carceral, is not the driving force.

7. Media Personality Jian Ghomeshi

The Ghomeshi case is interesting because it went to trial, lasted for months and leaves a trove of legal and media texts to analyse, including court transcripts and the day-by-day chronicling of the trial by the *Toronto Star*, the *National Post* and *The Global and Mail*. The primary allegations emerged just prior to #MeToo but unfolded during its height and, in contrast to the previous cases, involved a person of colour. The fact that it took place in Canada is also of note, as is the role of BDSM and explicit discussions about consent both at the trial and in public discourse. By way of background, Jian Ghomeshi is a prominent media figure who worked for the Canadian Broadcasting Corporation (CBC) and hosted a popular music and culture radio programme called *Q* that I myself listened to semi-regularly. Like Louis C.K. and Aziz Ansari, Ghomeshi used his platform to tackle social issues like rape culture, racism and social change. In 2016, after more than fifteen women came forward with claims of assault and harassment, Ghomeshi was charged with five counts of sexual assault and one count of overcoming resistance by choking on behalf of four women (CBC News 2016; Kassam 2016). It should be noted that rumours had followed Ghomeshi for years; I had personally heard about him as a PhD student living in Toronto between 2004 and 2008.

Ghomeshi was ultimately acquitted of all charges (the later charge of assault was settled out of court). He was also fired from his job. The judge found that the prosecution had not made their case beyond a reasonable doubt and, in his judgement, made clear that it was the reliability of the witnesses, who were aggressively cross-examined by the defence, that was the deciding factor. The fact that the case relied entirely on 'witness' accounts that were less than consistent was cited as a fundamental problem by the media as well. The women were criticised for 'holes in their memory' (about, for example, the kind of car Ghomeshi drove), their sending of emails and/or flowers after the event, and their telling of 'half truths' about other instances of sexual contact.

The testimony and behaviour of Lucy DeCoutere, the one woman who agreed to give her name, was seen by the judge as especially problematic:

> It is difficult for me to believe that someone who was choked as part of a sexual assault, would consider kissing sessions with the assailant both before and after the assault not worth mentioning when reporting the matter to the police . . . I can understand being reluctant to mention it, but I do not understand her thinking that it was not relevant. (*Maclean's* 2016)

By and large, it was the complainants who had been put on trial, which is consistent with the revictimisation thesis articulated by Susan Ehrlich (2003) wherein women who do not conform to normalised gender roles and sexual behaviours are seen as suspect. Cross-examination, Ehrlich contends, does ideological work to support and reify expectations around sexual propriety, utmost resistance, the seeking of help, and appropriate exercise of agency. Complainants were made to feel as if they were on trial, with DeCoutere characterising the experience as follows:

> The degradations of the assault were, at least, private. Imposed on me, but in my power to process. But the trial has been public and I've never lived through anything more harmful or humbling than having a spotlight shone on my frailties and being mocked in open court. (DeCoutere as cited by Spencer 2016)

Media coverage of the trial tended to support these gendered tropes and focus on the women rather than Ghomeshi himself. While these case studies are not meant to focus on media coverage specifically, it bears noting how quickly the media turned on these women. Research conducted by Sovdi (2016) as well as Coulling and Johnston (2018) demonstrates endemic bias against women in cases of assault. Weir also makes this argument in her reading of media accounts of this case in which, once the trial began, a palpable shift in coverage could be discerned as it related to inconsistencies in witness testimony such that, 'For several journalists, the inconsistencies and lies in the complainants' account made it impossible for the judge to do anything other than acquit' (Weir 2020: 150). My own reading of media coverage found the same. National outlets like the *Toronto Star*, the *National Post*, *The Globe and Mail*, as well as some local papers in large urban centres like the *Ottawa Citizen*, the *Vancouver Sun* and the *Montreal Gazette*, tended to err on the side of scepticism, with controversial columnist Christie Blatchford stating:

> Horkins [the judge], properly but nonetheless bravely in the current climate, placed the responsibility for the collapse of the case squarely where it belongs – with the three women who were Ghomeshi's accusers. (Blatchford 2016)

There were, however, a few pieces of media that highlighted the problems associated with how rape and assault trials are conducted – that is, by putting survivors on trial. Also discussed is how dominant social norms perpetuate sexual scripts and stereotypes about women and 'appropriate sexual behaviour' in a harmful manner (Charles 2016; BBC News 2016).

The subject of race as it relates to #MeToo is important – particularly in light of the criticism that its carceral and punitive focus will, as with most criminal justice-related initiatives, lead to the disproportionate incarceration of men of colour (and in particular Black men) (Pettit and Western 2004; Marcus Bell 2017). This is particularly the case when the women doing the accusing are white and the men Black, which has echoes of the racial stereotyping of Black men as sexually aggressive and dangerous (Hodes 2014; Apel 2004). Ghomeshi, being of Iranian descent, would have been thought to have been subject to a similar kind of treatment as a non-white Other, a Muslim Other and an Iranian Other.

Yet, as it relates to mainstream media and in this particular instance, it was the women who bore most of the public opprobrium and race was less of an explicit factor. Perhaps it was Ghomeshi's celebrity and years of being touted as a model of Canadian inclusiveness and egalitarianism that mitigated the treatment he received. Throughout his life, this had not always been the case. Having immigrated from Iran by way of Britain as a child, Ghomeshi suffered from racism and stigma growing up in the suburbs of Toronto (which he recounts in his memoirs) (Ghomeshi 2014). Most of the overt racism directed towards Ghomeshi during the trial came from social media and included harassment and racism directed at 'his Iranian heritage' (Ahearn and Bresge 2018). The Othering of a non-white man believed to have assaulted white women usually brings with it discourses of violation, the assertion of protective masculinity, and Islamophobia. This is because white women tend to represent 'the border of territory, family, race, culture, and identity', such that those that are racialised are demonised when sexual boundaries are crossed (Horsti 2017: 1,449).

In being held up as an ideal or what is often called a 'model' immigrant, Ghomeshi seems to have suffered less of the institutional racism experienced by other men of colour without his celebrity, cultural capital and means. The precariousness of the 'model minority' myth is reflected in the belonging that comes with education and wealth accumulation coupled with fear of stigmatisation as a result of racial and religious difference. It would appear that Ghomeshi felt much less of the latter as he became more recognisable (Shams 2019; Sharma 2016). One woman in particular recounts how Ghomeshi was well aware of his power after being told by him that 'he was better than me because he followed his dreams and look how successful he was and what he's done for minorities everywhere' (Donovan 2014). This played into how the women who accused him were judged (most of whom did not fit into the 'ideal victim' stereotype), and explains, at least partially, why race might not have played an overt role. Also of note is that race was not part of the suit Ghomeshi's lawyers filed (and then dropped) against the CBC over his firing. Rather, the basis for the suit was on bad faith, breach of confidence and defamation (Kane 2014).

Although the verdict hinged specifically on the reliability of the accusers, another publicised aspect of the defence had to do with discussions around consent, with all three women claiming that at no time did Ghomeshi ask for consent. These accounts were similar in describing sexual acts that took them by surprise and included 'nonconsensual' choking, slapping and biting (Donovan 2014). As the initiator, not ensuring consent would violate all standards of permissibility whether we are operating on the basic, affirmative/enthusiastic or communicative models. This illegality would persist even if other interactions were deemed consensual. Remember that in Canadian law, consent is interpreted in line with an affirmative ethic wherein agreement must be expressed by words or actions. Moreover, any engagement in sexual relations cannot involve the abuse of power and can be terminated at any time (Criminal Code 1985).

It is also important to emphasise the significance of BDSM since it, as a form of sexual practice Ghomeshi enjoyed, was generally constructed throughout the trial as morally suspect, non-normative, and outside the bounds of what is traditionally permissible (Khan 2014; Brown 2010). One of the reasons for this is its potential for bodily harm – which is why BDSM cases are often taken forward as assault rather than sexual assault (since it is easier to prosecute). Ghomeshi's claim that he was being singled out due to his sexual preferences, however, sits uneasily with the traditions of BDSM subcultures which have established strong shared norms and expectations including clear consent talk:

> Communication and negotiation is an integral part of the majority of kink/BDSM interactions . . . Participants in kink or BDSM activities usually set aside time to communicate before their interactions, and these discussions can cover anything including STD status and safer sex methods that will be used, the type of play/interaction that will take place during the activity, how long the activity will take, any health concerns (including triggers, allergies, disability issues, medication needs), what toys may be used during the time together, as well as any potential safety issues that should be planned for as part of this interaction. (Kattari 2015: 887; see also Kukla 2018)

Moreover, within BDSM, consent has to be explicit rather than implied and, as such, it functions as a line of demarcation separating consensual sex from rape and violence (Pitagora 2013). A common refrain amongst BDSM practitioners is Safe, Sane, Consensual (SSC) (Nielsen 2010). In addition to consent, sexual autonomy also plays a role in BDSM practices with respect for the co-determination of sexual relations. Criminalising BDSM is seen by some scholars as potentially constraining sexual autonomy in that doing so weakens one's capacity for sexual exploration while also reifying heteronormativity as *the* permissible form of sexual self-expression (Fischel and O'Connell 2015; Bloom 2015). However, none of the women who made allegations against Ghomeshi or who testified called what occurred consensual, nor, they maintain, did any conversations occur about boundaries, expectations and mutual desire. Lucy DeCoutere, the most vocal of the women, testified that the violence was not consensual but that some of their interactions, even after the assault, were:

> Women can be assaulted and still having positive feelings for them afterward, DeCoutere said Friday . . . According to the CBC, she added: 'That doesn't change the fact that he assaulted me and I never gave consent to him.' (Redden 2016)

However, it is also significant that, as discussed in Chapter 1, the ability to give consent freely implies the existence of a fully transparent, choosing neoliberal subject removed from structures of power and experiences of oppression. Ghomeshi's gender, celebrity, popularity and public platform placed him in a position of power vis-à-vis the women he was accused of assaulting, which for radical feminists renders free consent all but impossible. A weak version of this thesis would draw attention to the structural inequalities within which women must make these choices, while that strong interpretation, best articulated by Catharine MacKinnon, makes the case that sex is always 'a social construct of male power: defined by men, forced on women, and constitutive of the meaning of gender' (MacKinnon 1989: 113). It is thus important to identify and consider the role the myth of the liberal choosing subject performed throughout the trial as it relates to questions like 'why didn't you leave or say no?' or statements like 'you ought to have known better' (Wente 2016).

In all of the #MeToo cases discussed in this book, celebrity, power (both cultural and economic) and attractiveness are important factors to consider as they relate to consent and sexual autonomy. The accusers themselves relayed that Ghomeshi was a charismatic and powerful person, with one stating that he 'was flirtatious . . . He's funny, he's intelligent, he opens doors, a perfect gentleman' (Donovan and Hasham 2016). Another, even more delicate factor is the mixture of embodied desire and aversion expressed by the complainants wherein loving emails and sexy photos were exchanged and meetings (e.g. karaoke, tapings of his show, drinks) took place even after the fact (Miller 2016; Bess 2016).

However, placing an inordinate amount of stock in the assertion that women are devoid of power and agency, and thus were taken in by Ghomeshi's charms, risks playing into gendered stereotypes linking femininity with innate passivity. It may also be the case that each of the women who did engage with Ghomeshi after the alleged assaults took place did so in order to regain a sense of control, thereby asserting a form of strategic agency (something often left underexplored). Alternatively, their behaviour might be explained as a product of internalised gender scripts that encourage nonconfrontation as a result of 'disciplinary practices that engender the "docile bodies" of women, bodies more docile than the bodies of men' (Bartky 1997: 95; see also Ehrlich 2003).

Ghomeshi himself, after being fired from the CBC, wrote about the subject of consent and sexual autonomy in a Facebook post in which he states that he had only ever participated in 'sexual practices that are mutually agreed upon, consensual, and exciting for both partners'. He also asserts that his proclivities towards 'rough sex (BDSM)' were shared. Mutuality and shared pleasure are reflective of sexual autonomy discourse as it relates to self-determination – namely, the ability to freely choose with whom and under what conditions to have sex (Schulhofer 1998). Also of note is Ghomeshi's aside that one of his accusers often initiated said BDSM and that she 'encouraged our role-play', which speaks to sexual autonomy's core tenet that 'an act counts as sexually autonomous only if it is sexually self-expressive, engaging the sexual desire of the agent' (Gauthier 2011: 176). The post goes on to talk about the use of 'safe words' and 'comfort levels', and characterises sexual preferences as a 'human right'. Ghomeshi then details what he maintains is the building of a fabricated case against him and closes by taking a swipe against his accusers – who he claims are lying. He concludes with the assertion that all of this, particularly his firing, was a result of 'what I do in my private life' (*Toronto Star* 2014).

At the time, the media played into the more salacious aspects of this case in ways that betrayed a preference for coverage about unconventional sex rather than the intersections of sex, consent, pleasure, pain and desire. For example, there was little media coverage of the often contentious debate in legal circles around the ability to consent to potential injury as it relates to

BDSM versus sports wherein consent can be given despite the potential for head injuries and other physical damage. Perhaps, as Fischel argues, this is because the injuries associated with sport are not seen as an affront to dignity as transgressive sex is (Fischel 2019). Thus, a distinction needs to be made between the BDSM and consent practice, which is strong, and routine sex, in which consent is required but often does not occur with the level of enthusiasm required of other practices. As such, the defence of 'agreed upon sexual kink', wherein BDSM is seen to affirm agency and eroticise a 'disguised expression for the longing for surrender', does not have a strong standing since it assumes a level of discourse that does not appear to have occurred in this case (Ghent 1990: 119).

While #MeToo still had to gain traction during the trial, the hashtag having not yet gone viral, its impact on the Ghomeshi case took hold when his 'apology' letter was published in *The New York Review of Books* (Ghomeshi 2018). Prior to this, the impact and publicity of the trial produced #MeToo-adjacent hashtags like #RapedNeverReported and #IBelieveWomen, as well as heightened media attention around cases of sexual misconduct in the realms of politics, sport and the judiciary in Canada (Kingston 2018). Writers of popular books that chronicled the height of #MeToo and assessed its future, like Robyn Doolittle's (2019) *Had It Coming: What's Fair in the Age of #MeToo*, position the Ghomeshi allegations and trial as propulsive and overlapping with the movement temporally via its aftereffects.

It was the publication of that apology essay that brought this case directly into the purview of #MeToo conversations. This makes it even more relevant as a case study since it was an instigator of cathartic confessions early on as well as an exemplar case of outrage during #MeToo's height. In the essay, titled 'Reflections from a hashtag', Ghomeshi chronicles his feelings around being the butt of jokes, being an outcast, and becoming a 'metonym for everything from male privilege to the need for due process'. He reflects on his career, his progressive bona fides (even positioning himself as a #MeToo pioneer) and all the celebrities he interviewed, before turning to the allegations and trial that had turned him into a 'poster boy for men who are assholes'. While never fully offering a full mea culpa as it relates to the allegations of violence, Ghomeshi does admit 'leveraging his status to entice women', and expresses regret for being moody and dismissive. The remainder of the essay discusses his own feelings at the 24-7 sensational media coverage, social media opprobrium, feelings of loneliness, and possibility of financial ruin. Notably he also, for the first time, addresses the subject of race by stating that 'I abhorred the racist implication that bad behaviour would be seen as correlated with my ethnic background – just another Iranian guy channeling some ancestral Middle Eastern brand of Asiatic misogyny'. This, of course, was aimed pointedly at the media and public prejudices rather than at the structural racism that usually applies to and shapes the experiences of men of colour caught in the criminal justice system. Finally, Ghomeshi discusses his conversations with other men fearful that what happened to him could happen to them and closes with an anecdote about hitting it off with a woman who had no idea who he was.

The essay itself was roundly condemned for being self-involved, arrogant and solipsistic, and for never once directly addressing the allegations or the individual women who made them (Ahearn and Bresge 2018). An article in *The Cut* describes the essay as a self-obsessed 'attempt to try to blind us into accepting his version of truth, without acknowledging the depth of the pain he's caused' (Spencer 2018). Following its publication and a barrage of critical commentary launched at the *Review*, its editor, Ian Buruma, took to the media to defend himself. In justifying the publication of the letter, Buruma also took a swipe at #MeToo, arguing that, 'like all well-intentioned and good things, there can be undesirable consequences. I think, in a general climate of denunciation, sometimes things happen and people express views that can be disturbing.' His primary argument was that the Ghomeshi trial and its aftermath represented a 'murky' case in which, as Buruma puts it, 'people are not found to have broken the law but have misbehaved in other ways nonetheless. How do you deal with such cases? Should that last forever?' (Chotiner 2018). Buruma eventually resigned from his post but not without taking a parting shot at the media and the *Review* in an interview with a Dutch publication in which he defended his decision to publish the piece, lamenting that he had 'now . . . been convicted on Twitter, without any due process' (Cohen 2018). Overall, this rather messy constellation of allegation, investigation, trial, essay, response, resignation and media fallout is representative of the core entanglements I am carefully trying to unpick in this case study. In analysing the case for further options and opportunities for progressive change, some more discussion of consent is warranted before moving on to the opportunities offered by my model of just sexual ethics and of restorative justice.

In this case of gender-based violence made infamous by #MeToo, consent still forms the crux of conversations held online, offline, on social media and in academic circles. All of the consent and consent-adjacent options in this case, including communicative, affirmative and enthusiastic consent as well as sexual autonomy, collapsed at the trial into a 'he said, she said' morass that placed the women on trial. The presence of BDSM as a practice further complicated the role of consent and permissibility by functioning not as a way in which to further probe the limits and potentialities of consent as law, but as a source of prurient spectacle – or what has come to be known as the 'kinky defence' (Grinberg 2014).

The continued juridical impoverishment of sexual assault and rape trials silences survivor voices and minimises accountability and repair. #MeToo has been able to fill at least part of this gap through what Leigh Gilmore calls 'democratised survivor speech' (Gilmore 2017). It is unclear, in these circumstances, how a higher bar of consent, or one mitigated by appeals to bodily integrity or wantedness/desirability, would improve things. The impact of the trial on the women whose characters were impugned and integrity questioned was immense – particularly DeCoutere, who, in subsequent interviews, describes feeling as though her memory was on trial, remarking that she 'never felt so bad about being myself than I do now' and confessing, in a CBC interview, that 'Personally, it's not been worth it, the years that I've lost to this' (Boesveld 2016; *Out in the Open* 2016).

Ghomeshi, in 2017 and 2018, launched short-lived 'comebacks' (plural) including a video series titled *The Ideation Project* and then a podcast called *Roque* (which focused on the stories of the Iranian diaspora) (Thiessen 2020). Suffice to say they were not well received and added to the injury faced by Ghomeshi's accusers given their coverage in the media.

A more fruitful process, I contend, would result from drawing on the 'pleasure and care-centred ethic of embodied and relational sexual Otherness' and restorative justice I have put forth. When analysed through this lens, it is clear from the women's accounts that Ghomeshi's behaviour violates this framework of sexual relationality on a number of levels. To begin with, the sex was neither pleasurable nor wanted – particularly in those instances where the initial act was unexpected. As stated, a number of women reported being punched, their hair being pulled, being whipped and being bitten under circumstances that had not been discussed, mutually agreed upon and/or desired (Woolf 2014). Despite the model's focus on emergence, prohibition and non-representational modes of communication, it is clear from the allegations that Ghomeshi transgressed ethical permissibility and violated democratic sexual co-constitution.

Second is the capacity for a sexual interaction to actualise self-care through investment in a kind of autonomy that involves the 'ongoing, interactive, creation of our selves – our relational selves' and our sexual selves (Nedelsky 2011: 45). This requires confidence that the verbal and bodily cues one communicates are being respected and understood. To rely on the miscommunication trope is to obviate the responsibility to attend to and read basic social cues while also risking reinscribing the male gaze as inherently desiring and women as blameworthy due to unclear communication (Cowan 2007; Conaghan and Russell 2014). A 'pleasure and care-centred ethic of embodied and relational sexual Otherness' must also consider that the interactions, as they are described, took place in a context in which celebrity, embedded asymmetries of power, gender norms and structural misogyny are mediating contextual factors worthy of discussion and debate. This might entail that differences are ignored or cast aside if desire and pleasure are seen as paramount. Sexual self-care, also important to this model, requires that connection to one's body and the Other's, consistent with an ethos of responsiveness and radical self-preservation, is established and nurtured. All of these possibilities and expectations were negated by Ghomeshi's actions and behaviour and are in conflict with the feminist, prosocial and justice-oriented platform he publicly ascribed to and which a number of the women stated was important to them (Brown 2015).

Finally, there is the element of Otherness inclusive of sexual Otherness (e.g. BDSM), relational Otherness, desirous Otherness, and the Otherness of the gift which demands the mutual recognition of vulnerability and reciprocity. Here, sex is seen as a form of social communication and, in relation to the gift, can be freely given. Sex that is routine, instrumental or not fully desired (for conception, to please one's partner, etc.) is also acceptable (Kukla 2018). The Otherness of relationality is arguably more applicable to the Ghomeshi case than the gift in that it centres the reciprocal sharedness of the act. Given the number of women who described Ghomeshi's behaviour as abusive, it is clear that even this basic condition was absent (Li 2014; Kingston 2018). It is important to underline that Otherness is emergent and affective, not purely rational, and is also sufficiently open to allow for discomfort and hesitancy as long as the basic ethic is respected. It is also sufficiently capacious to allow for BDSM as well as sex work as long as discrete acts reflect an ethos of understanding of self and Other as well as an equitable distribution of positive and negative autonomy (Finch and Monro 2006). Again, Ghomeshi's actions are violative of these principles and values inclusive of capabilities, sexual pleasure, autonomy and intimacy (Fischel and O'Connell 2015). Remember that the 'pleasure and care-centred ethic of embodied and relational sexual Otherness' is regulative and idealised (an ideal type) and therefore to be strived for even within a context constituted by structural inequalities, misogyny and unequal power relations. As such, it is also best placed to be operationalised within a programme and culture of restorative justice.

The critical question, as in all the cases covered in this book, is whether Ghomeshi would enter into a programme of restorative justice in which he would have to admit to causing harm. Ghomeshi's early statement arguably suggests some openness to a more fulsome apology – even if it is just in order to avoid media intrigue and public opprobrium. Being given an opportunity to grow, learn and repair the harm caused can serve as a strong incentive to enter into a restorative process. As for the women, there are strong indications that they might have preferred this option. DeCoutere, for example, when asked whether there was anything Ghomeshi could do to make things right, stated: 'I guess show some kind of sincere understanding that some damage was done and it can't continue . . . But he would have to call me. We would have to have a conversation. If he just gave some interview or wrote something – no, f-ck no' (Doolittle 2019b). Linda Redgrave, another complainant whom Ghomeshi allegedly punched, lamented that 'The legal system does not address trauma and its effects such as fear or possible re-traumatization' (Krishnan 2017).

The use of a healing or peacemaking circle would not be oriented to ascertaining Ghomeshi's guilt or innocence but, as in all restorative rituals, would 'offer hope for healing not only the wrongdoing between individuals . . . [and also] lift the heavy burden of human history and open up a future in which all life may flourish' (Vogel 2006: 595). Having this norm as a touchstone, I argue, could work to orient the circle sessions wherein the women harmed could state clearly how far Ghomeshi's actions were from the values of care, Otherness, relationality and embodiment. Moreover, while Vogel's demand for flourishing might seem lofty on its surface, it is important to remember that the telos of the circle is to find ways to repair the harm caused not only in the specific case, but also with an eye towards changing structures, values and norms that permit such actions to take place in the first place. Ostensibly, this is what #MeToo wants to achieve as well.

This process would also allow the CBC to be involved as the institution in which some of the harassment occurred and which did nothing to address the 'culture of fear' and disrespect at the show or the complaints of sexual assault made by Kathryn Borel (CBC Radio 2016; Bradshaw and McArthur 2014). Holding institutions responsible is an essential part of restorative justice. Furthermore, creating the conditions in which Ghomeshi is made to listen to and account for precisely how he harmed these women in an environment that does not hinge on the determination of guilt or innocence, consent or nonconsent, and where the complainants are not retraumatised, can be revelatory for all parties involved. Of course, its parameters would have to be carefully circumscribed and, as I have argued, contain an educative component beginning in the classroom as part of sex education about what is ideal as it relates to sexual intimacy. Repair might include careful listening, an apology, financial compensation, the forgoing of professional opportunities, therapy, education or community service, before the difficult subject of redemption and reintegration could be considered. Taken together, and given the specificities of this case, I would submit that the arguments I have proposed form a strong case for the consideration of restorative justice and the 'pleasure and care-centred ethic of embodied and relational sexual Otherness' as an alternative to the courts within which little justice was actually done.

8. New York University Professor Avital Ronell

The case of Avital Ronell, NYU Professor of German and Comparative Literature and Jacques Derrida Chair and Professor of Philosophy at The European Graduate School, serves as another example of #MeToo asserting itself in ways that challenge the boundaries of sexual normativity and restorative justice. In this case, Ronell, whose reputation as a forward-thinking and provocative public philosopher preceded her, was suspended without pay after being found guilty of sexually harassing her PhD student, Nimrod Reitman. Specifically, the Title IX investigation launched by the university found Ronell responsible for 'sexually charged physical and verbal coercion' against Reitman (Small 2018).

Under Title IX, Reitman had lodged a complaint against Ronell in 2018 for alleged unwanted sexual contact, stalking and harassing behaviour (Ronell was only found culpable for the harassment due to lack of evidence). The inciting incidents included a stay with Reitman in Paris in 2012 and events that occurred over a few days when Ronell stayed at Reitman's apartment in New York during Hurricane Sandy. Gifts between the two with inscriptions that conveyed their 'mutual affection' for one another were cited and submitted, as were emails including one that Reitman sent to Ronell about their time in Paris which stated: 'Sending tender love and kisses, I too remember and reminded of our beautiful scenery in Paris – vivid and always occurring I send you music, love, and kisses' (Ronell 2018). Ronell, for her part, is alleged to have 'groped' and 'kissed' Reitman repeatedly as well as pushed herself on him sexually in Paris and in his apartment. Ronell denied that any of their contact was nonconsensual and produced other emails conveying reciprocal fondness, including one which referred to her as 'Mon Avital' and read, 'beloved and special one . . . You are the best, my miracle. Sending you infinite love, kisses, and devotion' – which Reitman claimed he felt pressured to send (Wiener 2018; Greenberg 2018).

What makes this case particularly unique is that (1) it became a media story despite the fact that it does not involve celebrities or known personalities; (2) the alleged perpetrator is female and the complainant male; (3)

the body determining culpability is a university tribunal, not a conventional court; (4) the relationship of thesis supervisor-supervisee is rarely discussed outside of academic contexts; and (5) Ronell self-identifies as queer/lesbian and Reitman as gay. It is likely the culmination of all these particularities that resulted in amplified media interest.

A twist in the case came when a letter of support for Ronell was penned by Judith Butler and signed by a veritable who's who of intellectual superstars including Slavoj Zizek, John Searle, Gayatri Chakravorty Spivak, Jean-Luc Nancy and others who defended Ronell on the basis of her scholarly contributions, reputation and potential:

> We testify to the grace, the keen wit, and the intellectual commitment of Professor Ronell and ask that she be accorded the dignity rightly deserved by someone of her international standing and reputation. If she were to be terminated or relieved of her duties, the injustice would be widely recognized and opposed. (Leiter Reports 2018)

In addressing the accusations made by Reitman the letter states that 'the allegations against her do not constitute actual evidence, but rather support the view that malicious intention has animated and sustained this legal nightmare'. Following a public outcry, including think and hit pieces from a number of media outlets, Butler penned a letter of clarification and regret addressing many of the critiques. She, on behalf of herself and many of the signatories, conceded that the letter was written in haste and without complete information, that they should not have implied that Ronell's reputation somehow made her less accountable, and that all claims of harassment within the university deserve a fair hearing:

> claims of sexual harassment have too often been dismissed by discrediting the complainant, and that nefarious tactic has stopped legitimate claims from going forward and exacerbated the injustice. When and where such a claim proves to be illegitimate, it should be demonstrated on the basis of the evidence alone. (Butler 2018)

Further public criticism of the letter focused on the need for accountability and on on the difficulty of what to do when the accused is a friend, a feminist, a woman, a lesbian. Media coverage addressing perceived feminist hypocrisy was widespread. An article written for *The New Republic*, for example, questioned 'What a pair of scandals says about a movement that is now being accused of hypocrisy' (Livingston 2018), while *The New York Times* came out with a piece titled 'What happens to #MeToo when a feminist is the accused?' (Greenberg 2018). *The Atlantic*, in a similar vein, wrote about academia specifically in 'When academics defend colleagues accused of harassment'

(Harris and Wong 2018). Finally, Sharrona Pearl penned a widely read blog post, 'When a queer feminist professor is accused of harassment', which raised similar concerns and asked: 'If women can't be held accountable in the #metoo movement, then what is the movement for?' (Pearl 2018).

There were, however, pockets of support for Ronell that persisted despite Butler's clarification. Lisa Duggan, a fellow NYU Professor, wrote a lengthy article for *Bully Bloggers* in which she criticised liberal, social justice feminism for its carceral and corporate leanings. Her article, however, is more analytic than defensive in that she examines structures rather than the veracity of the allegations themselves. Importantly, Duggan argues that the relationship between Reitman and Ronell is atypical because it is queer and thus should not be judged using a heteronormative lens:

> A queer woman and a gay man in a romantic relationship? Romantic language that does not signify sexual desire? Forms of intimacy well outside the parameters of heterosexual (and, homosexual) courtship and marriage are commonplace among queers who not clearly separate friendship and romance, partnership and romantic friendship. The correspondence between Ronell and Reitman, full of literary allusions as well, can be read literally as an indicator of a sexual relationship. This is a culture clash. (Though that is not to say the correspondence is not 'problematic' as we academics like to say . . . and it does not establish that there was not a sexual relationship either). (Duggan 2018)

This is an interesting argument and one that is consistent with work in queer studies (Browne and Nash 2016). Duggan also takes a swipe at #MeToo for its neoliberal and sensationalist tendencies that tend to be expressed through individualised shaming and one-off firings rather than through structural changes. She closes by calling for a more capacious understanding of feminism – one that is anti-carceral, sex radical and socialist. Noted queer scholar John Halberstam tweeted a link to Duggan's piece, asserting that 'This is a clear, politically savvy take on the Ronell case by Lisa Duggan. Enough of the he said/she said, let's move to the analysis. Enough twitter outrage, and facebook high horse, read this, circulate and get real!!' (Macharia 2018). I share, quite strongly, Duggan's critique of carceral feminism, her assessment of misogyny within academic spaces, her assessment of advisor/advisee relations as it relates to boundaries, her calling out of the double standard applied to marginalised (queer) communities as it relates to (un)fair treatment by institutions, and her demand for a more expansive understanding of queer sexuality. What I find problematic with regard to #MeToo, however, is Duggan's tendency to essentialise 'queer kinship' and her assertion that some of these accusations are the result of sexual confusion or acts of projection and revenge – something which I am not sure there is sufficient evidence to support. These arguments, however, raise interesting questions about permissible sexual expression and whether, in cases like this and within higher education specifically, an institutional conversation needs to take place about the university's heteronormativity as it relates to faculty/graduate student relations.

Ronell, in later interviews and in a public statement, doubled down on the queer sensibility argument, stating:

> Our communications – which Reitman now claims constituted sexual harassment – were between two adults, a gay man and a queer woman, who share an Israeli heritage, as well as a penchant for florid and campy communications arising from our common academic backgrounds and sensibilities. These communications were repeatedly invited, responded to and encouraged by him over a period of three years. (Greenberg 2018)

In the German publication *Welt*, she referred to this kind of communication as a 'hyperbolic gay dialect' (Wang 2018).

Much of the scholarly work on female-driven harassment and abuse has tended to focus on the analysis of dominant sexual scripts wherein allegations made against women are taken less seriously than sexual assaults committed by men. One such frame that informs this assumption is the 'women as sexual gatekeepers' and 'men as sexual aggressors' trope which persists and is present in this case, especially as it relates to allegations of #MeToo hypocrisy. These sexual scripts are widespread in media, have been reflected in criminal convictions and sentencing, and have 'aided in both the under-recognition and reporting of female sex offending' (Hayes and Baker 2014: 3; Boyce 2013; Holmes 2010; Quintero Johnson and Miller 2016). It is possible that some of this is at play in the Ronell case but the largest factor explaining the attention it received, I contend, is that both parties identified as gay/queer, which initial media coverage did not quite know what to do with. *Salon*, for example, first reported the story under the title 'The strange case of Avital Ronell', in which the author spent a significant amount of time examining 'sexual orientation . . . as a mitigating factor' vis-à-vis the politics of language and sexual norms (O'Hehir 2018). *The Cut* offered a similar reading of non-normative sexuality but also drew attention to how important it is to consider larger structures of inequality within higher education. The author, Corey Robin, writes:

> Depending on whom you believe, Ronell's claims on Reitman may or may not have been for sex, but the sex was only one part of the harassment . . . Ronell's largest claims were on his time, on his life, on his attention and energy, well beyond the legitimate demands of an adviser on an advisee. (Arnold 2018)

Overwork, casualisation and the lack of funding faced by graduate students, the article contends, form the context within which exploitation of this kind is made possible.

Returning to the subject of gender, sexual assault/harassment and heteronormative scripts, Arnestad et al., writing about harassment by female aggressors, determined that men in particular considered so-called #HeToo cases to be less serious and female-driven assaults less likely to cause long-lasting suffering and harm (Arnestad et al. 2020). For example, when the media does cover stories of female-perpetrated sexual assault, they tend to focus on Mary Kay Letourneau-like cases of female teachers becoming sexually involved with their students and highlight the oddity of the cases since they challenge assumptions about female sexuality (Grimm and Harp 2011). Media narratives also tend to reconstruct and retrofit instances of female-driven sexual assault into narratives in which the purported victim, male in this case, is sexually precocious and the primary pursuer (Frankel 1998; Edwards 1998). Because age is not the central factor in this example, however, what remains of particular concern – and a matter of much public conversation – is the subject of power.

Analysis of the purported female offender (Ronell) and male victim (Reitman) roles in this case have revolved around the subject of power as it relates to the supervisor-supervisee relationship. Ethical norms, as well as the specifics of Title IX and governing university policies, are thus of particular import. Most university rules on relationships between students and supervisors (at the graduate level) tend to be governed by conflict of interest and sexual violence principles wherein consensual relations are permitted 'with the understanding that consent must be affirmative and ongoing and that consent cannot be obtained through the abuse of a position of power, trust or authority' (Harol and Zackodnik 2019: 209). NYU's policy, however, prohibits romantic relationships between professors and their students, especially when they are in the same programme and, relevant to the Ronell-Reitman case, between an advisor and advisee.

Also important is how this case is read through the lens of professional ethics. *The Chronicle of Higher Education* and *Inside Higher Ed*, for example, ran a number of articles from scholars exploring various dimensions of ethical decision-making. An especially compelling piece from the perspective of graduate students argued that academia had become a rarefied space in which reputation, lack of rules, shifting power relations and institutional sedimentation had 'empower[ed] our colleagues and superiors to suddenly feel entitled, seemingly at random' (Gerdsen and Walker 2019: 164). This includes entitlements to their time, their labour, and increasingly their friendship. My ability to speak to the uniqueness of this relationship comes out of my own experience with my PhD supervisor, with whom I spent long hours at their home, even renting from them at one point, working on papers, projects and my own scholarly research. This was representative of most of my colleagues' working relationships with their supervisors for whom the description 'close friend and mentor' does not seem out of place. The length of a PhD, in Canada and the US, is four years but it usually takes upwards of six and involves comprehensive exams, a proposal defence, a dissertation defence and intense primary research. This means that you inevitably establish a very close relationship with your supervisor during that time. Andrea Long Chua, in an article for *The Chronicle of Higher Education*, delivers a scathing assessment of the Ronell case rooted in a more general critique of graduate school:

> Graduate students know this intuitively; it is written on their bones. They've watched as their professors play favorites, as their colleagues get punished for citing an adviser's rival, as funding, jobs, and prestige are doled out to the most obedient and obsequious. The American university knows only the language of extortion. 'Tell,' it purrs, curling its fingers around your IV drip, 'and we'll eat you alive.' (Chua 2018)

While this was not my experience, I freely admit that it is not an exceptional or particularly hyperbolic characterisation. In the best-case scenario, the advisor/student relationship can be nurturing and mutually beneficial. In the worst case, of which I have known many, the relationship can be one of labour exploitation, neglect, denial of support, interpersonal and research-oriented conflict and, in this case, alleged abuse (Chua 2018). And yet I also know many former PhD students whose first or second supervisors became, at some point, their significant others. Some continue to be in those relationships.

Sullivan and Ogloff, however, maintain that the supervisor-supervisee relationship is not unlike that of a therapist, rendering the power supervisors have over their students' progress, reputation and day-to-day life disproportionate. They state:

> So long as a graduate student's consent may be unduly influenced by the power differential that exists, the consent cannot be seen to be voluntary, and hence it is not valid. Therefore, it is our position . . . that students generally are not free to give full voluntary consent to activities suggested by their supervisor. (Sullivan and Ogloff 1998: 231; see also Quatrella and Wentworth 1995; Stites 1996)

On the other hand is the position that prohibiting such relations infantilises students, who are adults, by denying them sexual agency and autonomy. It can also have the effect of driving the relationships underground and silencing those who might have a valid complaint.

Turning to the 'pleasure and care-centred ethic of embodied and relational sexual Otherness' and the objectives of #MeToo, the way this case unfolded leaves much to be desired. To begin with, consent, as a marker of permissibility, poses the intractable problem it does in all of the cases discussed thus far. Reitman's contention that the relationship was not consensual, and Ronell's argument that it was, reduces judgement of the case to which side of the 'he said, she said' binary you believe. If we take Reitman at his word, consent in all of its permutations (affirmative, enthusiastic, communicative) is lacking since there is no indication that active steps to establish ground rules, needs and/or desires were taken by Ronell. It is also far from clear that verbal or bodily expressions of willingness were conveyed or solicited. Remember that for affirmative consent to be enacted, the 'burden of proof . . . does not require that a woman prove she [*sic*] did not consent, but instead asks what happened to show and demonstrate consent' (Beres 2007: 103). The question then becomes: what did Ronell, as the initiator, do to establish consent and on what basis did she proceed (i.e. what cues – verbal or other – did Reitman express to communicate an unambiguous 'yes')? According to Reitman, 'reasonable steps' had not been taken by Ronell to ascertain affirmative consent, willingness or desire.

Further, any abuse of power and trust is often considered to be a factor in cases like this – particularly as it relates to the subject of consent. Whether or not power has been abused depends on the respective law or the regulations which, in this case, had been violated vis-à-vis NYU's own statutes. Moreover, with respect to consent, it is important to underline that the miscommunication defence, wherein the accused asserts that they genuinely believed consent had been given, has been largely debunked. As stated previously, extensive empirical work on this subject has established that the 'I genuinely thought she was into it' defence is spurious: 'The root of the problem', as Kitzinger and Frith argue, 'is not that men do not understand sexual refusals, but that they do not like them' (Kitzinger and Frith 1999: 310; see also Tuerkheimer 2015; Beres, Senn and McCaw 2014). This extends to women as well.

The philosophical problems associated with consent are present here also – particularly relating to the notion that individuals are liberal, autonomous and free agents capable of asserting their desires in spite of coercive structures and relations of power. This is a particularly salient factor in the context of graduate school. If we take Andrea Long Chua's interpretation of the advisor-advisee relationship at face value, consent, whether communicative, affirmative or enthusiastic, becomes all but impossible. The fracturing of desire and the complicated ways in which these desires become manifest conflict with the requirement that they be demonstrated in ways that are equivocal (i.e. by demonstrating clear and consistent refusal). The continued exchange of gifts, emails and meetings, for example, exposes the consent model as one that individualises crime and responsibilises sexual subjects for 'inconsistent' behaviour instead of addressing systemic and structural problems related to gender, power and sexual agency (Gotell 2008).

Finally, the subject of queer sexual epistemologies highlighted by this case requires that we rethink the 'masculine sexual agent seeking consent/feminine sexual subject acquiescing to it' dichotomy since neither Ronell nor Reitman fits these categories. It is clear that a rethink of how gender scripts operate in queer contexts is needed. However, it is also important to consider that the taking on of traditionally masculine-identified values and behaviours by women is also possible and that given the right conditions, such as a system in which aggression and exploitation are valued, masculine-identified script can be internalised and performed by anyone – including Ronell.

Turning to sexual autonomy, the other central model for the governing of sexual relations of interest to this case, according to Reitman his had been diminished. Reitman maintains that his options and ability to self- and/or co-determine sexual choice and exercise relational decision-making had been severely curtailed by Ronell. His lawsuit against NYU and Ronell stated that her actions had 'devastated him and caused serious damage that he will likely suffer for years to come' as a result of her creating 'a false romantic relationship . . . and by threat of, among other things, not allowing him to advance his Ph.D . . . assert[ing] complete domination and control over his life' (Reitman 2018). Sexually autonomous decision-making requires that the person deciding is well-informed of their options and equipped with 'the freedom to determine one's own sexual experiences, to choose how and with whom one expresses oneself sexually' (Lacey 1998b). The unstated norms of the institution, coupled with Ronell's behaviour, prevented the exercise of sexual autonomy in that it impeded the 'conscious reflection about preferences and a deliberate choice of one's goals' (Schulhofer 1998: 106; Oliver 1996).

As in other cases, the possibility to exercise clear, rational, unconstrained decision-making needs to be interrogated since coercive structures can also form a part of sexual autonomy. Additionally, it is also the case that sexual ethics, inclusive of the consent and autonomy frameworks, need to do a better job of contending with the complexity and boundary-breaking nature of sex qua sex. Yet, on the basis of Reitman's characterisation of the events, it would appear that Ronell's actions did curtail his sexual autonomy on a personal level.

The fact that Reitman launched a lawsuit against Ronell and NYU is telling as it relates to the university's tribunal process which, according to Reitman, was not satisfactory. Reitman's sense of validation and justice, the institution's desire for transparency, Ronell's need for due process, and #MeToo's call for all three were not met by this quasi-judicial hearing. The norm of a 'pleasure and care-centred ethic of embodied and relational sexual Otherness', I argue, offers a potentially transformative reframing – particularly when explored within the context of restorative justice.

On the face of it, Reitman's account speaks to and describes a concatenation of interactions and conversations within an institutional framework that is itself exploitative. The university system, coupled with the way graduate school and the student/supervisor relationship is structured, appears to have left open space for power to be exerted on Reitman, whose entire career and success in the programme depended on the say-so of one person. A 'pleasure and care-centred ethic of embodied and relational sexual Otherness' often requires that the ethic of care for the Other be fostered. Often this requires formulation of clear boundaries if anything intimate is taking place between colleagues or between individuals whose access to material or institutional power is unequal. This is a structural argument that cannot be separated from the experience of graduate students as it relates to labour in the form of teaching and research (often for their supervisors), as well as interpersonal dynamics that can range from negligence or sabotage to harassment (Harbin 2017; Anderson and Swazey 1998). Studies of the poor mental health status of graduate students speak to these realities (Jaschik 2015; Evans et al. 2018). The Ronell-Reitman case is one of many that needs to be assessed in light of this. The ideal of a 'pleasure and care-centred ethic of embodied and relational sexual Otherness' requires that the analysis of context, institutions and power relations form a large part of the adjudication of whether a sexual interaction meets the bar of being just for both/all parties. It is unlikely that trials and/or hearings like this one, set up to ascertain clear guilt or innocence, are able to address these issues, let alone the complex dynamics of sexual identity, self-representation and sexual norms that lie outside of heteronormative expectations.

The approach I have articulated, however, does provide more space than traditional frameworks by, in the first instance, allowing for a discussion of nonheteronormative sexual practices that might include bodily pleasure but do not have to be penetrative. The fact that neither Reitman nor Ronell self-identifies as heterosexual is accounted for in this approach since its focus on Otherness in a dual sense (i.e. relation to the Other and to *Otherness*) is capacious enough to account for diverse kinds of queer subjectivity. Namely, that they are 'exposed to queer politics that promote subversion of normative constructions of intimate life, while, at the same time, they are embedded in a culture that promotes a particular vision of romance, love, and family life' (Lamont 2017: 625). In this case, Ronell's contention that their relationship was reciprocal and subversive is supported by this approach. However, for Reitman, Ronell violated the Otherness of mutual recognition and intersubjectivity, what Elizabeth Anderson calls a 'democracy of equals', by failing to query, ascertain and accommodate his needs and desires (i.e. Otherness the other way around) (Anderson as cited by Wong 2019). The power dynamics in this case are decidedly unequal, with no attempt to mitigate or address them as the 'pleasure and care-centred ethic of embodied and relational sexual Otherness' approach requires.

This model is also capacious enough to account for the push and pull of the first stages of relationships that might reflect attraction and hesitancy by allowing for the consideration of the non-discrete (i.e. unfolding) dimensions of intimacy. Any discussion of this in a reflective capacity, however, is unlikely to take place in the kind of tribunal set up by NYU in which ascertaining consent is the ultimate goal. Even if it were permitted, it is likely to hinge on a presence/absence determination rather than through considered dialogue. Embodied communication, another key dimension of the 'pleasure and care-centred ethic of embodied and relational sexual Otherness', is also disregarded according to Reitman's account since not only was his sense of self, connection and desire not attended to, but it also did not reflect the 'ongoing state of alertness', 'mutuality of desire' or concern for the 'ends of [the] partner' that it requires (Pineau 1989: 234).

According to Reitman's explanation, particularly in his lawsuit which details numerous other instances of alleged assault, coercion, manipulation and jealousy, his relationship with Ronell was characterised by overwork and the use of his research without attribution. It is important to consider how care for the self and Other requires a level of respect that goes beyond sex qua sex to encompass reciprocity and trust (Supreme Court of the State of New York 2018). Finally, this model also allows for the experience of both parties to be taken up and addressed simultaneously in a manner that does not presume ideal conditions including full agency, transparent communication and dispositive decision-making. Proof of Reitman returning Ronell's affections through texts, gifts and agreement does not necessarily serve as evidence that no harm was done. The approach I have put forth allows for sex to be wanted and willing (ideally), willing but not wanted, or unwilling and unwanted but acquiesced to within the same relationship (Levand and Zapien 2019).

Overall, the outcome of this case leaves much to be desired. I contend that had a tribunal been conducted using a restorative framework (as in a healing circle) based on a 'pleasure and care-centred ethic of embodied and relational sexual Otherness', the outcome would have been more satisfactory and less litigious. Provided with a choice of mediation, circles or a reparative board, Reitman would have had a powerful platform with which to voice his experience requiring that Ronell hear and acknowledge his pain with the university acting as a community. This kind of restorative approach could use the 'pleasure and care-centred ethic of embodied and relational sexual Otherness' as a barometer or ideal type, building this model of sexual relationality into university norms and practices. Remember that restorative justice is aimed at 'address[ing] harms, needs, and obligations, in order to heal and put things as right as possible', and has as much chance of success as the Title IX process, if not more – particularly if the goal is to repair harm and encourage accountability (Zehr 1990: 37; Cameron 2006). From reading the accounts, counter accounts, media statements and formal complaints from Reitman and Ronell, it is clear that what is paramount is to have harms addressed by allowing Reitman's experience and perspective to be heard while also working towards the transformation of structures that gave rise to this kind of behaviour in the first place.

Whether Ronell would agree to such a process and consent to Reitman's requirements vis-à-vis restoration cannot be determined with any certainty. However, the option of avoiding an adversarial and reductive process, as well as the media storm that followed, might have been sufficiently attractive to warrant her buy-in. In addition to this cost-benefit analysis, a restorative process would also provide Ronell with the opportunity to engage in the critical self-reflection, learning and growth needed to stop this kind of behaviour and make amends. Restorative justice provides a framework through which Reitman could have set the terms and conditions, in the community, for the process itself and the steps required for repair to take place. The tribunal process makes this all but impossible in the way that it both incentivises denial and sidelines the survivor.

The use of restorative justice in this case also lines up with the objectives of #MeToo at least in so far as its purpose, on a larger scale, is to transform how sexual norms, scripts and expectations are structured. A continuation of this process, as it stands, has very little chance of resulting in positive outcomes for either party or for the #MeToo movement since, while changing the cultural conversation, it has

> left those affected searching for consequences and next steps . . . it has stalled because it lacks a sense of resolution, satisfaction, and justice for those involved as well as any means of assuring that offenders understand their actions and will not continue exactly as before after an indeterminate [for Ronell an eleven-month suspension] period of social banishment. (Stewart 2018: 1,712)

Overall, I contend that restorative justice, together with the norm of a 'pleasure and care-centred ethic of embodied and relational sexual Otherness' and a centring of relationality, rational and bodily desire, communication, and care for the Other in a relation of co-constitution, offers a novel and more repair-oriented way forward. One that aims at transforming the oppressive structures that give rise to abusive behaviour, this time with respect to the university system and vis-à-vis the student/supervisor relationship, and promotes perpetrator accountability and survivor agency and healing. Moreover, as Ptacek argues, decreasing the role of dominant institutions in 'responding to crime and increas[ing] the involvement of personal, familial, and community networks in repairing the harm caused by crime' offers a way in which to get at the root causes of oppression while also facilitating healing and ensuring transformative change (Ptacek 2010: ix).

9. Actor and Comedian Aziz Ansari

The Aziz Ansari case is particularly fascinating in light of its so-called 'greyness'. It is also a suitable candidate for a process of restorative justice with a 'pleasure and care-centred ethic of embodied and relational sexual Otherness' acting as the ideal typical sexual norm. Ansari is an American actor and comedian of South Asian descent (his parents are originally from Tamil Nadu, India) who gained fame in television shows like *Parks and Recreation*, movies like *I Love You, Man*, and through his standup comedy shows. Ansari's television show *Master of None*, which he co-created, co-wrote and starred in, won him acclaim for, amongst other things, its progressiveness by taking on issues like representation, racism, sexuality, ableism and sexism. It also won him numerous awards including a Golden Globe and several Emmys. Ansari also co-wrote a book in 2015 called *Modern Romance: An Investigation* with sociologist Eric Klinenberg which discussed similar themes – particularly sexism and racism. His wry, self-deprecating and social justice-oriented humour made Ansari the darling of the progressive left and of Hollywood. He also challenged traditional hegemonic masculinity through his characters and his public persona, which tended to be stylish, cultured, urbane and a little awkward when it came to women. In a 2014 interview with David Letterman, Ansari gained plaudits for proclaiming that he had always been a feminist:

> Some people wrote: 'Er, Aziz's girlfriend turned him into a feminist,' and that's not true, I've been a feminist my whole life. There wasn't a period where I was really against women and then started dating one and was like, 'You know what? Men and women are equal.' (Iqbal 2015)

In 2015, Ansari was nominated to be 'Feminist Celebrity of the Year' by the left feminist *Ms. Magazine*. He was also applauded for calling out Hollywood's racial diversity problem in another interview:

> That's a real thing that happens. When they cast these shows, they're like, 'We already have our minority guy or our minority girl.' There would never be two Indian people in one show. With Asian people, there can be one, but there can't be two. Black people, there can be two, but there can't be three because then it

> becomes a black show. Gay people, there can be two, women there can be two; but Asian people, Indian people, there can be one, but there can't be two. (Hagi 2015)

Scholars of feminism and celebrity culture supported this analysis but also articulated early concerns, including that Ansari represented a particularly problematic form of postfeminist masculinity. They argued that his interpretation of feminism was stripped of its capital 'P' political objectives since it focused on 'safe' subjects like diversity and equal pay (Hamad and Taylor 2015). Others took on the subjects of masculinity and race specifically, with Harpalani pointing to the invisibility of race in many of Ansari's characters as well as around his public identity (Owens 2016; Harpalani 2013). I give all this background in order to establish the progressive bona fides Ansari had carefully cultivated prior to an especially explosive article that came out in 2018 challenging many of the assumptions about him and other similarly situated 'woke' men.

In January 2018, an article was published on *Babe.net*, a now defunct spin-off of *The Tab*, a Rupert Murdoch-supported series of university publications across the US and the UK. *Babe*'s coverage, according to *Slate*'s Ruth Graham, included subjects like 'feminism, celebrities, "fuckboys," star signs, and fuckboys' star signs. The color palette is millennial pink. Its manifesto is headlined "babe is for girls who don't give a fuck." According to a piece in *Mashable*, its oldest editorial staffer is 25' (Graham 2018). The article itself, titled 'I went on a date with Aziz Ansari. It turned into the worst night of my life', was written by Katie Way and chronicled what happened to a twenty-three-year-old, female-identifying, Brooklyn-based photographer, pseudonymously called 'Grace', who had been on a date with Ansari a year earlier.

Grace, through Way, begins by describing a rather routine date of dinner and drinks after which they returned to Ansari's apartment in Tribeca. It was during her time in Ansari's apartment that Grace claims she was assaulted. She describes a quick escalation, soon after they arrived, from kissing to grabbing a condom, oral sex, and repeatedly being pulled towards his penis: 'It was 30 minutes of me getting up and moving and him following and sticking his fingers down my throat again. It was really repetitive. It felt like a fucking game.' By way of resistance, Grace claims that both verbal and non-verbal cues were given: 'Most of my discomfort was expressed in me pulling away and mumbling. I know that my hand stopped moving at some points,' she said. 'I stopped moving my lips and turned cold.'

After a brief visit to the bathroom, Grace returned to Ansari, who asked if she was okay and stated that he did not want her to feel forced before returning to the same behaviour including pointing, repeatedly asking where she wanted him to 'fuck her', aggressively kissing her, and 'moving to undo her pants'. After Grace left (Ansari called her a taxi) she texted him a message communicating how 'uneasy' his behaviour had made her feel and later sent the following message: 'You ignored clear non-verbal cues; you kept going with advances . . . I want to make sure you're aware so maybe the next girl doesn't have to cry on the ride home' – to which Ansari replied, 'I'm so sad to hear this . . . Clearly, I misread things in the moment and I'm truly sorry.'

When the story went live, media and public reactions came quickly. Perhaps unexpectedly this case uncovered a much more polarised set of opinions that got to the heart of some of the contradictions around #MeToo as it relates to consent, responsibility, agency and misogyny. On the one hand were those who were critical of both Ansari and the sensationalist way in which Grace's story had been told. Others addressed the tensions between sexual and gender norms and misogyny that the article revealed. Pieces in outlets as diverse as *Cosmopolitan* and *The Guardian*, for example, made the case that 'Coercive sex is still harmful even if no physical violence is involved, and it is uniquely harmful coming from men who make public claims of feminist allyship' (Young 2018). Those that took this approach concluded that our sexual politics need to shift in order to 'recogn[ise] the smaller abuses of power too' (Farmer 2018). Emma Gray, in a nuanced piece for *Huffpost*, pointed out that the encounter chronicled in the *Babe.net* essay had brought to the fore the need to 'renegotiate the sexual narratives we've long accepted. And that involves having complicated conversations about sex that is violating but not criminal' (Gray 2018). Finally, Jessica Valenti distilled the argument made by supporters of Grace in a widely circulated tweet which stated that 'A lot of men will read that post about Aziz Ansari and see an everyday, reasonable sexual interaction. But part of what women are saying right now is that what the culture considers "normal" sexual encounters are not working for us, and are oftentimes harmful' (Valenti 2018). Taken together, scholars, activists, journalists, and everyday people that saw harm in the story appear to be of the opinion that while Ansari's actions may not be criminal, they were injurious. The pressure, disrespect and aggression Ansari displayed were thus not only wrong, but indicative of larger, more structural problems in which women, due to power dynamics, sexual norms and persistent social conditioning, feel unable to demand that their own desires and needs be attended to.

On the other hand, critics of the essay like Caitlin Flanagan (who has been critical of #MeToo) called the allegations dangerous for eliding real rape with a 'complicated' situation. She places a considerable amount of blame on Grace for not being honest about what she wanted (love, affection) but did not get from Ansari, resulting in '3,000 words of revenge porn'. According to Flanagan, women need to take some responsibility for the situations they place themselves in and assert agency in spite of a society that may have socialised them not to. That Grace did not just say no and leave is thus seen as the sticking point: 'Apparently there is a whole country full of young women who don't know how to call a cab, and who have spent a lot of time picking out pretty outfits for dates they hoped would be nights to remember' (Flanagan 2018b). In an interview for NPR, Flanagan conveys frustration that the strides made by women have not translated into the kinds of agency that would have brought a stop to Ansari's bad, but not criminal, behaviour. She laments that, 'in this one core area, they're so weak, which is they jump into these, you know, hookup situations' (NPR 2018). Flanagan also, in her essay for *The Atlantic*, takes a swipe at the mostly privileged white women criticising Ansari for their hypocrisy, chastising them for 'open[ing] fire on brown-skinned men . . . on the basis of [their self-professed] intersectionality and all that' (Flanagan 2018b).

Bari Weiss, writing for *The New York Times*, is also critical of Grace and, similar to Flanagan, argues that she should have asserted her agency and exercised common sense: 'If you are hanging out naked with a man,' Weiss argues, 'it's safe to assume he is going to try to have sex with you.' Weiss is clear that even though we live in a sexual culture that is unequal and often unfair, this was in line with other cases of regrettable, bad sex (Weiss 2018). Lucia Brawley, in a piece for CNN, goes further, arguing that the story risks trivialising actual sexual crimes, and advocates for initiatives to train young women to say no. She concludes that 'Ansari is not Harvey Weinstein. He's not even on the same planet. We have to differentiate between the two if our #MeToo movement is to succeed. If we don't, no one will take our valid claims seriously and things will get worse for women' (Brawley 2018).

Detractors took aim at Flanagan's comments, arguing that it reinscribed forceful rape as the norm and failed to address the subject of power, which Ansari, as a wealthy male celebrity, had in spades (Gash and Harding 2018). Dubrofsky and Levina pointed out that survival in a situation that is potentially harmful is itself agentic and that the yes/no of consent always takes place in an affective economy shaped by patriarchy (Dubrofsky and Levina 2020). Grace's story, they argue, should be judged on these terms. Also of note is the argument around coercion and wrongdoing in which the question of whether Ansari's behaviour had impaired Grace's ability to give consent, and thus whether he should benefit from the minimal consent given by someone who is coerced (vis-à-vis the oral sex specifically), needs to be interrogated (Ferzan 2018). For Ferzan, the answer is yes, Grace's ability to give consent had been impaired, but no, Ansari is not an offender of the kind we tend to associate with the early cases of #MeToo (e.g. Harvey Weinstein and Bill Cosby).

Challenges to the way the story was told by way of style and journalistic ethics became another bone of contention. Stylistically, it was written in a tabloid form focusing on the physical and sensational with very little by way of analysis. Spratt, for example, declared that '*Babe*'s reporting was a sensationalized hatchet job which left Grace's story wide open to the inevitable criticism that followed' (Spratt 2018). It was also seen as suspect that the reporter, only twenty-two, had sought Grace out but did not make this clear in the article – leaving Grace open to the charge of opportunism. The fact that Way wrote the piece in the first person was also troubling, as was her focus on seemingly trivial details (e.g. the choice of wine), her editorialising, her continual use of the term 'girl', and the fact that she gave Ansari only five hours to respond to the piece. This opened *Babe.net* up to accusations of reckless reporting (Tiffany 2018; Filipovic 2018).

Soon after the article was published, Ansari issued a statement through his publicist in which he confirmed that they met at a party and that he and the woman in question went on a date, but maintained that all sexual activity was 'by all indications . . . completely consensual'. He went on to admit that she (Grace) may have been uncomfortable, that he took her words to heart, and that he is supportive of the movement (#MeToo) and the 'necessary and long overdue' changes it has brought (*Variety* 2018). Much of the publicised response to the press release mirrored reactions to the story itself, with supporters decrying the overreach, thus taking Ansari at his word, versus critics like comedian Samantha Bee, whose response summarised the feelings of many critics: 'A lot of people are worried about Aziz's career – which no one is trying to end, because again, we know the difference between a rapist, a workplace harasser, and an Aziz Ansari . . . That doesn't mean we have to be happy about any of them' (Bradley 2018).

Ansari's more full-throated mea culpa was made in his Netflix special over a year later in which he discloses that the whole ordeal made him feel scared and humiliated but also that he felt terrible 'that this person felt this way'. He tells the audience, off the top, that he had re-evaluated every date he had ever been on in the hope of becoming a 'more thoughtful' person going forward (Saad 2019). Ansari ends the show by relaying the fear he felt around the prospect of 'never get[ting] to do this again', remarking that 'it almost felt like I died' (North 2019a). The #MeToo response to this putative apology is summarised by an article in *Jezebel* which characterised it as insufficient for its focus on 'how the allegations affected him . . . how he's handled the situation thus far, how he hopes to keep growing', rather than tackling the issue head-on (Garza 2019). Others offered lukewarm defences of Ansari or, in their reviews of the show, spent very little time on it at all (Rao 2019; Bruney 2019; Pollard 2019). The *National Review*, a conservative outlet, lauded Ansari for his sincerity and complimented him for learning from his 'past poor behaviour' despite the 'public shaming' (Verbruggen 2019).

Since then, Ansari has refocused his standup and returned to the cultural subjects he used to engage with. Public opposition to his presence in roles and on the public stage has largely abated. Grace herself never did respond to the fallout although her identity was leaked online. Way did the media rounds defending her reporting, and Grace even appeared on an episode of a show called *Crime and Justice* after personally attacking its host for their criticism of the piece, calling the coverage despicable.

Taken as a whole, Way's story, for all of its faults, forced a necessary conversation about sexual norms and gender roles. The Ansari case, being the least clear-cut, is significant because of this greyness and for how it drew out conversations, during the peak of #MeToo, about sexual interactions that fall into the space between 'no' and 'yes' and which feel 'violating even when [they] may not be deemed criminal in a legal sense' (Chiara Cooper 2018: 7).

Having provided this description, we can now turn to a deeper analysis of the role played by the various consent(s) discussed in Chapter 1 (enthusiastic, affirmative, communicative) as well as notions of sexual autonomy, citizenship and integrity. Contextually, it is important to note that the date and its aftermath took place in a sexual assemblage of asserted heteronormative and hegemonic masculinity, celebrity and affluence in which Grace objectively holds less of all of these things. It is also necessary to consider how assemblages coalesce to push particular interpretations and expectations while also leaving room for resistance. As Tsing states, 'Assemblages are open-ended gatherings. They allow us to ask about communal effects without assuming them. They show us potential histories in the making' (Tsing 2015: 22).

Consent represents the most knotty of the frameworks in this particular case. On a general level, the shortcomings of the consent model are clear in its assumption of static temporality, its demand for consistency, its opacity and its partiality (Loick 2020). Remember that consent does not always express itself in dispositive ways. Nor is it consistently asserted, meaning that consenting to one act at one point in time does not entail agreement to engage in later acts. Consent is also not always transparent – even to those involved – since desire and wantedness are often in flux. Grace, for example, reported feeling a mixture of emotions and conflicting desires throughout the night. This partiality of consent means that it has to be ethically and substantively co-determined in order to function properly and, in this case, it would appear that a mutual ethic of co-determination was not present.

Also not present was the clear communication required of communicative consent as evidenced by Grace's description of 'mumbling' resistance and pulling away coupled with her reluctantly performing oral sex. Communicative consent requires, a priori, that the liberal model of an atomistic self be cast aside in favour of one that is dynamic and where communication is ongoing and clear. On the other hand, communicative consent risks reifying the 'woman as sexual gatekeeper' trope by placing her behaviour on trial which, when interpreted as a verbal act (as it is in this case), renders Grace's 'unclear' communication the problem. This is particularly true within #MeToo discourse wherein the ability to say no in individual circumstances is often focused on at the expense of larger conversations about coercive structures, asymmetrical relations of power, and the reality of sex itself. The Ansari case makes it clear that a more nuanced framework is needed.

This brings us to a discussion of the role played by two further dimensions of consent discourse, beginning with the 'yes means yes' and 'no means no' features of EC and AC. First, it is important to emphasise that for both EC and AC, silence and/or passive yielding do not imply consent (Anderson 2005; Botnick 2018). This begs the question of whether Grace exercised 'reasonable resistance' thereby rendering Ansari's actions, if not criminal, at least ethically damaging. Again, it is Grace whose actions are placed under the microscope – did she say 'no'? And if she did, how emphatic was she? Finally, if she did resist, did she do so in a manner that a reasonable person would understand? On the other hand, if we draw on a more 'thick' understanding of EC and AC, the question becomes one of Ansari's actions – namely, did *he* do enough to obtain clear consent in an ongoing fashion? From Grace's description, it does not appear that Ansari did enough to meet this standard whether we define AC/EC discretely or as an ongoing process. This, again, ushers in some problematic implications vis-à-vis gender roles wherein Grace is again framed as the gatekeeper from whom pleasure is extracted, rather than an agent or desiring co-actor herself (Jozkowski, Marcantonio and Hunt 2017).

Second is the potentially more contentious issue of AC and EC's inability to navigate and bring clarity and justice to a practice that exceeds society's strictures. As the Ansari case illustrates, and as I have argued throughout this book, sex is a complicated and relational act that resists the 'boxing' consent discourse demands. It also assumes a heteronormative conception of sexuality that eschews the erotic and the unknown for the certain and the dispositive (Pereira 2009; Butler 1990). This view poses a challenge to some second wave feminist understandings of male sexuality as inherently aggressive and female sexuality as colonised by male power (Franke 2001). Uncertainty, desire and spontaneity, as they relate to AC and EC, are therefore delimited in ways that may work to make sex legible juridically, but do not serve women well. Sex and female desire, when understood as excessive, fluid and contingent, becomes a constitutive part of a 'formlessness that engulfs all form, a disorder that threatens all order' (Grosz 1994: 203). As such, AC and EC, as a gauge for sexual permissibility, are simultaneously too broad and too narrow. This case, as compared with all others, brings this tension to the fore in the form of difficult questions that AC and EC, thus far, have been unable to answer.

Finally, Grace's sexual integrity and autonomy can also be seen to have been violated in that her boundaries were crossed by Ansari, who impinged on her interests as an intact emotional, corporeal and conscious person. This includes the violation of trust as well as Grace's feeling of humiliation and shame: 'It really hit me that I was violated. I felt really emotional all at once when we sat down there. That that whole experience was actually horrible' (Way 2018; see also Lacey 1998b; Chiara Cooper 2018). Sexual autonomy, in its focus on sexual choice and agency, should function to challenge the power of coercive norms. When asked why she did not just leave, Grace responds: 'I didn't leave because I think I was stunned and shocked . . . This was not what I expected. I'd seen some of his shows and read excerpts from his book and I was not expecting a bad night at all, much less a violating night and a painful one.' Sexual autonomy can still play a productive role when sex is understood in this way, that is, as embodied and co-constituted.

An important additional subject that is important to consider is that of race. As stated, Ansari is of South Asian descent and has centred advocacy around race and representation in his comedy and the roles he chooses. Race comes up in this case in a number of ways which shape and condition how it has played out in conversations around #MeToo. First, it is important to emphasise Ansari's commitment, in his comedy, acting and writing, to push for diversity in media specifically. In a 2015 article for *The New York Times*,

Ansari wrote about the first time he saw an Indian character in an American movie (in brownface), decrying the lack of space given to Indian actors – even for those roles written as Indian – and calling on casting directors and writers to do more (Ansari 2015). The subject of racism in this case, oddly enough, was first brought up by Flanagan who, as discussed above, drew attention to the image of privileged white women going after a brown-skinned man as inimical to the intersectionality white women profess to hold. She also, in a backhanded insult, remarked that she thought 'they'd stay laser focused on college-educated white men for another few months' (Flanagan 2018b). Flanagan's point about white women making spurious accusations against men of colour (particularly Black men) goes back to slavery and is relevant to the extent that it draws attention to how historical racism frames how non-white defendants are treated, judged and sentenced (Wriggins 1983; Hodes 2014). An intersectional lens would draw out these insights. I, however, do not think this is what Flanagan was going for here – the sarcasm is quite evident.

Nadya Agrawal, in an article for *HuffPost*, broaches the subject of race by challenging Flanagan's assumptions and arguing that by bringing up race she detracts from the real issue: sexual coercion. In framing Ansari as a model to emulate (i.e. the kind of brown person we can get behind and other South Asians should look up to) Flanagan risks 'invoking society's stereotypes about dark-skinned and Muslim men being sexually deviant and misogynistic, while also trying to subvert those same stereotypes. She can't have it both ways.' This double characterisation is present in the media coverage of Jian Ghomeshi as well. Agrawal draws attention to the fact that because Flanagan assumes Grace is white, itself a problematic move, she further perpetuates the innocent white woman/sexually aggressive man of colour stereotype – albeit inadvertently. Agrawal writes that 'By crying racism where it doesn't exist, an analysis like Flanagan's distracts from real conversations about consent, and forces brown people to defend the person we once thought was so cool and refreshing who now leaves a bitter taste in our mouths' (Agrawal 2018).

It is notable that Ansari's ascribed race does not appear to have been a major topic in legacy media or of general public discussion. In a content analysis of responses to Bari Weiss's *New York Times* editorial, race does not come up at all. Rather, according to Worthington, issues of consent, privacy and the distinction between assault and bad behaviour dominates the majority of the responses and conversations around the article (Worthington 2020). Nor does his Muslim identity form a major part of public discourse – aside from it being conflated with race.

It can also be argued, in line with #MeToo, that Ansari's discernible 'preference' for white women is reflective of a culture that privileges the white female body and that his behaviour, as Bhandaru contends, is simply a 'product of this white supremacist culture' as well 'as patriarchal bro culture' (Bhandaru 2018). Read in this way, Ansari's aggressiveness is in some part a result of wanting, as many children of immigrants can attest, to fit into a sexual culture that is inimical to that of our parents. What I think is most salient about Bhandaru's argument is his point that whiteness is imbricated with patriarchy and therefore, through a perverse kind of intersectionality, can result in the production of further incentives for misogynistic behaviour – even amongst men of colour. Grace herself adopts gendered expectations including wanting to please and avoid generating discomfort, 'opting for apparent passivity as the best course of action to get through the encounter' (Dubrofsky and Levina 2020: 10).

Finally, it is worth commenting on the aspects of race, #MeToo and this case through what Ali Na calls 'Desi masculinity', which is constituted by the characterisation of brown men as (1) a terror threat; (2) desexualised and disempowered; and (3) a model minority. The trope of the 'funny cute' Desi man fits Ansari's persona as a fumbling, infantile, harmless and often feminised character. This made it all the more frustrating for his fans upon learning that Ansari was not quite what he seemed. However, as Na argues, this manifestation of 'funny cute' works only in so far as it can be controlled. It can very quickly, as responses critical of Ansari's behaviour demonstrate, revert to fear in the form of Islamophobia (which was less manifest in this case) and by 'rekindl[ing] the implicit threat of nonnormative non-white sexuality as aberrant. In [Ansari's] divergence from the white masculine norm, fear and disgust at his sexuality is ever ready to emerge' (Na 2019: 323). This understanding, when added to the greyness around consent, explains the inordinate amount of scrutiny this case continues to engender. Which is not to say that Ansari's conduct does not deserve analysis and criticism, but that the degree to which it continues to permeate conversations around #MeToo is notable.

Turning to the 'pleasure and care-centred ethic of embodied and relational sexual Otherness' and the potential for restorative justice, a number of important points need to be considered. First is the sexual assemblage out of which this event emerges and the various ways in which it reflects asymmetries of status, race, class and gender. Also important to consider are the finer points of context and place – for example, Grace mentions eating (with Ansari) at an oyster bar on the Hudson River, drinking wine, which she did not choose, and feeling excited. It is the entanglement of all these factors that constitutes the event and must be engaged with. Put another way, how we 'cut' and think of this interaction requires the evaluation of 'all manner of questions regarding the nature of mattering com[ing] together here – that is, questions of matter in the multiple senses of meaning, being, and valuing' (Barad 2012: 77).

As I have done in all other #MeToo case studies, it is important to examine how the details of this case stack up against the regulative norm of a 'pleasure and care-centred ethic of embodied and relational sexual Otherness'. First, it is patently clear that the ideal that sexual relations should centre pleasure and care for self and Other is undermined by Ansari's behaviour in that he instrumentalises and objectifies Grace throughout the night. Grace describes how quickly things escalated and the way in which Ansari's persistent gesturing towards his penis and dismissal of nonverbal messaging (like her consistent moving away from him) made her feel denigrated: 'I know I was physically giving off cues that I wasn't interested. I don't think that was noticed at all, or if it was, it was ignored' (Way 2018). Grace's pleasure and desire were thus entirely divorced from Ansari's. Yet, contrary to AC and EC, which I argue can be overdetermining and restrictive, this approach does permit that pleasure need not be exuberant and overwhelming all the time. It can also be pleasant, okay, bad or paid for but still permissible in so far as it emerges out of a co-constituted ethic of mutual respect and contextualised agreement. Even by this standard, Grace's experience does not fulfil the mutuality this model requires.

While Ansari's behaviour does not rise to the level of rape or even assault (I come back to this point below), I would posit he should have to answer for the pain he caused Grace and the degree to which his actions reflected a disregard for her personhood – which can be seen most starkly as it relates to the values of Otherness and care (Savigny 2020). For an ethic of Otherness to take hold and persist as a sexual norm, it has to extend far beyond generalised respect and reason, residing in 'a moment of justice . . . superimpos[ing] itself on the "extravagant" generosity of the "for the other," on its infinity' (Levinas 1998: 195–6). Care for Grace is not attended to by Ansari except in the most minimal way (through the performance of concern by stating 'Oh, of course, it's only fun if we're both having fun' and 'Let's just chill over here on the couch') – before he resumes his pressurising behaviour (Way 2018).

Grace, in staying, perversely demonstrates a level of care for the Other exacted through gendered expectations consistent with the female duty to placate men and their sexual desires (Schippers 2007; Kiefer and Sanchez 2007). Kate Manne refers to this as Himpathy, a neologism meant to refer to a kind of unearned care for the Other (i.e. men) by women, even after an assault, as well as the general privileging of aggressive and violent men and boys over women and girls by society (Manne 2020). Manne writes about this vis-à-vis the Ansari case and asks why it is 'we regard many men's potentially hurt feelings as so important, so sacrosanct? And, relatedly, why do we regard women as so responsible for protecting and ministering to them?' (Manne 2020: 60). The model I have proposed challenges this kind of unearned care for the Other, or what I call a kind of asymmetrical gift-giving, while also allowing for non-normative sex and the desire to attend to the embodied needs of one's counterpart.

Grace's care for self, similar to almost all the cases discussed above, was enacted through staying – which may have been the best choice for her at the time – and later receiving support from her friends, and agreeing to speak to Way. Genuine care for self, of the kind Grace could not access, would have enabled her to act for herself in ways that centred her psychic well-being. Not being able to bring this into fruition with Ansari – and thus forcing a societal reckoning with these contradictions and uncertainties around heteronormative sexuality – perhaps constitutes a unique kind of self-care reflecting what Sarah Ahmed describes as 'finding ways to exist in a world that is diminishing' (Ahmed 2016). This would make Grace a 'feminist killjoy' who pursues her own care for the self and becomes the problem when she dares to describe it, thereby making the concealed manifest (Ahmed 2016).

Finally, as part of the 'pleasure and care-centred ethic of embodied and relational sexual Otherness', Grace's sexual autonomy – namely her freedom to act free from pressure – is also attenuated. Remember that autonomy requires respect for the sexual subjectivity of the Other inclusive of the pleasure and desire necessary for their sexual self-making (Alcoff 2018). Embodied sexuality, of which autonomy is one part, was asymmetrically enacted since Grace, by her own account, made her desires clear both verbally and nonverbally. Additionally, in this case pleasure was not mutually experienced, since the sexual interaction itself was uncomfortable and unwanted, and the context in which it occurred was constituted by unaddressed power differentials. While all of these issues need not come up on a first date, thinking about their role in a sexual assemblage draws attention to the need to cultivate what Fischel (2019) calls a 'democratic hedonic culture' in which women no longer feel compelled to engage in unwanted sex. Taken together, on each of the elements of the 'pleasure and care-centred ethic of embodied and relational sexual Otherness', the experience articulated by Grace fails. Moreover, while it may not have been the level of violation committed by Weinstein or Ghomeshi, it has caused harm – harms I argue can be addressed through restorative practices where the 'pleasure and care-centred ethic of embodied and relational sexual Otherness' acts as a regulative ideal.

Before moving to a discussion of restorative justice, it is important to point out how the Ansari case acts as a boundary object in that it skirts the line between the criminal and the unethical or socially unacceptable. In doing so, it draws attention to the danger of over-criminalising sex. Over-criminalisation, as Vance argues, risks negating pleasure by being overly prescriptive and we should, instead, balance reducing the dangers women face with 'expand[ing] the possibilities, opportunities, and permissions for pleasure that are open to them' (Vance 1993). In pursuit of this, it is important to address specific harms but also the conditions that gave rise to them. It is here where restorative justice can provide solutions other avenues cannot. First, it is clear, apart from a few legal opinions, that Grace's ordeal is not prosecutable – that it was not rape, did not occur in a workplace and, by her own admission, did not rise to the level of assault (she states that she was only 'able to validate this as sexual assault' months later (Way 2018)). Her objective in disclosing this event is thus more about being heard, to be able to articulate the harms she faced, and to seek some kind of apology and recompense. #MeToo has proven effective in providing a forum for the rage, community and catharsis traditional forms of legal redress cannot. It has also acted as a means by which to express frustration at a sexist and patriarchal social order in which women's pleasure and desire are ignored.

I argue that a restorative justice process that centres the norm of a 'pleasure and care-centred ethic of embodied and relational sexual Otherness' offers a far more robust and ethical means by which to seek the kind of repair Grace and #MeToo desire while offering Ansari an opportunity to repair relations, make good on his public statements against misogyny and sexism, and put a stop to the public 'back and forth' about him, his feminist bona fides, and what he 'really' thinks.

Ansari, from his public persona via interviews and his writing, would appear to be the most amenable to this kind of process of all the men involved in the #MeToo scandals I have discussed. His claim to be a feminist on David Letterman (albeit a 'safe' one – limiting his feminism to issues of pay and formal rights) and the subject matter of his shows (I am reminded of a scene in *Master of None* which focuses on the fear women have walking home at night) are indicative of the likelihood that he might participate. Ansari's text to Grace, his formal apology and the subject matter of his comedy since (which has been better than some of the 'comeback' material and apologies made by others) make this case ideal for a restorative process. Ansari also, in his more public apology, states that he 'took her words to heart and responded privately after taking the time to process what she had said' (Green 2019: 141). If this concern is genuine, and the desire to learn and grow sincere, a restorative process offers a principled way to move forward.

A restorative approach would also offer Grace an opportunity to bring to fruition what is most important to her – namely, to be heard, to have her rights respected, to get an apology, and to ensure that Ansari's behaviour, which she characterised as that of a 'horny, rough, entitled 18-year-old', does not continue (Way 2018). The much-derided *Babe.net* story provided an imperfect vehicle for Grace to get some of this by affording her a space to assert her own narrative with the support of a #MeToo community. However, apart from a period of public scrutiny and a few rescinded offers, Ansari has basically been accepted back into the celebrity/comedic fold. He recently (August 2020) appeared in a Zoom reunion special for the hit show *Parks and Recreation* without much pushback.

Concretely, a healing circle similar to that offered by RESTORE or even private mediation, more could be done for Grace. As I have argued, for gender-based violence, healing circles are the most productive in that they are oriented specifically towards finding ways to promote survivor agency, demand offender accountability, and address social injustice (Ptacek 2010). Grace could have a platform to state clearly *to Ansari* how her pleasure had been denied and the myriad ways in which the ethic of embodied and relational sexual Otherness had been appropriated and ignored. Ansari would be made to listen, internalise this and apologise.

In this way, restorative justice gets at the roots of harm where power, behaviour, culture, values, institutions and assumptions are all on the table and where Grace is in the driving seat (Strait 2020; Van Wormer 2009). Ansari would also be given the opportunity to formulate a response in the form, first and foremost, of an apology, but also through a fulsome and considered reflection on his own misogyny, internalised sexism, and the harms he caused. Neither the state nor the social media echo-sphere need be part of this process (Frederick and Lizdas 2003; Van Wormer 2009). Yet having a community present, whether in the form of friends, colleagues, confidants or family members, helps to solidify the commitment to repair (since they would be part of the accountability structure and act as witnesses to the pledges and promises made). Transformative practices ensure popular access to and participation in 'all aspects of transitional justice processes (design, implementation, evaluation)' and encourage 'culturally resonant mechanisms that resist global models' by providing survivors like Grace with the 'opportunity to challenge a range of exclusions and power relations' (Gready and Robins 2014: 349).

Repair in this case might include monetary compensation, donations, a commitment to learn through classes and/or therapy, a pledge to hire more women, and tangible steps towards changing the practices that give rise to this behaviour (through talks, public engagement, etc.). Building a 'pleasure and care-centred ethic of embodied and relational sexual Otherness' into the educational part of the process will help cultivate a more democratic sexual culture, one where Grace is seen as a desiring, pleasure-seeking woman deserving of care and respect. This approach, as Jolly, Cornwall and Hawkins state, '"expand[s] the analysis of pleasure" and return[s] us to the erotic embodied agency that is a central part of women's lived experience – a part that patriarchal culture tries to muffle, circumscribe and reduce to passivity through a litany of violations and intrusions' (Jolly, Cornwall and Hawkins 2013: 35). If we compare this prospective outcome to the one we have now, which remains stuck on the subject of consent and where Grace and Ansari are seen by #MeToo proponents and detractors as entirely victimised or victimising, I would argue that the restorative approach coupled with a new, more capacious model of sexuality offers a fruitful way forward – importantly, one which speaks to #MeToo's purported goals of care, sexual equality, responsibility and transformed gender norms. As Page and Arcy put it, for #MeToo to meet these objectives, it has to centre healing, the politics of care, and pent-up feminist rage. I argue that these are best met through restorative, sex positive processes rather than solely through digital labour or through carceral logics that uphold rape culture (Page and Arcy 2020). If any of the cases discussed has a chance of succeeding using this framework, it is this one.

Conclusion: #MeToo: New Models and New Possibilities

What I have attempted to do throughout this book is to articulate a novel and robust framework of sexual ethics that attends to the singular nature of sex and presents restorative justice as the framework that is best placed to deal with gender-based violence inclusive of microaggressions, assault, harassment and even rape. This has required that I grapple with complex questions that have been made urgent by #MeToo, including: What is the most just way in which to approach sexual relations? What are the forces and structures that impinge on mutually pleasurable sex? How do we judge the spectrum of gendered violations of sexual integrity? And what do we do with the (largely but not exclusively) men who are guilty of those violations?

In the preceding chapters, I have provided a mixture of information, pedagogy, analysis and argument to sort through this shifting assemblage of controversies. One of the most important throughlines of the book is the transformative nature of sex and the persistence of gender-based violence. As I have argued, sexual violence has been the focus of public conversations for centuries beginning, for the purposes of this book, with the biblical story of Judith beheading the enemy general Holofernes as depicted by seventeenth-century artist Artemisia Gentileschi (Straussman-Pflanzer 2013). The painting, as I explained earlier on, is widely interpreted as a representation of Gentileschi's own rape and trial wherein charges were brought by her father at a time when women were seen as possessions and rape a violation of property. Throughout the centuries, we have moved from women being seen as property (and virginity as one of several acquired assets) to various permutations of sex as consent, namely 'consent to sex' based on a judgement of force, consent where coercion is central, affirmative consent, enthusiastic consent and communication consent, as well as sexual autonomy, queer sexuality, sexual integrity and embodied sexuality (Evans and Chamberlain 2015; Whelehan 1995; Subotnik 2008). Each of the norms and frameworks has been taken up and deployed by women to push for social and legal change through feminist movements, beginning with first and second wave liberal feminists who demanded recognition of marital rape, stronger consent laws, harsher sentences and a more robust understanding of force, to radical feminists for whom oppression and patriarchal norms rendered giving consent all but impossible. It also includes third wave feminists who advocated for sex positivity in which women's autonomy, choice and pleasure took centre stage (Gerhard 2001; Ferguson 1984). Later feminist formations, inclusive of fourth wave feminism, postfeminism and feminist materialism, played with the strictures around technology, agency and engaged embodiment further and complexified our understanding of pleasure, sex and agency (Burkett and Hamilton 2012; Anderson 2018; Allen 2018).

I remind the reader of these formations here because of their importance in tracing the genesis of #MeToo. They also set the stage for #MeToo's embrace of carceral feminism which, retrospectively, has evolved in a counterproductive direction – namely, one that is unlikely to meet its objectives over and above generalised consciousness raising such as the elimination of gender-based violence, the sexual empowerment of women and the advancement of just solutions. As such, I argue that #MeToo has some very real tactical shortcomings in that it relies on social media-driven acts of cathartic confession (which are perfectly reasonable given the paucity of options but insufficient as a robust plan of action) and is decisively carceral with respect to the solutions it provides (Mack and McCann 2018; Cossman 2019). As I have maintained, this form of carceral feminism leaves much to be desired given its imbrication with a state-led model of justice that is rarely successful (if we see imprisonment as success), disproportionately criminalises racialised and sexual minorities, and does not facilitate the accountability, survivor agency and repair demanded by those that have been victimised.

My criticisms of the traditional modalities of sexual ethics include: (1) their inability to adequately consider structures and norms that attenuate choice for women; (2) their assumption that decision-making around sex is transparent and dispositive; (3) their perpetuation of the 'woman as passive sexual gatekeeper' stereotype; and (4) their weaponisation against minority groups by using consent as a cudgel (Gruber 2015, 2016; Fischel 2016, 2019; Wriggins 1995). On the other hand, I have suggested a view of sex that, in practice, can be quotidian and routine, transactional and functional, *and/or* excessive, boundary pushing and overwhelming depending on context and cultural factors (Vance 1984). Affect and embodied subjectivity have always existed alongside discourse and cultural (re)articulations of ethical sex – yet this is rarely highlighted in discussions around #MeToo.

It is from these shortfalls that I crafted my alternative approach: the 'pleasure and care-centred ethic of embodied and relational sexual Otherness' which is simultaneously material and social and aspires to capture how sexual desire often resists juridical and normative control 'by obliterating the boundary between self and other while retaining the autonomy of self'. Sex is thus seen as constituted by a hodgepodge of 'sexual affects, thoughts, fantasies, acts, or bodily sensations' that can be desiring and hesitant at the same time (Cherkasskaya and Rosario 2019: 1,660–1).

The 'pleasure and care-centred ethic of embodied and relational sexual Otherness' framework entails co-determination, embodied communication, and respect for the self and Other, and functions as a regulative, as opposed to determinative, norm that is strived for and lofty, but commodious enough to accommodate routine sex, sex for another (i.e. in a committed relationship), unpleasurable sex and sex work. #MeToo, in its current iteration, has yet to take on such 'out of the box' thinking. #MeToo also continues to rely on and strive for a form of justice that is firmly rooted in traditional jurisprudence and carceral punishment. The shortcomings of this approach, as noted above and throughout this book, centre around its inability to provide the healing, accountability, repair and control desired by survivors, as well as its production of a system of punishment that is based on retribution over repair and which disproportionally criminalises the marginalised.

Restorative justice, in the form of healing circles, mediation or boards, together with the 'pleasure and care-centred ethic of embodied and relational sexual Otherness', offers a more just and progressive way forward – one that is resonant with #MeToo's stated objectives and those of survivors all over the world. Restorative justice is flexible, survivor-centred, embodied and ongoing. It platforms those aspects of justice that victims of crime have demanded for decades, including 'victim voice and participation . . . victim validation and offender responsibility . . . communicative and flexible environment[s] . . . [and] relational repair' (Daly and Stubbs 2006: 9; Hudson 1998). The emotionality involved, as Maruna and Pali argue, does not render restorative justice 'soft', as is often claimed by detractors who hold tight to the feminisation of emotion which is placed in opposition to reason, masculinity and the law (Maruna and Pali 2020).

The case studies in the latter part of this book are meant to function as felt examples drawn on to demonstrate how this process might work. Taking on the cases that triggered #MeToo as the site of analysis was valuable in that this work can now act as a lodestar to guide further research. On the one hand, we have the strong case of gender-based violence committed by Harvey Weinstein who was alleged to have assaulted dozens of women in a quasi-professional capacity before being charged. The impunity with which he committed these crimes, coupled with the media storm and a painful trial, led to a less than ideal outcome in which Weinstein was jailed but the conditions that gave rise to his assaults were not addressed. The healing that might have occurred from a victim-led process in which offender accountability is required is absent, as is an ethic of sexual relationality grounded in values like care, pleasure and co-determination that are central to the #MeToo movement. This is also true vis-à-vis the Jian Ghomeshi case, which was complexified by a host of factors like his apology, his attempted 'comebacks', a controversial essay and BDSM, all of which became part of the conversation. Unlike in the Weinstein case, Ghomeshi was found not guilty and his victims, by their own accounts, have been left feeling revictimised as a result of the difficult trial and the fact that little has been done to effect substantive change. Avital Ronell's alleged harassment and assault against her PhD student led to her suspension, but the 'trial' itself was held behind closed doors without victim input. Moreover, the entire case was made even more complicated by the introduction of complex sexual and gender dynamics with Ronell, a woman, being the transgressor and both parties identifying as queer. The power differentials of an advisor-advisee relationship were also heightened in this case, as was the need for a process that centred the survivor and produced an outcome that enabled learning and healing.

The Louis C.K. and Aziz Ansari sagas unfolded entirely removed from formal judicial proceedings and, instead, played out mostly via media conversations and online debates. For C.K., his repeated placing of women in situations in which his sexual gratification came first, like those of all the preceding cases as well as Ansari's, renders it even more clear that there is something fundamentally wrong in the way we conceptualise and enact sexual norms. The greyness of the Ansari case draws attention to how powerful gender scripts are in curtailing a woman's ability to centre her own pleasure while magnifying the entitlement that can result from normative male sexuality. In both cases, the outcomes are less than ideal with little having been done to facilitate the kinds of productive conversations and justice-oriented processes that would be of use to the victims as well as Ansari and C.K. in the long run.

In each of these cases consent, as the prevailing ethic, fails to provide a robust and sufficiently capacious set of principles in which sex can be transformed into something that is mutually advantageous despite structural conditions that might work against it. More dynamic forms of consent, inclusive of its affirmative, enthusiastic and communicative iterations, as well as associated frameworks like sexual autonomy and integrity, are improvements but remain insufficient. I think we can do better. The 'pleasure and care-centred ethic of embodied and relational sexual Otherness' framework, when coupled with a process of restorative justice, offers a transformative way in which to enact the values and objectives that form the rationale of #MeToo as a movement. One that centres women and other sexual and racialised groups, where cycles of violence and poverty are broken, and through which a process of ethical reconstruction can occur. As Kim argues, the shift from 'an adversarial binary of victim and perpetrator to one that acknowledges the impact of harm not only on individuals but on broader communities' is a prerequisite for gender-based violence to be addressed in a survivor-centred way. It is also needed to begin to challenge the inadequacy, biases and violence of our current criminal justice system (Kim 2018: 225).

The 'pleasure and care-centred ethic of embodied and relational sexual Otherness' approach can then function as a ideal to infuse this process with an ethic of care, non-normative Otherness, mutually constituted pleasure, and communication capable and provide the basis for evaluation *and* education. In each of the #MeToo cases I have analysed, this ethical ideal is unmet to various degrees (with the Weinstein and Ghomeshi examples being more clear-cut and the complexity increasing vis-à-vis Ronell, C.K. and Ansari), with their 'unmet-edness' being illuminated when examined through this ideal and with respect to the opportunities afforded by restorative justice. In addition, the subjects of gender, non-normative sexuality and racialisation constitute other factors I have tried to attend to throughout this book. What is left is the further articulation of an ambitious project of de- and re-construction in which, ideally, movements like #MeToo and #BLM align to articulate shared goals, fight for anti-carceral and restorative forms of justice, expand sex education to draw on a 'pleasure and care-centred ethic of embodied and relational sexual Otherness', infuse this ethic into public scholarship, and challenge the media to do so as well. Facilitating and working towards this is daunting but not impossible. If anything, #MeToo has drawn attention to the injustices of our present system and the anger victims of harassment and assault feel at being overlooked and silenced. It also, in calling for carceral forms of justice, has put a spotlight on the inadequacies of the criminal justice system by revealing, in practice, how it has not reduced harassment and assault or attended to the systems of marginalisation and oppression that have given rise to these behaviours in the first instance. It also does not address the needs of survivors who 'deserve a response to the wrongdoing they experienced intrinsically and not just because or only if a response will facilitate broader societal change' (Wexler, Robbennolt and Murphy 2019: 104). I believe strongly that the reconstructed sexual ideal I have articulated, when coupled with restorative justice, provides the basis from which this is possible. We now need to do this work.

References

ABC News (2017). 'Harvey Weinstein: Full transcript of the "horrifying" exchange with Ambra Gutierrez.' *ABC News*, 10 October, <https://www.abc.net.au/news/2017-10-11/harvey-weinstein-full-transcript-of-audio-with-ambra-gutierrez/9037268> (last accessed 23 March 2021).

Abdulali, Sohaila (2018). *What We Talk About When We Talk About Rape*. Oxford: Myriad Editions.

Abrams, Kathryn (1995). 'Sex wars redux: Agency and coercion in feminist legal theory.' *Columbia Law Review* 95, no. 2: 304–76.

Abrams, Kathryn (1999). 'From autonomy to agency: Feminist perspectives on self-direction.' *William & Mary Law Review* 40, no. 3: 805–46.

Adams-Curtis, Leah E., and Gordon B. Forbes (2004). 'College women's experiences of sexual coercion: A review of cultural, perpetrator, victim, and situational variables.' *Trauma, Violence, & Abuse* 5, no. 2: 91–122.

Adetiba, Elizabeth (2017). 'Tarana Burke says #MeToo should center marginalized communities.' *The Nation*, 17 November, <https://www.thenation.com/article/archive/tarana-burke-says-metoo-isnt-just-for-white-people> (last accessed 23 March 2021).

Afzal, Sarah, and Paige Wallace (2019). 'Entangled feminisms: #MeToo as a node on the feminist mesh.' *South Central Review* 36, no. 2: 131–55.

Agrawal, Nadya (2018). 'It's time to talk about race and the Aziz story.' *Huffpost*, 25 January, <https://www.huffpost.com/entry/opinion-agrawal-aziz-race_n_5a65f7c0e4b0e5630071b7aa> (last accessed 23 March 2021).

Agustín, Laura María (2007). *Sex at the Margins: Migration, Labour Markets and the Rescue Industry*. London: Zed Books.

Ahearn, Victoria, and Adina Bresge (2018). 'Ghomeshi reflects on fall-out from trial in The New York Review of Books.' *iNFOnews.ca*, 14 September, <https://infotel.ca/newsitem/jian-ghomeshi/cp777396272> (last accessed 23 March 2021).

Ahmed, Sara (2014). 'Selfcare as warfare.' feministkilljoys, 25 August, <https://feministkilljoys.com/2014/08/25/selfcare-as-warfare> (last accessed 23 March 2021).

Ahmed, Sara (2016). *Living a Feminist Life*. Durham, NC: Duke University Press.

Airey, Jennifer L. (2018). '#MeToo.' *Tulsa Studies in Women's Literature* 37, no. 1: 7–13.

Alabi, Olabisi Adurasola (2019). 'Sexual violence laws redefined in the "Me Too" era: Affirmative consent & statutes of limitations.' *Widener Law Review* 25: 69.

Alaggia, Ramona, and Susan Wang (2020). '"I never told anyone until the #MeToo movement": What can we learn from sexual abuse and sexual assault disclosures made through social media?' *Child Abuse & Neglect* 103: 104,312.

Alcoff, Linda Martín (1997). 'The politics of postmodern feminism, revisited.' *Cultural Critique* 36: 5–27.

Alcoff, Linda Martín (2018). *Rape and Resistance*. New York: John Wiley & Sons.

Alexander-Floyd, Nikol G. (2010). 'Critical race Black feminism: A "jurisprudence of resistance" and the transformation of the academy.' *Signs: Journal of Women in Culture and Society* 35, no. 4: 810–20.

Alldred, Pam, and Miriam E. David (2007). *Get Real about Sex: The Politics and Practice of Sex Education*. Maidenhead: McGraw-Hill Education (UK).

Allen, Louisa (2018). *Sexuality Education and New Materialism: Queer Things*. New York: Springer.

Anders, Allison Daniel, and James M. DeVita (2014). 'Intersectionality: A legacy from critical legal studies and critical race theory.' In Donald Mitchell Jr, Charlana Y. Simmons and Lindsay A. Greyerbiehl (eds), *Intersectionality & Higher Education: Theory, Research, & Praxis*. New York: Peter Lang Publishing, pp. 31–44.

Andersen, Mille Cecilie (2018). 'Getting to the root of #MeToo – through the fourth wave of feminism.' Master's dissertation, University of Copenhagen, doi: 10.13140/RG. 2.2. 20534.14403.

Anderson, Ben, Matthew Kearnes, Colin McFarlane and Dan Swanton (2012). 'On assemblages and geography.' *Dialogues in Human Geography* 2, no. 2: 171–89.

Anderson, Elizabeth (1995). *Value in Ethics and Economics*. Cambridge, MA: Harvard University Press.

Anderson, Grant (2018). '"Why can't they meet in bars and clubs like normal people?": The protective state and bioregulating gay public sex spaces.' *Social & Cultural Geography* 19, no. 6: 699–719.

Anderson, Melissa S., and Judith P. Swazey (1998). 'Reflections on the graduate student experience: An overview.' *New Directions for Higher Education* 101: 3–13.

Anderson, Michelle J. (2002). 'From chastity requirement to sexuality license: Sexual consent and a new rape shield law.' *George Washington Law Review* 70, no. 1: 51–162.

Anderson, Michelle J. (2005). 'Negotiating sex.' *Southern California Law Review* 78, no. 6: 1,401–38.

Anderson, Michelle J. (2010). 'Diminishing the legal impact of negative social attitudes toward acquaintance rape victims.' *New Criminal Law Review: An International and Interdisciplinary Journal* 13, no. 4: 644–64.

Anderson, Michelle J. (2015). 'Campus sexual assault adjudication and resistance to reform.' *Yale Law Journal* 125: 1,940.

Anonymous (2020). 'I was touched without my consent, but I won't be speaking out on social media.' *The Guardian*, 26 June, <https://www.theguardian.com/commentisfree/2020/jun/26/touched-without-my-consent-speaking-out-social-media-harassment-assault> (last accessed 24 March 2021).

Ansari, Aziz (2015). 'Aziz Ansari on acting, race and Hollywood.' *The New York Times*, 10 November, <https://www.nytimes.com/2015/11/15/arts/television/aziz-ansari-on-acting-race-and-hollywood.html> (last accessed 24 March 2021).

Ansari, Aziz, and Eric Klinenberg (2015). *Modern Romance*. London: Penguin Random House.

Apel, Dora (2004). *Imagery of Lynching: Black Men, White Women, and the Mob*. New Brunswick, NJ: Rutgers University Press.

Armatta, Judith (2018). 'Ending sexual violence through transformative justice.' *Interdisciplinary Journal of Partnership Studies* 5, no. 1: 1–38.

Armstrong, Cory L., and Jessica Mahone (2017). '"It's on us." The role of social media and rape culture in individual willingness to mobilize against sexual assault.' *Mass Communication and Society* 20, no. 1: 92–115.

Arnestad, Mads, Anna Studzinska, Magnus Nordmo and Stig Berge Matthiesen (2020). '#HeToo? Men trivialize cases of sexual harassment by a female aggressor toward a male victim, but women do not.' <https://psyarxiv.com/q2zhg> (last accessed 24 March 2021).

Arnold, Amanda (2018). 'What's going on with Avital Ronell, the prominent theorist accused of harassment?' *The Cut*, 21 August, <https://www.thecut.com/2018/08/avital-ronell-professor-accused-of-harassment-what-to-know.html> (last accessed 24 March 2021).

Aron, Raymond (2018). *Main Currents in Sociological Thought, Volume 2: Durkheim, Pareto, Weber*. Abingdon: Routledge.

Associated Press (2018). '"Bill Cosby took my spirit and crushed it": Andrea Constand speaks out on sexual assault.' *The Guardian*, 25 September, <https://www.theguardian.com/world/2018/sep/25/bill-cosby-sexual-assault-andrea-constand> (last accessed 25 March 2021).

Associated Press (2020). 'Weinstein accuser's account grilled during cross examination.' *Associated Press*, 3 February, <https://www.crainsnewyork.com/entertainment/weinstein-accusers-account-grilled-during-cross-examination> (last accessed 24 March 2021).

Bachman, Ronet, and Raymond Paternoster (1993). 'A contemporary look at the effects of rape law reform: How far have we really come?' *Journal of Criminal Law & Criminology* 84: 554–74.

Backhouse, Constance (1983). 'Nineteenth-century Canadian rape law 1800–1892.' *Essays in the History of Canadian Law* 1: 212–48.

Backhouse, Constance (2012). 'A feminist remedy for sexual assault: A quest for answers.' In Elizabeth Sheehy (ed.), *Sexual Assault Law, Practice, and Activism in a Post-Jane Doe Era*. Ottawa: University of Ottawa Press, pp. 725–39.

Baehr, Amy R. (ed.) (2004). *Varieties of Feminist Liberalism*. Lanham, MD: Rowman & Littlefield.

Baer, Nicholas (2018). 'The liberal sexual subject: A conversation with Damon R. Young.' *Film Quarterly* 72, no. 2: 100–5.

Bailey, Marlon M. (2019). 'Whose body is this? On the cultural possibilities of a radical Black sexual praxis.' *American Quarterly* 71, no. 1: 161–9.

Baker, Katharine K. (2001). 'Dialectics and domestic abuse (reviewing Elizabeth M. Schneider, *Battered Women and Feminist Lawmaking*).' *Yale Law Journal* 110, no. 8: 1,459–91.

Baker, Katharine K., and Michelle Oberman (2016). 'Women's sexual agency and the law of rape in the 21st century.' In *Special Issue: Feminist Legal Theory* (*Studies in Law, Politics, and Society* 69). Bingley: Emerald Group Publishing Limited, pp. 63–111.

Baldwin, Keith (2020). 'I believe what Louis C.K. claims in his new special – but it's not enough.' *Popdust*, 4 June, <https://www.popdust.com/louis-c-k-special-2645651083.html> (last accessed 15 April 2021).

Ball, Carlos A. (2005). 'This is not your father's autonomy: Lesbian and gay rights from a feminist and relational perspective.' *Harvard Journal of Law & Gender* 28: 345.

Banakar, Reza, and Max Travers (eds) (2005). *Theory and Method in Socio-Legal Research*. London: Bloomsbury Publishing.

Banerjee, Pompi, Raj Merchant and Jaya Sharma (2018). 'Kink and feminism – breaking the binaries.' *Sociology and Anthropology* 6, no. 3: 313–20.

Banks, Olive (1986). *Becoming a Feminist: The Social Origins of 'First Wave' Feminism*. Brighton: Wheatsheaf Books.

Barad, Karen (2007). *Meeting the Universe Halfway: Quantum Physics and the Entanglement of Matter and Meaning*. Durham, NC: Duke University Press.

Barad, Karen (2012). 'Intra-actions.' *Mousse* 34. Interview of Karen Barad by Adam Kleinman, <https://www.academia.edu/1857617/_Intra_actions_interview_ of_Karen_Barad_by_Adam_Kleinmann_> (last accessed 24 March 2021).

Barad, Karen (2014). 'Diffracting diffraction: Cutting together-apart.' *Parallax* 20, no. 3: 168–87.

Barnard, Ian (2020). *Sex Panic Rhetorics, Queer Interventions* (Rhetoric, Culture and Social Critique). Tuscaloosa: University of Alabama Press.

Barnsdale, Lee, and Moira Walker (2007). *Examining the Use and Impact of Family Group Conferencing*. Edinburgh: Scottish Executive, <https://www.fgcni.org/cmsfiles/files/fgc-scottish-exec-report-2007.pdf> (last accessed 24 March 2021).

Barr, Jeremy (2020). 'Why the Weinstein trial jurors are deliberating slowly.' *The Hollywood Reporter*, 19 February, <https://www.hollywoodreporter.com/thr-esq/why-weinstein-trial-jurors-are-deliberating-slowly-1279975> (last accessed 24 March 2021).

Barranco, Kyla (2016). 'Canadian sexual assault laws: A model for affirmative consent on college campuses.' *Michigan State International Law Review* 24: 801–40.

Barrett, Michèle (2014). *Women's Oppression Today: The Marxist/Feminist Encounter*. London: Verso.

Bartky, Sandra (1997). 'Foucault, femininity, and the modernization of patriarchal power.' In Irene Diamond and Lee Quinby (eds), *Feminism and Foucault: Reflections on Resistance*. Boston: Northeastern University Press, pp. 93–111.

Bauer, Fred (2019). 'Cancel culture impoverishes both the heart and the intellect.' *National Review*, 25 September, <https://www.nationalreview.com/2019/09/cancel-culture-impoverishes-heart-and-intellect> (last accessed 24 March 2021).

Bauer, Robin (2014). *Queer BDSM Intimacies: Critical Consent and Pushing Boundaries*. Basingstoke: Palgrave Macmillan.

Baumgardner, Jennifer, and Amy Richards (2010). *Manifesta: Young Women, Feminism, and the Future*. New York: Farrar, Straus and Giroux.

Bay-Cheng, Laina Y. (2012). 'Recovering empowerment: De-personalizing and re-politicizing adolescent female sexuality.' *Sex Roles* 66, nos. 11–12: 713–17.

Bazelon, Lara, and Aya Gruber (2020). '#MeToo doesn't always have to mean prison.' *The New York Times*, 2 March, <https://www.nytimes.com/2020/03/02/opinion/metoo-doesnt-always-have-to-mean-prison.html> (last accessed 24 March 2021).

BBC News (2016). 'Jian Ghomeshi trial rattles sexual assault survivors.' *BBC News*, 25 March, <https://www.bbc.co.uk/news/magazine-35884343> (last accessed 24 March 2021).

BBC News (2019). 'Harvey Weinstein scandal: Who has accused him of what?' *BBC News*, 10 January, <https://www.bbc.co.uk/news/entertainment-arts-41580010> (last accessed 24 March 2021).

BBC News (2020). 'Harvey Weinstein timeline: How the scandal unfolded.' *BBC News*, 29 May, <https://www.bbc.co.uk/news/entertainment-arts-41594672> (last accessed 24 March 2021).

Beard, Jeannie C. Parker (2020). 'Click bait, cancel culture, and the rhetoric of civic discourse.' 20 February, <http://dr.jeanniebeard.com/2020/02/click-bait-cancel-culture-the-rhetoric-of-civic-discourse> (last accessed 25 March 2021).

Beaumont, Elizabeth (2016). 'Gender justice v. the "invisible hand" of gender bias in law and society.' *Hypatia* 31, no. 3: 668–86.

Becker, Mary Ann, and Kathleen Barry (2003). 'The prostitution of sexuality, the global exploitation of women.' *Depaul Law Review* 52: 1,043–5.

Beinhorn, Jana, and Birgit Glorius (2018). 'Patterns of politicisation on refugees and policy responses: The case of Germany.' *Ceaseval*, <http://ceaseval.eu/publications/12_BeinhornGlorius_WP5_Germany.pdf> (last accessed 24 March 2021).

Bell, Allan (2011). 'Re-constructing Babel: Discourse analysis, hermeneutics and the interpretive arc.' *Discourse Studies* 13, no. 5: 519–68.

Bell, Derrick (2018). *Faces at the Bottom of the Well: The Permanence of Racism*. London: Hachette UK.

Bell, Elizabeth (2005). 'Sex acts beyond boundaries and binaries: A feminist challenge for self care in performance studies.' *Text and Performance Quarterly* 25, no. 3: 187–219.

Bell, Gabriel (2017). 'Louis C.K. admits to sexual misconduct in ultimately disingenuous confession.' *Salon*, 10 November, <https://www.salon.com/2017/11/10/louis-ck-statement-apology> (last accessed 24 March 2021).

Bell, Marcus (2017). 'Criminalization of Blackness: Systemic racism and the reproduction of racial inequality in the US criminal justice system.' In Ruth Thompson-Miller and Kimberley Ducey (eds), *Systemic Racism: Making Liberty, Justice, and Democracy Real*. New York: Palgrave Macmillan, pp. 163–83.

Benhabib, Seyla (1992). *Situating the Self: Gender, Community, and Postmodernism in Contemporary Ethics*. New York: Psychology Press.

Bennett, Christopher (2006). 'Taking the sincerity out of saying sorry: Restorative justice as ritual.' *Journal of Applied Philosophy* 23, no. 2: 127–43.

Bennett, Theodore (2018). '"Unorthodox rules": The instructive potential of BDSM consent for law.' *Journal of Positive Sexuality* 4, no. 1: 4–11.

Bennett, W. Lance (2012). 'The personalization of politics: Political identity, social media, and changing patterns of participation.' *The Annals of the American Academy of Political and Social Science* 644, no. 1: 20–39.

Bennington, Geoffrey, and Jacques Derrida (1993). *Jacques Derrida*. Chicago: University of Chicago Press.

Benoit, William L. (2014). *Accounts, Excuses, and Apologies: Image Repair Theory and Research*. Albany: State University of New York Press.

Berardino, Mike (2019). 'Black Lives Matter co-founder Opal Tometi encourages "unapologetic" activism.' *IndyStar*, 15 December, <https://eu.indystar.com/story/news/2019/01/21/black-lives-matter-co-founder-opal-tometi-speaks-notre-dame/2641487002> (last accessed 24 March 2021).

Beres, Melanie A. (2007). '"Spontaneous" sexual consent: An analysis of sexual consent literature.' *Feminism & Psychology* 17, no. 1: 93–108.

Beres, Melanie A., Charlene Y. Senn and Jodee McCaw (2014). 'Navigating ambivalence: How heterosexual young adults make sense of desire differences.' *The Journal of Sex Research* 51, no. 7: 765–76.

Berkseth, Leslie, Kelsey Meany and Marie Zisa (2017). 'Rape and sexual assualt.' *Georgetown Journal of Gender and the Law* 18: 743.

Berlant, Lauren (2000). 'The subject of true feeling: Pain, privacy and politics.' In Sara Ahmed, Celia Lury, Jane Kilby, Maureen McNeil and Beverley Skeggs (eds), *Transformations: Thinking Through Feminism*. London: Routledge, pp. 33–47.

Bernal, Kristen Lee (2019). 'All we have is each other: Restorative justice responses to sexual assault.' PhD dissertation, San Francisco State University.

Bernert, Donna J. (2011). 'Sexuality and disability in the lives of women with intellectual disabilities.' *Sexuality and Disability* 29, no. 2: 129–41.

Bernstein, Mary (2005). 'Identity politics.' *Annual Review of Sociology* 31: 47–74.

Bersani, Leo (2009). *Is the Rectum a Grave? And Other Essays*. Chicago: University of Chicago Press.

Bess, Gabby (2016). '"This is barbaric": Jian Ghomeshi accuser urges for sexual assault reform.' *Vice*, 28 March, <https://www.vice.com/en_us/article/bmwqkv/this-is-barbaric-jian-ghomeshi-accuser-urges-for-sexual-assault-reform> (last accessed 24 March 2021).

Bhandaru, Deepa (2018). 'Let's talk about sex, Ansari, and white women.' *The Stranger*, 22 January, <https://www.thestranger.com/slog/2018/01/22/25737858/lets-talk-about-sex-ansari-and-the-pursuit-of-white-women> (last accessed 24 March 2021).

Bidois, Louis Matthew (2016). 'The value of restorative justice.' *Commonwealth Law Bulletin* 42, no. 4: 596–613.

Bing, Janet M., and Victoria L. Bergvall (1996). 'The question of questions: Beyond binary thinking.' *Rethinking Language and Gender Research: Theory and Practice*: 1–30.

Blackstone, William (1830). *Commentaries on the Laws of England*. Vol. 2. New York: Collins & Hannay.

Blatchford, Christie (2016). 'Christie Blatchford: Ghomeshi verdict was magnificent, compared to trial by press or social media.' *National Post*, 24 March, <https://nationalpost.com/opinion/a-good-day-for-justice-watch-christie-blatchford-break-down-the-ghomeshi-verdict> (last accessed 24 March 2021).

Blatier, Catherine, C. Sellon, C. Gimenez and M. Paulicand (2016). 'The assessment of incarcerated sexual delinquents' risk of recidivism.' *European Review of Applied Psychology* 66, no. 4: 189–98.

Bloom, Chole Turner (2015). 'The regulation of sexual autonomy.' *Exeter Student Law Review* 1: 52.

Boesveld, Sarah (2016). 'Exclusive: Lucy DeCoutere on the Ghomeshi disaster.' *Chatelaine*, 24 March, <https://www.chatelaine.com/news/exclusive-lucy-decoutere-on-the-ghomeshi-disaster> (last accessed 24 March 2021).

Bondurant, Barrie (2001). 'University women's acknowledgment of rape:

Individual, situational, and social factors.' *Violence Against Women* 7, no. 3: 294–314.

Bonner, Hannah (2019). 'Performing archives in the present: Exploring feminist performance art, the politics of (in) visibility, and the archive in #MeToo and #TimesUp.' *South Central Review* 36, no. 2: 33–51.

Bordo, Susan (1993). 'Feminism, Foucault and the politics of the body.' In Caroline Ramazanoglu (ed.), *Up Against Foucault: Explorations of Some Tensions between Foucault and Feminism*. London: Routledge, pp. 179–202.

Botnick, Julie (2018). 'Archival Consent.' *InterActions: UCLA Journal of Education and Information Studies* 14, no. 2.

Bouffard, Jeff, Maisha Cooper and Kathleen Bergseth (2017). 'The effectiveness of various restorative justice interventions on recidivism outcomes among juvenile offenders.' *Youth Violence and Juvenile Justice* 15, no. 4: 465–80.

Boutilier, Sophia, and Lana Wells (2018). 'The case for reparative and transformative justice approaches to sexual violence in Canada: A proposal to pilot and test new approaches.' University of Calgary, Shift: The Project to End Domestic Violence, <http://dx.doi.org/10.11575/PRISM/34971> (last accessed 7 April 2021).

Boyce, Jillian (2013). 'Adult criminal court statistics in Canada, 2011/2012.' *Juristat: Canadian Centre for Justice Statistics*: B1.

Bradley, Laura (2018). 'Sam Bee to Aziz Ansari: "If you say you're a feminist, then f--k like a feminist."' *Vanity Fair*, 18 January, <https://www.vanityfair.com/hollywood/2018/01/aziz-ansari-allegations-samantha-bee-metoo-backlash-shitty-media-men-list> (last accessed 24 March 2021).

Bradshaw, James, and Greg McArthur (2014). 'Ghomeshi's staff complained about "culture of fear".' *The Globe and Mail*, 6 November, <https://www.theglobeandmail.com/news/national/ghomeshis-staff-complained-about-culture-of-fear/article21473254> (last accessed 24 March 2021).

Brady, Geraldine, Pam Lowe, Geraldine Brown, Jane Osmond and Michelle Newman (2018). '"All in all it is just a judgement call": Issues surrounding sexual consent in young people's heterosexual encounters.' *Journal of Youth Studies* 21, no. 1: 35–50.

Braidotti, Rosi (2003). 'Cyberfeminism with a difference.' In Michael Peters, Mark Olssen and Colin Lankshear (eds), *Futures of Critical Theory: Dreams of Difference*. Lanham, MD: Rowman & Littlefield, pp. 239–59.

Braidotti, Rosi (2006). 'Posthuman, all too human: Towards a new process ontology.' *Theory, Culture & Society* 23, nos. 7–8: 197–208.

Brajanac, Amina (2019). 'Addressing intersectionality in the #MeToo movement: A case study of women's mobilization under the #MeToo movement in the postcolonial context of South Africa.' Master's thesis, University of Gothenburg.

Bratskeir, Kate (2018). 'Language experts on Christine Blasey Ford's testimony – and how words impact if women are believed.' *MIC*, 28 September, <https://mic.com/articles/191555/language-experts-on-christine-blasey-fords-testimony-and-how-words-impact-if-women-are-believed> (last accessed 24 March 2021).

Braun, Bruce (2011). 'Book review forum: *Vibrant Matter: A Political Ecology of Things*.' *Dialogues in Human Geography* 1, no. 3: 390–3.

Braun, Virginia, Johanna Schmidt, Nicola Gavey and John Fenaughty (2009). 'Sexual coercion among gay and bisexual men in Aotearoa/New Zealand.' *Journal of Homosexuality* 56, no. 3: 336–60.

Brawley, Lucia (2018). 'Let's be honest about Aziz Ansari.' *CNN*, 19 January, <https://edition.cnn.com/2018/01/17/opinions/lets-be-honest-about-aziz-ansari-brawley/index.html> (last accessed 24 March 2021).

Breslin, Mark (2019). 'Breslin: Why I brought Louis C.K. back from the dead.' *The Canadian Jewish News*, 8 November, <https://www.cjnews.com/culture/entertainment/breslin-why-i-brought-louis-c-k-back-from-the-dead> (last accessed 24 March 2021).

Brewster, Mary P. (2013). 'Children and stalking.' *Family and Intimate Partner Violence Quarterly* 5, no. 3: 247–70.

Brodie, Meghan (2019). 'Lysistrata, #MeToo, and consent: A case study.' *Theatre Topics* 29, no. 3: 183–96.

Brown, Jesse (2015). 'Why some of Jian Ghomeshi's accusers don't want to "tell all".' *The Guardian*, 5 May, <https://www.theguardian.com/commentisfree/2015/may/05/why-some-of-jian-ghomeshis-accusers-dont-want-to-tell-all> (last accessed 15 April 2021).

Brown, Michelle, and Judah Schept (2017). 'New abolition, criminology and a critical carceral studies.' *Punishment & Society* 19, no. 4: 440–62.

Brown, Toni O. L. (2010). '"If someone finds out you're a perv": The experience and management of stigma in the BDSM subculture.' PhD dissertation, Ohio University.

Browne, Kath, and Catherine Nash (eds) (2016). *Queer Methods and Methodologies*. Abingdon: Routledge.

Brownmiller, Susan (1975). *Against Our Will*. New York: Simon & Schuster.

Brownmiller, Susan (1986). *Against Our Will*. London: Bantam, Doubleday, Dell.

Bruney, Gabrielle (2019). 'Aziz Ansari's new Netflix special trades apologies for exhausted anti-PC messages.' *Esquire*, 10 July, <https://www.esquire.com/entertainment/a28338800/aziz-ansari-netflix-special-right-now-metoo-review-allegations-response> (last accessed 24 March 2021).

Bryden, David P. (2000). 'Redefining rape.' *Buffalo Criminal Law Review* 3, no. 2: 317–479.

Brysk, Alison (2017). 'Violence against women: Law and its limits.' *Deusto Journal of Human Rights* 1: 145–73.

Buchanan, Nicole T., and Alayne J. Ormerod (2002). 'Racialized sexual harassment in the lives of African American women.' *Women & Therapy* 25, nos. 3–4: 107–24.

Buchwald, Emilie, Pamela Fletcher and Martha Roth (eds) (1993). *Transforming a Rape Culture*. Minneapolis: Milkweed Editions.

Buckley, Cara (2017). 'Asking questions Louis C.K. doesn't want to answer.' *The New York Times*, 11 September, <https://www.nytimes.com/2017/09/11/movies/louis-ck-rumors-wont-answer.html> (last accessed 24 March 2021).

Burgess, Sarah K. (2018). 'Between the desire for law and the law of desire: #MeToo and the cost of telling the truth today.' *Philosophy & Rhetoric* 51, no. 4: 342–67.

Burgess-Jackson, Keith (ed.) (1999). *A Most Detestable Crime: New Philosophical Essays on Rape*. Oxford: Oxford University Press on Demand.

Burgin, Rachael (2018). 'Submission to terms of reference in relation to consent and knowledge of consent.' New South Wales Law Reform Commission, <https://www.lawreform.justice.nsw.gov.au/Documents/Current-projects/Consent/Preliminary-submissions/PCO72.pdf> (last accessed 8 April 2021).

Burkett, Melissa, and Karine Hamilton (2012). 'Postfeminist sexual agency: Young women's negotiations of sexual consent.' *Sexualities* 15, no. 7: 815–33.

Burmakova, Olga (2013). '50 shades of yes: Feminist re-conceptualization of sexual consent as affirmative, communicative, enthusiastic.' Unpublished thesis, Central European University, Budapest.

Butler, Judith (1990). 'Feminism and the subversion of identity.' *Gender Trouble* 3: 1–25.

Butler, Judith (1993a). *Bodies that Matter: On the Discursive Limits of Sex*. London: Routledge.

Butler, Judith (1993b). 'Critically queer.' *GLQ: A Journal of Lesbian and Gay Studies* 1, no. 1: 17–32.

Butler, Judith (2011a). *Gender Trouble: Feminism and the Subversion of Identity*. Abingdon: Routledge.

Butler, Judith (2011b). 'Sexual consent: Some thoughts on psychoanalysis and law.' *Columbia Journal of Gender and Law* 21: 3.

Butler, Judith (2018). 'Judith Butler's statement about the letter in support of Avital Ronell.' *Remaking the University*, 20 August, <http://utotherescue.blogspot.com/2018/08/judith-butlers-statement-about-letter.html> (last accessed 24 March 2021).

Butler, Judith, and Joan W. Scott (eds) (2013). *Feminists Theorize the Political*. Abingdon: Routledge.

Butler, Mary (2011). *Clicktivism, Slacktivism, or 'Real' Activism: Cultural Codes of American Activism in the Internet Era*. Boulder: University of Colorado.

Byrnes, Craig T. (1998). 'Putting the focus where it belongs: Mens rea, consent, force, and the crime of rape.' *Yale Journal of Law and Feminism* 10: 277–306.

C.K., Louis (2017). 'Louis C.K. responds to accusations: "These stories are true."' *The New York Times*, 10 November, <https://www.nytimes.com/2017/11/10/arts/television/louis-ck-statement.html> (last accessed 24 March 2021).

C.K., Louis (2020). 'Sincerely Louis C.K.' <https://louisck.com/collections/sincerely-louis-ck> (last accessed 7 April 2021).

Cacho, Lisa Marie (2012). *Social Death: Racialized Rightlessness and the Criminalization of the Unprotected*. Vol. 7. New York: New York University Press.

Cahill, Ann J. (2001). *Rethinking Rape*. Ithaca, NY: Cornell University Press.

Cahill, Damien, and Martijn Konings (2017). *Neoliberalism*. Cambridge: Polity.

Calder, Martin C. (ed.) (2007). *Working with Children and Young People who Sexually Abuse: Taking the Field Forward*. Lyme Regis: Russell House.

California Education Code 67386(a)(1) (2020). Education Code. *California Legislative Information*, 31 May, <http://leginfo.legislature.ca.gov/faces/codes_displaySection.xhtml?lawCode=EDC§ionNum=67386> (last accessed 24 March 2021).

Calogero, Rachel M., and Jaclyn A. Siegel (2019). 'Widening understandings of women's sexual desire: A social-ecological lens.' *Archives of Sexual Behavior* 48, no. 6: 1,693–8.

Cameron, Angela (2006). 'Sentencing circles and intimate violence: A Canadian feminist perspective.' *Canadian Journal of Women and the Law* 18, no. 2: 479–512.

Campbell, Bradley, and Jason Manning (2018). 'Trigger warnings, safe spaces, and the language of victimhood.' In *The Rise of Victimhood Culture*, London: Palgrave Macmillan, pp. 71–104.

Campoamor, Danielle (2018). 'I'm not a sexual assault "survivor" – I'm a victim.' *Harper's Bazaar*, 21 May, <https://www.harpersbazaar.com/culture/features/a20138398/stop-using-survivor-to-describe-sexual-assault-victims> (last accessed 24 March 2021).

Carbin, Maria, and Sara Edenheim (2013). 'The intersectional turn in feminist theory: A dream of a common language?' *European Journal of Women's Studies* 20, no. 3: 233–48.

Carey, James W. (2008). *Communication as Culture: Essays on Media and Society* (rev. edn). Abingdon: Routledge.

Caringella, Susan (2008). *Addressing Rape Reform in Law and Practice*. New York: Columbia University Press.

Carlson, Gretchen (2020). Twitter post, 24 February, 5.18 pm, <https://twitter.com/GretchenCarlson/status/1231991715663417348> (last accessed 24 March 2021).

Carlström, Charlotta, and Catrine Andersson (2019). 'The queer spaces of BDSM and non-monogamy.' *Journal of Positive Sexuality* 5, no. 1: 14–19.

Carmody, Moira (2003). 'Sexual ethics and violence prevention.' *Social & Legal Studies* 12, no. 2: 199–216.

Caruso, Gregg D. (2016). 'Free will skepticism and criminal behavior: A public health-quarantine model.' *Southwest Philosophy Review* 32, no. 1: 25–48.

Cavalieri, Shelley (2019). 'On amplification: Extralegal acts of feminist resistance in the #MeToo era.' *Wisconsin Law Review*: 1,489.

CBC News (2016). 'Jian Ghomeshi trial: Read highlights and judge's full decision.' *CBC News*, 24 March, <https://www.cbc.ca/news/canada/toronto/horkins-decision-ghomeshi-1.3505808> (last accessed 24 March 2021).

CBC Radio (2016). 'CBC apologizes to former employee, says "things have changed".' *CBC Radio*, 11 May, <https://www.cbc.ca/radio/asithappens/as-it-happens-wednesday-edition-1.3577228/cbc-apologizes-to-former-

employee-says-things-have-changed-1.3577232> (last accessed 24 March 2021).

Central MN Sexual Assault Center (2020). Facts About Sexual Assault, <https://cmsac.org/facts-and-statistics> (last accessed 24 March 2021).

Chamallas, Martha (1987). 'Consent, equality, and the legal control of sexual conduct.' *Southern California Law Review* 61: 777–862.

Chamberlain, Prudence (2017). *The Feminist Fourth Wave: Affective Temporality*. London: Palgrave Macmillan.

Charles, Ron (2016). 'Jian Ghomeshi trial could deter women from reporting sexual assault.' *CBC News*, 10 February, <https://www.cbc.ca/news/canada/toronto/ghomeshi-trial-sexual-assault-chill-1.3441059> (last accessed 24 March 2021).

Chemaly, Soraya (2018). *Rage Becomes Her*. London: Simon & Schuster.

Chen-Wishart, M. (2006). 'Undue influence: Vindicating relationships of influence.' *Current Legal Problems* 59, no. 1: 231–66.

Cherkasskaya, Eugenia, and Margaret Rosario (2019). 'The relational and bodily experiences theory of sexual desire in women.' *Archives of Sexual Behavior* 48, no. 6: 1,659–81.

Chi, Luu (2019). 'Cancel culture is chaotic good.' *JSTOR Daily*, 18 December, <https://daily.jstor.org/cancel-culture-is-chaotic-good> (last accessed 24 March 2021).

Cho, Sumi, Kimberlé Williams Crenshaw and Leslie McCall (2013). 'Toward a field of intersectionality studies: Theory, applications, and praxis.' *Signs: Journal of Women in Culture and Society* 38, no. 4: 785–810.

Chotiner, Isaac (2018). 'Why did the New York Review of Books publish that Jian Ghomeshi essay? We asked the editor.' *Slate*, 14 September, <https://slate.com/news-and-politics/2018/09/jian-ghomeshi-new-york-review-of-books-essay.html> (last accessed 24 March 2021).

Christie, Nils (1986). 'The ideal victim.' In Ezzat A. Fattah (ed.), *From Crime Policy to Victim Policy*. London: Palgrave Macmillan, pp. 17–30.

Chua, Andrea Long (2018). 'I worked with Avital Ronell. I believe her accuser.' *The Chronicle of Higher Education*, 30 August, <https://www.chronicle.com/article/i-worked-with-avital-ronell-i-believe-her-accuser> (last accessed 24 March 2021).

Clark, Rosemary (2016). '"Hope in a hashtag": The discursive activism of #WhyIStayed.' *Feminist Media Studies* 16, no. 5: 788–804.

Clark-Parsons, Rosemary (2019). '"I see you, I believe you, I stand with you": #MeToo and the performance of networked feminist visibility.' *Feminist Media Studies*: 1–19.

Clarke, Jessica A. (2019). 'The rules of #MeToo.' *University of Chicago Legal Forum* 1: 3.

Clarke-Vivier, Sara, and Clio Stearns (2019). 'MeToo and the problematic valor of truth: Sexual violence, consent, and ambivalence in public pedagogy.' *Journal of Curriculum Theorizing* 34, no. 3.

Cobb, Shelley, and Tanya Horeck (2018). 'Post Weinstein: Gendered power and harassment in the media industries.' *Feminist Media Studies* 18, no. 3: 489–91.

Cockburn, Helen (2012). 'The impact of introducing an affirmative model of consent and changes to the defence of mistake in Tasmanian rape trials.' PhD dissertation, University of Tasmania.

Cohen, Mischa (2018). 'Ian Buruma reacts: "I still stand behind my decision to publish."' *Vrij Nederland*, 20 September, <https://www.vn.nl/reaction-ian-buruma> (last accessed 24 March 2021).

Colbert, Stephen (StephenAtHome) (2017). Twitter post, 10 November, 'Louis CK's apology leaves a lot to be desired. For example, I "desire" a time machine so I can go back and tell him not to masturbate in front of those women.'

Cole, Elizabeth R. (2009). 'Intersectionality and research in psychology.' *American Psychologist* 64, no. 3: 170.

Cole, Kevin (2019). 'Affirmative consent.' In Larry Alexander and Kimberly Kessler Ferzan (eds), *The Palgrave Handbook of Applied Ethics and the Criminal Law*, Cham: Palgrave Macmillan, pp. 47–68.

Coleman, Brooke D. (2018). '#MeToo justice (review of "#MeToo, Time's Up, and theories of justice" by Lesley Wexler, Jennifer Robbennolt and Colleen Murphy).' *Jotwell: The Journal of Things We Like (Lots)*, <https://digitalcommons.law.seattleu.edu/faculty/799> (last accessed 7 April 2021).

Coleman, Michelle (2019). 'What about my rights? #MeToo and the presumption of innocence.' In SLSA 2019: Socio-Legal Studies Association Annual Conference, 3–5 April, University of Leeds, <https://eprints.mdx.ac.uk/id/eprint/27764> (last accessed 24 March 2021).

Collins, Patricia Hill (1990). 'Black feminist thought in the matrix of domination.' In *Black Feminist Thought: Knowledge, Consciousness, and the Politics of Empowerment*. Boston: Unwin Hyman, pp. 552–64.

Collins, Patricia Hill (2004). *Black Sexual Politics: African Americans, Gender, and the New Racism*. New York: Routledge.

Collins, Patricia Hill, and Sirma Bilge (2020). *Intersectionality*. 2nd edn. Cambridge: Polity Press.

Comaroff, John L., and Jean Comaroff (2001). 'On personhood: An anthropological perspective from Africa.' *Social Identities* 7, no. 2: 267–83.

Combahee River Collective (2014). 'A black feminist statement.' *Women's Studies Quarterly* 4, nos. 3–4: 271–80.

Comeau, Natasha (2019). 'Restorative justice lets sexual-assault survivors take back their power.' *The Globe and Mail*, 4 November, <https://www.theglobeandmail.com/opinion/article-restorative-justice-lets-sexual-assault-survivors-take-back-their> (last accessed 24 March 2021).

Conaghan, Joanne, and Yvette Russell (2014). 'Rape myths, law, and feminist research: "Myths about myths"?' *Feminist Legal Studies* 22, no. 1: 25–48.

Consent Respect (2020). 'Affirmative consent laws (yes means yes) state by state', 4 May, <http://affirmativeconsent.com/affirmative-consent-laws-state-by-state> (last accessed 24 March 2021).

Cooper, Brittney (2018). *Eloquent Rage: A Black Feminist Discovers her Superpower*. New York: St. Martin's Press.

Cooper, Chiara (2018). 'Article – speaking the unspeakable? Nicola Lacey's unspeakable subjects and consent in the age of #MeToo.' *feminists@law* 8, no. 2.

Cooper, Davina (2006). 'Active citizenship and the governmentality of local lesbian and gay politics.' *Political Geography* 25, no. 8: 921–43.

Cooper, Davina (2007). '"Well, you go there to get off": Visiting feminist care ethics through a women's bathhouse.' *Feminist Theory* 8, no. 3: 243–62.

Coppock, Vicki, Deena Haydon and Ingrid Richter (2014). *The Illusions of Post-Feminism: New Women, Old Myths*. Abingdon: Routledge.

Cornell, Drucilla (1998). *At the Heart of Freedom: Feminism, Sex, and Equality*. Princeton: Princeton University Press.

Corry, Rebecca (2018a). 'Louis C.K. put me in a lose-lose situation.' *Vulture*, 24 May, <https://www.vulture.com/2018/05/louis-c-k-put-me-in-a-lose-lose-situation.html> (last accessed 24 March 2021).

Corry, Rebecca (HippoloverCorry) (2018b). Twitter post, 22 October, 'To be real clear, CK had "nothing to offer me" as I too was his equal on the set the day he decided to sexually harass me. He took away a day I worked years for and still has no remorse. He's a predator who victimized women for decades and lied about it.'

Corsilles, Angela (1994). 'No-drop policies in the prosecution of domestic violence cases: Guarantee to action or dangerous solution.' *Fordham Law Review* 63, no. 3: 853–81.

Cossman, Brenda (2003). 'Sexuality, queer theory, and "feminism after": Reading and rereading the sexual subject.' *McGill Law Journal* 49, no. 4: 847–76.

Cossman, Brenda (2019). '#MeToo, Sex Wars 2.0 and the power of law.' In Javaid Rehman, Ayesha Shahid and Steve Foster (eds), *The Asian Yearbook of Human Rights and Humanitarian Law*. Vol. 3. Leiden: Brill Nijhoff, pp. 18–37.

Coulling, Ryan, and Matthew S. Johnston (2018). 'The criminal justice system on trial: Shaming, outrage, and gendered tensions in public responses to the Jian Ghomeshi verdict.' *Crime, Media, Culture* 14, no. 2: 311–31.

Cowan, Sharon (2007). '"Freedom and capacity to make a choice": A feminist analysis of consent in the criminal law of rape.' In Vanessa E. Munro and Carl F. Stychin (eds), *Sexuality and the Law: Feminist Engagements*. Abingdon: Routledge-Cavendish, pp. 69–90.

Cowan, Sharon (2019). 'Sense and sensibilities: A feminist critique of legal interventions against sexual violence.' *Edinburgh Law Review* 23, no. 1: 22–51.

Coy, M., L. Kelly, F. Vera-Gray, M. Garner and A. Kanyeredzi (2016). 'From "no means no" to "an enthusiastic yes": Changing the discourse on sexual consent through sex and relationships education.' In V. Sundaram and H. Sauntson (eds), *Global Perspectives and Key Debates in Sex and Relationships Education: Addressing Issues of Gender, Sexuality, Plurality and Power*. London: Palgrave Macmillan, pp. 84–99.

Crawford, Bridget J. (2007). 'Toward a third-wave feminist legal theory: Young women, pornography and the praxis of pleasure.' *Michigan Journal of Gender & Law* 14, no. 1: 99–168.

Crenshaw, Kimberlé (1989). 'Demarginalizing the intersection of race and sex: A black feminist critique of antidiscrimination doctrine, feminist theory and antiracist politics.' *University of Chicago Legal Forum* 1: 139–67.

Crenshaw, Kimberlé (1991). 'Mapping the margins: Intersectionality, identity politics, and violence against women of color.' *Stanford Law Review* 43, no. 6: 1,241–99.

Crenshaw, Kimberlé (2015). 'Intersectional feminism.' Interview at the Women's and Gender Studies Conference, Lafayette, <https://www.youtube.com/watch?v=ROwquxC_Gxc> (last accessed 8 April 2021).

Creutzfeldt, Naomi, Marc Mason and Kirsten McConnachie (eds) (2019). *Routledge Handbook of Socio-Legal Theory and Methods*. London: Routledge.

Criminal Code – General (2012). Canadian Legal FAQs. *Criminal Code – General*, April, <https://www.law-faqs.org/national-faqs/criminal-code/criminal-code> (last accessed 8 April 2021).

Criminal Code, RSC (1985), c C-46 s 273.1, <http://laws-lois.justice.gc.ca/eng/acts/C-46> (last accessed 24 March 2021).

Crnkovich, Mary (1996). 'A sentencing circle.' *The Journal of Legal Pluralism and Unofficial Law* 28, no. 36: 159–81.

Croskery-Hewitt, Sarah (2015). 'Rethinking sexual consent: Voluntary intoxication and affirmative consent to sex.' *NZ Universities Law Review* 26, no. 3: 614–41.

Crosthwaite, Jan (1987). 'Feminist criticism of liberalism.' *Political Science* 39, no. 2: 172–84.

Cullors, Patrisse (2018). 'Abolition and reparations: Histories of resistance, transformative justice, and accountability.' *Harvard Law Review* 132: 1,684.

Curtis-Fawley, Sarah, and Kathleen Daly (2005). 'Gendered violence and restorative justice: The views of victim advocates.' *Violence Against Women* 11, no. 5: 603–38.

D'Cruze, Shani (1992). 'Approaching the history of rape and sexual violence: Notes towards research.' *Women's History Review* 1, no. 3: 377–97.

Dadas, Caroline (2020). 'Making sense of #MeToo: Intersectionality and contemporary feminism.' *Peitho* 22, no. 3, <https://cfshrc.org/article/making-sense-of-metoo-intersectionality-and-contemporary-feminism> (last accessed 8 April 2021).

Daly, Kathleen (2016). 'What is restorative justice? Fresh answers to a vexed question.' *Victims & Offenders* 11, no. 1: 9–29.

Daly, Kathleen, and Julie Stubbs (2006). 'Feminist engagement with restorative justice.' *Theoretical Criminology* 10, no. 1: 9–28.

Daly, Mary (1999). *Quintessence . . . Realizing the Archaic Future: A Radical Elemental Feminist Manifesto*. Boston: Beacon Press.

Daly, Mary (2016). *Gyn/ecology: The Metaethics of Radical Feminism*. Boston: Beacon Press.

Darby, Luke (2018). 'Louis C.K. targets trans people and Parkland shooting survivors in a leaked set.' *GQ*, 31 December, <https://www.gq.com/story/louis-ck-garbage-comeback-jokes> (last accessed 24 March 2021).

Davis, Angela Y. (2011). *Are Prisons Obsolete?* New York: Seven Stories Press.

Davis, Fania E. (2019). *The Little Book of Race and Restorative Justice:*

Black Lives, Healing, and US Social Transformation. New York: Simon & Schuster.

Davis, Kathy (ed.) (1997). *Embodied Practices: Feminist Perspectives on the Body*. Vol. 1. London: Sage.

Davis, Kathy (2008). 'Intersectionality as buzzword: A sociology of science perspective on what makes a feminist theory successful.' *Feminist Theory* 9, no. 1: 67–85.

de Lauretis, Teresa (1987). *Technologies of Gender: Essays on Theory, Film, and Fiction*. Bloomington: Indiana University Press.

de Lauretis, Teresa (1991). *Queer Theory: Lesbian and Gay Sexualities*. Bloomington: Indiana University Press.

Dean, Jodi (2005). 'Communicative capitalism: Circulation and the foreclosure of politics.' *Cultural Politics* 1, no. 1: 51–74.

Dean, Tim (2003). 'Lacan and queer theory.' In Jean-Michel Rabaté (ed.), *The Cambridge Companion to Lacan*. Cambridge: Cambridge University Press, pp. 238–52.

Deer, Sarah, and Abigail Barefoot (2018). 'The limits of the state: Feminist perspectives on carceral logic, restorative justice and sexual violence.' *Kansas Journal of Law & Public Policy* 28: 505.

Del Russo, Maria (2017). 'Could Louis C.K. face jail time?' *Refinery29*, 10 November, <https://www.refinery29.com/en-us/2017/11/180565/masturbation-illegal-sexual-misconduct-louis-ck> (last accessed 24 March 2021).

Delgado, Richard (2010). 'Rodrigo's reconsideration: Intersectionality and the future of critical race theory.' *Iowa Law Review* 96: 1,247.

Department of Justice (2014). 'Rape and sexual assault victimization among college-aged females, 1995–2013.' <https://www.bjs.gov/content/pub/pdf/rsavcaf9513.pdf> (last accessed 8 April 2021).

Department of Justice (2020). 'A definition of consent to sexual activity.' Government of Canada, 4 May, <https://www.justice.gc.ca/eng/cj-jp/victims-victimes/def.html> (last accessed 24 March 2021).

Der Spiegel (2018). 'Is there truth to refugee rape reports?' *Spiegel International*, 17 January, <https://www.spiegel.de/international/germany/is-there-truth-to-refugee-sex-offense-reports-a-1186734.html> (last accessed 24 March 2021).

Derene, Steven, Steve Walker and J. D. John Stein (2007). 'History of the crime victims' movement in the United States.' *Senator Tommy Burks Victim Assistance Academy Participant Manual*: 1–32.

Derrida, Jacques (1992). 'Force of law: The "mystical foundation of authority".' In Drucilla Cornell, Michel Rosenfeld and David Gray Carlson (eds), *Deconstruction and the Possibility of Justice*. New York: Routledge, pp. 3–67.

Derrida, Jacques (1999). 'Justice, law and philosophy – an interview with Jacques Derrida.' *South African Journal of Philosophy* 18, no. 3: 279–86.

Derrida, Jacques (2001). *On Cosmopolitanism and Forgiveness*. New York: Psychology Press.

Derrida, Jacques (2016). *Of Grammatology*. Baltimore: Johns Hopkins University Press.

Dessem, Matthew (2018). 'Audio of a new Louis C.K. set has leaked, and it's sickening.' *Slate*, 31 December, <https://slate.com/culture/2018/12/louis-ck-leaked-set-governors-parkland-pronouns.html> (last accessed 24 March 2021).

Desta, Yohana (2017). 'Salma Hayek: Weinstein threatened to kill me, forced me to shoot a full-frontal scene.' *Vanity Fair*, 13 December, <https://www.vanityfair.com/hollywood/2017/12/salma-hayek-harvey-weinstein-allegations> (last accessed 24 March 2021).

Desta, Yohana (2018). 'Sarah Silverman opens up about Louis C.K.: "I believe he has remorse."' *Vanity Fair*, 22 October, <https://www.vanityfair.com/hollywood/2018/10/sarah-silverman-louis-ck-interview-remorse> (last accessed 24 March 2021).

Dhami, Mandeep K., and Penny Joy (2007). 'Challenges to establishing volunteer-run, community-based restorative justice programs.' *Contemporary Justice Review* 10, no. 1: 9–22.

Di Leonardo, Micaela (2018). '#MeToo is nowhere near enough.' *HAU: Journal of Ethnographic Theory* 8, no. 3: 420–25.

DiFonzo, Nicholas, and Prashant Bordia (2007). 'Rumor, gossip and urban legends.' *Diogenes* 54, no. 1: 19–35.

Dignan, James (2004). *Understanding Victims and Restorative Justice*. Maidenhead: McGraw-Hill Education (UK).

Dill, Bonnie Thornton, and Marla H. Kohlman (2012). 'Intersectionality: A transformative paradigm in feminist theory and social justice.' In Sharlene Nagy Hesse-Biber (ed.), *Handbook of Feminist Research: Theory and Praxis*, 2nd edn. Los Angeles: Sage, pp. 154–74.

Diprose, Rosalyn (1994). *The Bodies of Women: Ethics, Embodiment, and Sexual Difference*. New York: Routledge.

Dixon, Kitsy (2014). 'Feminist online identity: Analyzing the presence of hashtag feminism.' *Journal of Arts and Humanities* 3, no. 7: 34–40.

Donovan, Brian (2010). *White Slave Crusades: Race, Gender, and Anti-Vice Activism, 1887–1917*. Champaign: University of Illinois Press.

Donovan, Kevin (2014). 'Jian Ghomeshi did not ask for consent, accusers say.' *Toronto Star*, 28 November, <https://www.thestar.com/news/gta/2014/11/28/jian_ghomeshi_did_not_ask_for_consent_accusers_say.html> (last accessed 24 March 2021).

Donovan, Kevin, and Alyshah Hasham (2016). 'Ghomeshi defence pushes hard on inconsistencies in woman's account.' *Toronto Star*, 1 February, <https://www.thestar.com/news/crime/2016/02/01/jian-ghomeshi-goes-on-trial-for-sexual-assault.html> (last accessed 24 March 2021).

Doolittle, Robyn (2019a). *Had It Coming: What's Fair in the Age of #MeToo?* Toronto: Penguin.

Doolittle, Robyn (2019b). 'Robyn Doolittle on Jian Ghomeshi's failed comebacks.' *Chatelaine*, 26 September, <https://www.chatelaine.com/living/books/robyn-doolittle-book> (last accessed 24 March 2021).

dos Santos Bruss, Sara Morais (2020). 'Queering feminist solidarities.' *Open Gender Journal* 4.

Dripps, Donald A. (1992). 'Beyond rape: An essay on the difference between the presence of force and the absence of consent.' *Columbia Law Review* 92, no. 7: 1,780–1809.

Dripps, Donald A. (1993). 'More on distinguishing sex, sexual expropriation, and sexual assault: A reply to professor West.' *Columbia Law Review* 93, no. 6: 1,460–72.

Dripps, Donald A. (2008). 'After rape law: Will the turn to consent normalize the prosecution of sexual assault.' *Akron Law Review* 41, no. 4: 957–80.

Dubrofsky, Rachel E., and Marina Levina (2020). 'The labor of consent: Affect, agency and whiteness in the age of #MeToo.' *Critical Studies in Media Communication* 37, no. 2: 1–15.

Duggan, Lisa (2018). 'The full catastrophe.' *Bully Bloggers*, 18 August, <https://bullybloggers.wordpress.com/2018/08/18/the-full-catastrophe> (last accessed 24 March 2021).

Duggan, Lisa, and Nan D. Hunter (2006). *Sex Wars: Sexual Dissent and Political Culture*. New York: Taylor & Francis.

Duggan, Marian (ed.) (2018). *Revisiting the 'Ideal Victim': Developments in Critical Victimology*. Bristol: Policy Press.

Dukmasova, Maya (2017). 'Is it time to reimagine justice and accountability for sexual misconduct?' *The Bleader*, 22 November, <https://www.chicagoreader.com/Bleader/archives/2017/11/22/is-it-time-to-reimagine-justice-and-accountability-for-sexual-misconduct> (last accessed 24 March 2021).

Dutta, Debolina, and Oishik Sircar (2013). 'India's winter of discontent:

Some feminist dilemmas in the wake of a rape.' *Feminist Studies* 39, no. 1: 293–306.

Dutton, Edward (2020). 'The return of heresy.' The National Policy Institute, 26 March, <https://nationalpolicy.institute/2020/03/26/the-return-of-heresy> (last accessed 24 March 2021).

Dworkin, Andrea (1981). 'Men possessing women.' New York: Perigee.

Dworkin, Andrea (1987). *Intercourse*. New York: Free Press.

Dworkin, Andrea (2006). *Intercourse*. New York: Basic Books.

Dwyer, Angela (2011). '"It's not like we're going to jump them": How transgressing heteronormativity shapes police interactions with LGBT young people.' *Youth Justice* 11, no. 3: 203–20.

Dwyer, Colin, and Vanessa Romo (2020). 'Harvey Weinstein found guilty of rape, sexual abuse in mixed verdict.' *NPR*, 24 February, <https://www.npr.org/2020/02/24/805258433/harvey-weinstein-found-guilty-of-rape-but-acquitted-of-most-sexual-assault-charg> (last accessed 24 March 2021).

Eckert, Stine, and Linda Steiner (2018). 'Sexual harassment in media education.' *Communication, Culture & Critique* 11, no. 3: 484–8.

Edenfield, Avery C. (2019). 'Queering consent: Design and sexual consent messaging.' *Communication Design Quarterly Review* 7, no. 2: 50–63.

Edwards, Alan, and Susan Sharpe (2004). 'Restorative justice in the context of domestic violence: A literature review.' Mediation and Restorative Justice Centre, Edmonton, <https://s3.amazonaws.com/mrjc/restorative_justice_DV_Lit_Review.pdf> (last accessed 8 April 2021).

Edwards, Daphne (1996). 'Acquaintance rape and the force element: When no is not enough.' *Golden Gate University Law Review* 26, no. 2: 241–300.

Edwards, Tamala M. (1998). 'Mad about the boy.' *Time*, 16 February, <http://content.time.com/time/magazine/article/0,9171,987832,00.html> (last accessed 24 March 2021).

Ehrlich, Susan (1998). 'The discursive reconstruction of sexual consent.' *Discourse & Society* 9, no. 2: 149–71.

Ehrlich, Susan (2003). *Representing Rape: Language and Sexual Consent*. London: Routledge.

Ellickson, Robert C. (2000). 'Trends in legal scholarship: A statistical study.' *The Journal of Legal Studies* 29, no. S1: 517–43.

Ellis, Gayle M. (1994). 'Acquaintance rape.' *Perspectives in Psychiatric Care* 30, no. 1: 11–16.

Emejulu, Akwugo (2018). 'On the problems and possibilities of feminist solidarity: The Women's March one year on.' *IPPR Progressive Review* 24, no. 4: 267–73.

Engel, Beverly (2017). 'Why don't victims of sexual harassment come forward sooner?' *Psychology Today* 16.

Erdely, Sabrina Rubin (2014). 'A rape on campus.' *Rolling Stone*, 19 November, <http://web.archive.org/web/20141119200349/http://www.rollingstone.com/culture/features/a-rape-on-campus-20141119> (last accessed 24 March 2021).

Evans, Adrienne, and Sarah Riley (2013). 'Immaculate consumption: Negotiating the sex symbol in postfeminist celebrity culture.' *Journal of Gender Studies* 22, no. 3: 268–81.

Evans, David Trevor (1993). *Sexual Citizenship: The Material Construction of Sexualities*. New York: Psychology Press.

Evans, Elizabeth, and Prudence Chamberlain (2015). 'Critical waves: Exploring feminist identity, discourse and praxis in western feminism.' *Social Movement Studies* 14, no. 4: 396–409.

Evans, Greg (2020). 'Harvey Weinstein accusers speak out: "23 Years! We did it!"' *Deadline*, 11 March, <https://deadline.com/2020/03/harvey-weinstein-accusers-speak-out-mimi-haley-jessica-mann-1202879743> (last accessed 24 March 2021).

Evans, Sara M. (2002). 'Re-viewing the second wave.' *Feminist Studies* 28, no 2: 259–67.

Evans, Teresa M., Lindsay Bira, Jazmin Beltran Gastelum, L. Todd Weiss and Nathan L. Vanderford (2018). 'Evidence for a mental health crisis in graduate education.' *Nature Biotechnology* 36, no. 3: 282.

Fahs, Breanne, and Sara I. McClelland (2016). 'When sex and power collide: An argument for critical sexuality studies.' *The Journal of Sex Research* 53, nos. 4–5: 392–416.

Faludi, Susan (2020). '"Believe All Women" is a right-wing trap.' *The New York Times*, 18 May, <https://www.nytimes.com/2020/05/18/opinion/tara-reade-believe-all-women.html> (last accessed 24 March 2021).

Farmer, Victoria Reynolds (2018). 'Sexual ethics.' *American Book Review* 39, no. 4: 10–11.

Farrow, Ronan (2017). 'From aggressive overtures to sexual assault: Harvey Weinstein's accusers tell their stories.' *The New Yorker*, 10 October, <https://www.newyorker.com/news/news-desk/from-aggressive-overtures-to-sexual-assault-harvey-weinsteins-accusers-tell-their-stories> (last accessed 24 March 2021).

Fauble III, Bryce R. (2018). 'Implementing restorative justice programs in the Cal Poly community.' California Polytechnic State University, <https://digitalcommons.calpoly.edu/cgi/viewcontent.cgi?article=1070&context=laessp> (last accessed 8 April 2021).

Feagin, Joe R., Anthony M. Orum and Gideon Sjoberg (eds) (1991). *A Case for the Case Study*. Chapel Hill: University of North Carolina Press.

Federici, Silvia (2004). *Caliban and the Witch*. New York: Autonomedia.

Feldman, Kate (2017). 'Analysis | How Louis C.K. positioned himself as a champion of feminism.' *Pittsburgh Gazette*, 13 November, <https://www.post-gazette.com/ae/tv-radio/2017/11/12/Analysis-How-Louis-CK-positioned-himself-as-a-champion-of-feminism/stories/201711120232> (last accessed 15 April 2021).

Ferber, Abby L. (2007). 'The construction of Black masculinity: White supremacy now and then.' *Journal of Sport and Social Issues* 31, no. 1: 11–24.

Ferguson, Ann (1984). 'Sex war: The debate between radical and libertarian feminists.' *Signs: Journal of Women in Culture and Society* 10, no. 1: 106–12.

Fernández, Alexia (2020). 'Annabella Sciorra breaks silence on Weinstein verdict: "My testimony was painful but necessary."' *People*, 24 February, <https://people.com/movies/annabella-sciorra-breaks-silence-harvey-weinstein-verdict> (last accessed 24 March 2021).

Ferzan, Kimberly Kessler (2018). 'Consent and coercion.' *Arizona State Law Journal* 50, no. 4: 951–1,007.

Feuer, Alan (2020). 'A timeline of the Weinstein case.' *The New York Times*, 24 February, <https://www.nytimes.com/2020/02/24/nyregion/harvey-weinstein-case-sexual-assault.html>(last accessed 25 March 2021).

Fiebrich, Caitlyn Grey (2019). 'From #MeToo to #OnlyYou: Epic systems, collective arbitration, and sexual harassment in the workplace.' *Houston Law Review: Off the Record* 10: 26.

Fileborn, Bianca, and Rachel Loney-Howes (eds) (2019). *#MeToo and the Politics of Social Change*. Cham: Palgrave Macmillan.

Filipovic, Jill (2018). 'The poorly reported Aziz Ansari exposé was a missed opportunity.' *The Guardian*, 16 January, <https://www.theguardian.com/commentisfree/2018/jan/16/aziz-ansari-story-missed-opportunity> (last accessed 24 March 2021).

Financial Times (2020). 'Harvey Weinstein found guilty of sex crimes at trial.' *Financial Times*, 24 Februrary, <https://www.ft.com/content/d093489e-529e-11ea-8841-482eed0038b1> (last accessed 24 March 2021).

Finch, Emily, and Vanessa E. Munro (2006). 'Breaking boundaries? Sexual consent in the jury room.' *Legal Studies* 26, no. 3: 303–20.

Fine, Gary Alan (2007). 'Rumor, trust and civil society: Collective memory and cultures of judgment.' *Diogenes* 54, no. 1: 5–18.

Firestone, Shulamith (2000). 'The dialectic of sex.' In Barbara A. Crow (ed.), *Radical Feminism: A Documentary Reader*. New York: New York University Press, pp. 90–7.

Fischel, Joseph J. (2010). 'Per se or power? Age and sexual consent.' *Yale Journal of Law and Feminism* 22: 279.

Fischel, Joseph J. (2016). *Sex and Harm in the Age of Consent*. Minneapolis: University of Minnesota Press.

Fischel, Joseph J. (2019). *Screw Consent: A Better Politics of Sexual Justice*. Oakland: University of California Press.

Fischel, Joseph J., and Hilary R. O'Connell (2015). 'Disabling consent, or reconstructing sexual autonomy.' *Columbia Journal of Gender and Law* 30, no. 2: 428–528.

Flanagan, Caitlin (2018a). '*Babe* turns a movement into a racket.' *The Atlantic*, 19 January, <https://www.theatlantic.com/entertainment/archive/2018/01/how-a-movement-becomes-a-racket/551036> (last accessed 24 March 2021).

Flanagan, Caitlin (2018b). 'The humiliation of Aziz Ansari.' *The Atlantic*, 15 January, <https://www.theatlantic.com/entertainment/archive/2018/01/the-humiliation-of-aziz-ansari/550541> (last accessed 24 March 2021).

Flynn, Asher, and Nicola Henry (2012). 'Disputing consent: The role of jury directions in Victoria.' *Current Issues in Criminal Justice* 24, no. 2: 167–84.

Foucault, Michel (1972). *The Archaeology of Knowledge and The Discourse on Language*. New York: Pantheon Books.

Foucault, Michel (1978). *The History of Sexuality, Vol. 1: An Introduction*, trans R. Hurley. New York: Pantheon.

Foucault, Michel (1980). 'The confession of the flesh.' In *Power/Knowledge: Selected Interviews and Other Writings 1972–1977*, ed. Colin Gordon. New York: Pantheon Books, pp. 194–228.

Foucault, Michel (1986). *The Care of the Self: The History of Sexuality*. New York: Random House.

Foucault, Michel (1987). 'The ethic of care for the self as a practice of freedom: An interview with Michel Foucault on January 20, 1984.' *Philosophy & Social Criticism* 12, nos. 2–3: 112–31.

Foucault, Michel (1990). *The History of Sexuality: An Introduction*. New York: Vintage.

Foucault, Michel (2012). *The History of Sexuality, Vol. 3: The Care of the Self*. New York: Vintage.

Foucault, Michel (2019). *The History of Sexuality, Vol. 1: The Will to Knowledge*. London: Penguin.

Framke, Caroline (2017). 'The sexual harassment allegations against Louis C.K., explained.' *Vox*, 10 November, <https://www.vox.com/culture/2017/11/9/16629400/louis-ck-allegations-masturbation> (last accessed 24 March 2021).

Framke, Caroline (2018). 'Most harassment apologies are just damage control. Dan Harmon's was a self-reckoning.' *Vox*, 12 January, <https://www.vox.com/culture/2018/1/11/16879702/dan-harmon-apology-megan-ganz-community> (last accessed 24 March 2021).

Frank, Lily, and Sven Nyholm (2017). 'Robot sex and consent: Is consent to sex between a robot and a human conceivable, possible, and desirable?' *Artificial Intelligence and Law* 25, no. 3: 305–23.

Franke, Katherine M. (2001). 'Theorizing yes: An essay on feminism, law, and desire.' *Columbia Law Review*: 181–208.

Frankel, Bruce (1998). 'Family man.' *People*, 2 November, <https://people.com/archive/family-man-vol-50-no-16> (last accessed 24 March 2021).

Fraser, Nancy (2019). 'Response: For an anti-capitalist feminism.' *Rassegna Italiana di Sociologia* 60, no. 4: 862–8.

Frederick, Loretta, and Kristine C. Lizdas (2003). 'The role of restorative justice in the battered women's movement.' *Battered Women's Justice Project*, September, <https://www.bwjp.org/resource-center/resource-results/the-role-of-restorative-justice-in-the-battered-women-s-movement.html> (last accessed 24 March 2021).

Friedan, Betty (2010). *The Feminine Mystique*. New York: W. W. Norton & Company.

Friedman, Jaclyn (2010). 'Consent is not a lightswitch.' *Amplify*, 9 November.

Friedman, Jaclyn, and Jessica Valenti (eds) (2019). *Yes Means Yes! Visions of Female Sexual Power and a World without Rape*. New York: Seal Press.

Friedman, Marilyn (2003). *Autonomy, Gender, Politics*. Oxford: Oxford University Press.

Gajjala, Radhika, Ayesha Vemuri and Raya Sarkar (2019). 'Dialogue interlude #9: On #LoSHA.' In Radhika Gajjala, *Digital Diasporas: Labor and Affect in Gendered Indian Digital Publics*. New York: Rowman & Littlefield International, pp. 188–99.

Gan, Orit (2013). 'Contractual duress and relations of power.' *Harvard Journal of Law & Gender* 36: 171.

Gapper, John (2017). 'Harvey Weinstein is Hollywood's monster.' *Financial Times*, 11 October, <https://www.ft.com/content/c1db9732-acda-11e7-aab9-abaa44b1e130> (last accessed 24 March 2021).

Garibotti, María Cecilia, and Cecilia Marcela Hopp (2019). 'Substitution activism: The impact of #MeToo in Argentina.' In Bianca Fileborn and Rachel Loney-Howes (eds), *#MeToo and the Politics of Social Change*, Cham: Palgrave Macmillan, pp. 185–99.

Garland-Levett, Sarah (2018). 'Knowing-in-being: Traversing the mind/body dualism to dissolve sexuality education's "knowledge/practice gap".' *Gender and Education* 32, no. 1: 1–18.

Garrett, Abby (2019). '#WhyIDidntReport: Using social media as a tool to understand why sexual assault victims do not report.' University of Mississippi, eGrove, <https://egrove.olemiss.edu/hon_thesis/1072> (last accessed 24 March 2021).

Garza, Frida (2019). 'Aziz Ansari effectively interrogates others, but not himself, in Netflix standup.' *Jezebel*, 11 July, <https://themuse.jezebel.com/aziz-ansari-effectively-interrogates-others-but-not-hi-1836275380> (last accessed 24 March 2021).

Gash, Alison, and Ryan Harding (2018). '#MeToo? Legal discourse and everyday responses to sexual violence.' *Laws* 7, no. 2: 21.

Gauthier, Jeffrey (2011). 'Prostitution, sexual autonomy, and sex discrimination.' *Hypatia* 26, no. 1: 166–86.

Gavrielides, Theo (2017). 'The victims' directive and what victims want from restorative justice.' *Victims & Offenders* 12, no. 1: 21–42.

Gawker (2012). 'Which beloved comedian likes to force female comics to watch him jerk off?' *Gawker*, 19 March, <https://gawker.com/5894527/which-beloved-comedian-likes-to-force-female-comics-to-watch-him-jerk-off?comment=48089921#comments> (last accessed 24 March 2021).

Genz, Stéphanie, and Benjamin A. Brabon (2009). *Postfeminism: Cultural Texts and Theories*. Edinburgh: Edinburgh University Press.

George, Ronald M. (2006). 'Balanced and restorative justice: An information manual for California.' Judicial Council of California: Administrative Office of the Courts, <https://www.courts.ca.gov/documents/BARJManual3.pdf> (last accessed 24 March 2021).

Gerdsen, Jenna, and Jonelle Walker (2019). 'Who reports mandatory reporters?' *Theatre Topics* 29, no. 2: 161–8.

Gerhard, Jane (2001). *Desiring Revolution: Second-Wave Feminism and the*

Rewriting of Twentieth-Century American Sexual Thought. New York: Columbia University Press.

Gerring, John (2008). 'Case selection for case-study analysis: Qualitative and quantitative techniques.' In Janet M. Box-Steffensmeier, Henry E. Brady and Davis Collier (eds), *The Oxford Handbook of Political Methodology*. Oxford: Oxford University Press, pp. 645–84.

Gersen, Jacob, and Jeannie Suk (2016). 'The sex bureaucracy.' *California Law Review* 104: 881.

Ghadery, Farnush (2019). '#Metoo – has the "sisterhood" finally become global or just another product of neoliberal feminism?' *Transnational Legal Theory* 10, no. 2: 252–74.

Ghent, Emmanuel (1990). 'Masochism, submission, surrender: Masochism as a perversion of surrender.' *Contemporary Psychoanalysis* 26, no. 1: 108–36.

Ghomeshi, Jian (2014). *1982*. Toronto: Penguin Canada.

Ghomeshi, Jian (2018). 'Reflections from a hashtag.' *The New York Review of Books*, 11 October, <https://www.nybooks.com/articles/2018/10/11/reflections-hashtag> (last accessed 24 March 2021).

Gibson, Sara L. (2016). 'Can Enthusiastic Consent Be Sexy? The Influence of Consent Type on Perceived Enjoyment and Sexiness of Sexual Encounters Related to Sexual Scripts and Consent Attitudes.' Master's dissertation, University of Louisiana at Lafayette.

Gieseler, Carly (2019). *The Voices of #MeToo: From Grassroots Activism to a Viral Roar*. Lanham, MD: Rowman & Littlefield.

Gilbert, Sophie (2017). 'The movement of #MeToo: How a hashtag got its power.' *The Atlantic*, 16 October, <https://www.theatlantic.com/entertainment/archive/2017/10/the-movement-of-metoo/542979> (last accessed 24 March 2021).

Gill, Rosalind (2007). 'Postfeminist media culture: Elements of a sensibility.' *European Journal of Cultural Studies* 10, no. 2: 147–66.

Gill, Rosalind (2008). 'Culture and subjectivity in neoliberal and postfeminist times.' *Subjectivity* 25, no. 1: 432–45.

Gill, Rosalind, and Shani Orgad (2018). 'The shifting terrain of sex and power: From the "sexualization of culture" to #MeToo.' *Sexualities* 21, no. 8: 1,313–24.

Gill, Rosalind, and Christina Scharff (eds) (2013). *New Femininities: Postfeminism, Neoliberalism and Subjectivity*. Basingstoke: Palgrave Macmillan.

Gillespie, Tom (2020). '"I hope the handcuffs are tight": Reaction to

Weinstein's guilty verdict.' *Sky News*, 25 February, <https://news.sky.com/story/taking-out-the-trash-harvey-weinsteins-accusers-react-to-guilty-verdict-11942583> (last accessed 24 March 2021).

Gillis, Stacy, Gillian Howie and Rebecca Munford (eds) (2004). *Third Wave Feminism*. New York: Palgrave Macmillan.

Gilmore, Leigh (2017). 'He said/she said: Truth-telling and #MeToo.' *FORUM: University of Edinburgh Postgraduate Journal of Culture & the Arts*, no. 25.

Gilmore, Ruth Wilson (2007). *Golden Gulag: Prisons, Surplus, Crisis, and Opposition in Globalizing California*. Vol. 21. Berkeley: University of California Press.

Glick, Elisa (2000). 'Sex positive: Feminism, queer theory, and the politics of transgression.' *Feminist Review* 64, no. 1: 19–45.

Golder, Scott A., and Michael W. Macy (2011). 'Diurnal and seasonal mood vary with work, sleep, and daylength across diverse cultures.' *Science* 333, no. 6,051: 1,878–81.

Goldner, Virginia (2020). 'Pleasure can hurt: The erotic politics of sexual coercion.' *Psychoanalytic Dialogues* 30, no. 3: 239–50.

Gomez, Logan Rae (2017). 'Beyond survival: Embodied rhetoric and resistance to campus sexual violence.' Dissertation, Syracuse University, <https://surface.syr.edu/cgi/viewcontent.cgi?article=1141&context=thesis> (last accessed 24 March 2021).

Gong, Rachel (2015). 'Indignation, inspiration, and interaction on the internet: Emotion work online in the anti-human trafficking movement.' *Journal of Technology in Human Services* 33, no. 1: 87–103.

González, Thalia, and Annalise J. Buth (2019). 'Restorative justice at the crossroads: Politics, power, and language.' *Contemporary Justice Review* 22, no. 3: 242–56.

Goodman, Bonnie K. (2018). 'Clinton, Shavit, should there be #MeToo forgiveness?' *Medium*, 7 September, <https://medium.com/@BonnieKGoodman/clinton-shavit-should-there-be-metoo-forgiveness-4a932304c021> (last accessed 25 March 2021).

Goss, Katie (2019). 'Pornography, psychoanalysis and the sinthome: Ignorance and ethics.' *Porn Studies* 6, no. 1: 59–73.

Gotell, Lise (2008). 'Rethinking affirmative consent in Canadian sexual assault law: Neoliberal sexual subjects and risky women.' *Akron Law Review* 41, no. 4: 865–98.

Graham, Ruth (2018). 'Fun, free-wheeling, and kind of terrifying.' *Slate*, 17 January, <https://slate.com/culture/2018/01/a-deep-dive-into-the-

archives-of-babe-net-after-its-bombshell-piece-on-aziz-ansari.html> (last accessed 24 March 2021).

Grant, Jordan A. (2020). 'How restorative justice practices affect adolescent recidivism rates: An examination.' Honors thesis, Portland State University.

Grant, Melissa Gira (2020). 'No justice for Harvey Weinstein's victims.' *The New Republic*, 10 March, <https://newrepublic.com/article/156747/no-justice-harvey-weinsteins-victims> (last accessed 24 March 2021).

Gray, Emma (2018). 'On Aziz Ansari and sex that feels violating even when it's not criminal.' *Huffpost*, 16 January, <https://www.huffingtonpost.co.uk/entry/aziz-ansari-sex-violating-but-not-criminal_n_5a5e445de4b0106b7f65b346?ri18n=true> (last accessed 24 March 2021).

Gray, J. M., and M. A. H. Horvath (2018). 'Rape myths in the criminal justice system.' In Emma Milne, Karen Brennan, Nigel South and Jackie Turton (eds), *Women and the Criminal Justice System: Failing Victims and Offenders?* Cham: Palgrave Macmillan, pp. 15–41.

Gready, Paul, and Simon Robins (2014). 'From transitional to transformative justice: A new agenda for practice.' *International Journal of Transitional Justice* 8, no. 3: 339–61.

Green, Michael Z. (2019). 'A new #MeToo result: Rejecting notions of romantic consent with executives.' *Employee Rights and Employee Policy Journal* 23, no. 1: 115–64.

Greenberg, Zoe (2018). 'What happens to #MeToo when a feminist is the accused?' *The New York Times*, 12 August, <https://www.nytimes.com/2018/08/13/nyregion/sexual-harassment-nyu-female-professor.html> (last accessed 24 March 2021).

Greene, Linda S., Lolita Buckner Inniss, Bridget J. Crawford, Mehrsa Baradaran, Noa Ben-Asher, I. Bennett Capers, Osamudia R. James and Keisha Lindsay (2019). 'Talking about Black Lives Matter and #MeToo.' *Wisconsin Journal of Law, Gender and Society* 34: 109.

Grimm, Josh, and Dustin Harp (2011). 'Happily ever after: Myth, rape, and romance in magazine coverage of the Mary Kay Letourneau case.' *Journal of Magazine & New Media Research* 2, no. 12: 1–18.

Grinberg, Emanuella (2014). 'The issue with ousted CBC host Jian Ghomeshi's "kinky defense".' *CNN*, 2 November, <https://edition.cnn.com/2014/10/28/living/jian-ghomeshi-cbc-fired-bdsm/index.html> (last accessed 24 March 2021).

Groenhout, Ruth E. (2002). 'Essentialist challenges to liberal feminism.' *Social Theory and Practice* 28, no. 1: 51–75.

Grossman, Paul (2015). 'Mindfulness: Awareness informed by an embodied ethic.' *Mindfulness* 6, no. 1: 17–22.

Grosz, Elizabeth (1994). *Volatile Bodies: Toward a Corporeal Feminism*. Bloomington: Indiana University Press.

Gruber, Aya (2015). 'Not affirmative consent.' *University of the Pacific Law Review* 47: 683–707.

Gruber, Aya (2016). 'Consent confusion.' *Cardozo Law Review* 38: 683–706.

Gruber, Aya (2019). 'The complexity of college consent.' *Adjudicating Campus Sexual Misconduct and Assault (Cognella 2019)*, <https://papers.ssrn.com/sol3/papers.cfm?abstract_id=3527825> (last accessed 24 March 2021).

Gruber, Aya (2020). *The Feminist War on Crime: The Unexpected Role of Women's Liberation in Mass Incarceration*. Berkeley: University of California Press.

Haaretz (2020), 'The key issue Black Lives Matter and #MeToo have in common.' *Haaretz*, 27 June, <https://www.haaretz.com/us-news/.premium.MAGAZINE-the-key-issue-black-lives-matter-and-metoo-have-in-common-1.8949081> (last accessed 24 March 2021).

Haas, Susan (2019). 'Harvey Weinstein says, "I feel like the forgotten man"; accusers call him "an unrepentant abuser".' *USA Today*, 15 December, <https://eu.usatoday.com/story/entertainment/celebrities/2019/12/15/harvey-weinstein-says-he-deserves-more-credit-advancing-women/2659403001> (last accessed 24 March 2021).

Habermas, Jürgen (1998). *On the Pragmatics of Communication*. Cambridge, MA: MIT Press.

Hagi, Sarah (2015). 'Aziz Ansari calls out racism in Hollywood.' *Complex*, 26 October, <https://www.complex.com/pop-culture/2015/10/aziz-ansari-calls-hollywood-racis> (last accessed 24 March 2021).

Haider, Asad (2018). *Mistaken Identity: Race and Class in the Age of Trump*. London: Verso.

Hakimi, Dehnad, Thema Bryant-Davis, Sarah E. Ullman and Robyn L. Gobin (2018). 'Relationship between negative social reactions to sexual assault disclosure and mental health outcomes of Black and White female survivors.' *Psychological Trauma: Theory, Research, Practice, and Policy* 10, no. 3: 270–5.

Halley, Janet (2000). 'Sexuality harassment.' Faculty of Law, University of Toronto.

Halley, Janet (2016). 'The move to affirmative consent.' *Signs: Journal of Women in Culture and Society* 42, no. 1: 257–79.

Halperin, David M. (1990). *One Hundred Years of Homosexuality: And Other Essays on Greek Love*. New York: Psychology Press.

Halperin, David M., and Trevor Hoppe (eds) (2017). *The War on Sex*. Durham, NC: Duke University Press.

Hamad, Hannah, and Anthea Taylor (2015). 'Introduction: Feminism and contemporary celebrity culture.' *Celebrity Studies* 6, no. 1: 124–7.

Hames-García, Michael (2011). 'Queer theory revisited.' In Michael Hames-García and Ernesto Javier Martínez (eds), *Gay Latino Studies: A Critical Reader*. Durham, NC: Duke University Press, pp. 19–45.

Haraway, Donna J. (2001). '"Gender" for a Marxist dictionary: The sexual politics of a word.' In Elizabeth A. Castelli and Rosamond C. Rodman (eds), *Women, Gender, Religion: A Reader*. New York: Palgrave Macmillan, pp. 49–75.

Haraway, Donna (2004). *The Haraway Reader*. New York: Psychology Press.

Harbin, Allison (2017). 'Burn it down: A systemic crisis in academia.' *Post-PhD*, 13 August, <https://www.allisonharbin.com/post-phd/2017/8/11/burn-it-down-emails-of-advisor-professor-abuse-expose-a-crisis-in-academia> (last accessed 24 March 2021).

Harding, Kate (2015). *Asking for It: The Alarming Rise of Rape Culture – and What We Can Do about It*. Boston: Da Capo Press.

Harlow, Summer, and Lei Guo (2014). 'Will the revolution be tweeted or Facebooked? Using digital communication tools in immigrant activism.' *Journal of Computer-Mediated Communication* 19, no. 3: 463–78.

Harol, Corrinne, and Teresa Zackodnik (2019). 'Consenting to conflict.' *Tulsa Studies in Women's Literature* 38, no. 1: 205–14.

Harpalani, Vinay (2013). 'DesiCrit: Theorizing the racial ambiguity of South Asian Americans.' *NYU Annual Survey of American Law* 69: 77–184.

Harris, Adam, and Alia Wong (2018). 'When academics defend colleagues accused of harassment.' *The Atlantic*, 15 August, <https://www.theatlantic.com/education/archive/2018/08/why-do-academics-defend-colleagues-accused-of-harassment/567553> (last accessed 24 March 2021).

Harris, Kate Lockwood (2018). 'Yes means yes and no means no, but both these mantras need to go: Communication myths in consent education and anti-rape activism.' *Journal of Applied Communication Research* 46, no. 2: 155–78.

Harrison, Helena, Melanie Birks, Richard Franklin and Jane Mills (2017). 'Case study research: Foundations and methodological orientations.' *Forum: Qualitative Sozialforschung/Forum: Qualitative Social Research* 18, no. 1.

Harvey, David (2007). *A Brief History of Neoliberalism*. New York: Oxford University Press.

Hasday, Jill Elaine (2000). 'Contest and consent: A legal history of marital rape.' *California Law Review* 88: 1,373.

Hasinoff, A. A. (2016). 'How to have great sext: Consent advice in online sexting tips.' *Communication and Critical/Cultural Studies* 13, no. 1: 58–74.

Hayek, Salma (2017). 'Harvey Weinstein is my monster too.' *The New York Times*, 12 December, <https://www.nytimes.com/interactive/2017/12/13/opinion/contributors/salma-hayek-harvey-weinstein.html> (last accessed 24 March 2021).

Hayes, Dade, and Dawn C. Chmielewski (2018). 'Louis C.K. faces Twitter backlash after return to stand-up stage, raising questions about #MeToo road to redemption.' *Deadline*, 28 August, <https://deadline.com/2018/08/louis-c-k-faces-twitter-backlash-after-return-to-stand-up-stage-raising-questions-about-metoo-road-to-redemption-1202453748> (last accessed 15 April 2021).

Hayes, Sharon, and Bethney Baker (2014). 'Female sex offenders and pariah femininities: Rewriting the sexual scripts.' *Journal of Criminology* 1, no. 1: 1–8.

Heaney, Michael T. (2019). 'Intersectionality at the grassroots.' *Politics, Groups, and Identities*: 1–21.

Hearn, Jeff (2014). 'Men, masculinities and the material(-)discursive.' *NORMA: International Journal for Masculinity Studies* 9, no. 1: 5–17.

Heinämaa, Sara (2012). 'Sex, gender, and embodiment.' In Dan Zahavi (ed.), *The Oxford Handbook of Contemporary Phenomenology*. Oxford: Oxford University Press, pp. 216–42.

Hekman, Susan (1991). 'Reconstituting the subject: Feminism, modernism, and postmodernism.' *Hypatia* 6, no. 2: 44–63.

Hekman, Susan J. (2013). *Gender and Knowledge: Elements of a Postmodern Feminism*. Hoboken: John Wiley & Sons.

Held, Virginia (2006). *The Ethics of Care: Personal, Political, Global*. Oxford: Oxford University Press.

Henley, Nancy M., Michelle Miller and Jo Anne Beazley (1995). 'Syntax, semantics, and sexual violence: Agency and the passive voice.' *Journal of Language and Social Psychology* 14, nos. 1–2: 60–84.

Henninger, Amy L., Michiko Iwasaki, Marianna E. Carlucci and Jeffrey M. Lating (2020). 'Reporting sexual assault: Survivors' satisfaction with sexual assault response personnel.' *Violence Against Women* 26, no. 11: 1,362–82.

Henry, Nicola, and Anastasia Powell (2015). 'Embodied harms: Gender, shame, and technology-facilitated sexual violence.' *Violence Against Women* 21, no. 6: 758–79.

Hermann, Donald H. J. (2017). 'Restorative justice and retributive justice: An opportunity for cooperation or an occasion for conflict in the search for justice.' *Seattle Journal for Social Justice* 16: 71.

Hernandez, Tanya Kateri (2000). 'Sexual harassment and racial disparity: The mutual construction of gender and race.' *Journal of Gender, Race & Justice* 4: 183.

Hernroth-Rothstein, Annika (2017). '#MeToo and trial by mob.' *National Review*, 20 October, <https://www.nationalreview.com/2017/10/metoo-meeting-trial-mob> (last accessed 25 March 2021).

Herring, Jonathan (2005). 'Mistaken sex.' *Criminal Law Review*: 511–24.

Herring, Jonathan (2009). 'Relational autonomy and rape.' In Shelley Day Sclater, Fatemeh Ebtehaj, Emily Jackson and Martin Richards (eds), *Regulating Autonomy: Sex, Reproduction and Family*. Oxford: Hart Publishing, pp. 53–72.

Hesse, Monica (2020). '"Believe women" was a slogan. "Believe all women" is a strawman.' *The Washington Post*, 12 May, <https://www.washingtonpost.com/lifestyle/style/believe-women-was-a-slogan-believe-all-women-is-a-strawman> (last accessed 25 March 2021).

Heyes, Cressida J. (2012). 'Identity politics.' In *The Stanford Encyclopaedia of Philosophy*, <https://plato.stanford.edu/archives/fall2002/entries/identity-politics> (last accessed 8 April 2021).

Heywood, Leslie, and Jennifer Drake (eds) (1997). *Third Wave Agenda: Being Feminist, Doing Feminism*. Minneapolis: University of Minnesota Press.

Hibberd, Bill (2014). 'Bill Cosby breaks silence to thank 2 celebrity defenders.' *Entertainment Weekly*, 3 December, <https://ew.com/article/2014/12/03/bill-cosby-thank-defenders> (last accessed 25 March 2021).

Hillstrom, Laurie Collier (2018). *The #MeToo Movement*. Santa Barbara: ABC-CLIO.

Hodes, Martha (2014). *White Women, Black Men: Illicit Sex in the Nineteenth-Century South*. New Haven: Yale University Press.

Hohman, Maura (2018). 'Kathy Griffin and more celebs criticize Louis C.K.'s comeback after sexual misconduct scandal.' *People*, 28 August, <https://people.com/tv/kathy-griffin-criticizes-louis-ck-comeback> (last accessed 25 March 2021).

Holland, Janet, Caroline Ramazanoglu, Sue Sharpe and Rachel Thomson

(1994). 'Power and desire: The embodiment of female sexuality.' *Feminist Review* 46, no. 1: 21–38.

Holmes, Jessie (2010). *Female Offending: Has There Been an Increase?* Sydney: NSW Bureau of Crime Statistics and Research.

Holub, Christian (2018). 'Louis C.K. mocks Parkland survivors, gender-neutral pronouns in leaked stand-up audio.' *Entertainment Weekly*, 31 December, <https://ew.com/celebrity/2018/12/31/louis-ck-mocks-parkland-survivors-trans-pronouns-stand-up-audio> (last accessed 25 March 2021).

Honeychurch, Kenn Gardner (1996). 'Researching dissident subjectivities: Queering the grounds of theory and practice.' *Harvard Educational Review* 66, no. 2: 339–56.

Hornaday, Ann (2018). 'Enough with naming and shaming: It's time for restorative justice in Hollywood.' *The Washington Post*, 1 Februrary, <https://www.washingtonpost.com/lifestyle/style/enough-with-naming-and-shaming-its-time-for-restorative-justice-in-hollywood/2018/02/01/416ccf80-0518-11e8-b48c-b07fea957bd5_story.html> (last accessed 25 March 2021).

Horsti, Karina (2017). 'Digital Islamophobia: The Swedish woman as a figure of pure and dangerous whiteness.' *New Media & Society* 19, no. 9: 1,440–57.

Howard, Zehr (1990). *A New Focus for Crime and Justice*. Scottsdale: Herald Press.

Howarth, Joan W. (2004). 'Adventures in heteronormativity: The straight line from Liberace to Lawrence.' *Nevada Law Journal* 5: 260.

Howson, Richard (2006). *Challenging Hegemonic Masculinity*. New York: Routledge.

Hsu, V. Jo (2019). '(Trans)forming #MeToo: Toward a networked response to gender violence.' *Women's Studies in Communication* 42, no. 3: 269–86.

Hudson, Barbara (1998). 'Restorative justice: The challenge of sexual and racial violence.' *Journal of Law and Society* 25, no. 2: 237–56.

Hudson, Deborah (2018). 'Workplace harassment after #MeToo.' Queens University Industrial Relations Centre, <http://irc.queensu.ca/sites/default/files/articles/workplace-harassment-after-metoo.pdf> (last accessed 25 March 2021).

Huffer, Lynne (2010). *Mad for Foucault: Rethinking the Foundations of Queer Theory*. New York: Columbia University Press.

Hulsman, Louk (1991). 'The abolitionist case: Alternative crime policies.' *Israel Law Review* 25: 681.

Hunter, Nan D. (2006). 'Contextualizing the sexuality debates: A chronology 1966–2005.' In Lisa Duggan and Nan D. Hunter, *Sex Wars: Sexual Dissent and Political Culture*. New York: Routledge, pp. 15–28.

Hunter, Nan D. (2019). 'Feminism, sexuality and the law.' In Robin West and Cynthia Grant Bowman (eds), *Research Handbook on Feminist Jurisprudence*. Cheltenham: Edward Elgar Publishing, pp. 138–64.

Hunter, Rosemary, and Sharon Cowan (eds) (2007). *Choice and Consent: Feminist Engagements with Law and Subjectivity*. New York: Routledge.

Hurd, Heidi M. (1996). 'The moral magic of consent.' *Legal Theory* 2, no. 2: 121–46.

Hurley, Natasha (2018). 'Pornocracy's queer circulations.' *Cultural Critique* 100: 157–75.

Illouz, Eva (2020). 'The key issue Black Lives Matter and #MeToo have in common.' *Haaretz*, 27 June, <https://www.haaretz.com/us-news/.premium.MAGAZINE-the-key-issue-black-lives-matter-and-metoo-have-in-common-1.8949081> (last accessed 25 March 2021).

INCITE! (2020). 'Dangerous intersections.' *INCITE!*, 12 July, <https://incite-national.org/dangerous-intersections> (last accessed 25 March 2021).

Iqbal, Nosheen (2015). 'Aziz Ansari: "I've always been a feminist. There wasn't a period when I was against women and then started dating one."' *The Guardian*, 7 June, <https://www.theguardian.com/culture/2015/jun/07/aziz-ansari-comedy-politics-women> (last accessed 15 April 2021).

Ivanski, Chantelle, and Taylor Kohut (2017). 'Exploring definitions of sex positivity through thematic analysis.' *The Canadian Journal of Human Sexuality* 26, no. 3: 216–25.

Izadi, Elahe (2020). 'Louis C.K.'s sexual misconduct tanked his career. Now he's selling out theaters.' *The Washington Post*, 11 March, <https://www.washingtonpost.com/arts-entertainment/2020/03/11/louis-ck-new-standup> (last accessed 25 March 2021).

Jackson, Sarah, Moya Bailey and Brooke Foucault Welles (2019). 'Women tweet on violence: From #YesAllWomen to #MeToo.' *Ada: A Journal of Gender, New Media, and Technology* 15.

Jaffe, Sarah (2018). 'The collective power of #MeToo.' *Dissent* 65, no. 2: 80–7.

Jaggar, Alison M., and Susan Bordo (eds) (1989). *Gender/Body/Knowledge: Feminist Reconstructions of Being and Knowing*. New Brunswick, NJ: Rutgers University Press.

Jagose, Annamarie (1996). *Queer Theory: An Introduction*. New York: New York University Press.

Jaschik, Scott (2015). 'The other mental health crisis.' *Inside Higher Ed*, 22 April, <https://www.insidehighered.com/news/2015/04/22/berkeley-study-finds-high-levels-depression-among-graduate-students> (last accessed 25 March 2021).

Jayapalan, N. (2001). *Sociological Theories*. New Delhi: Atlantic Publishers and Distributors.

Johnson, K. C., and Stuart Taylor, Jr (2018). *The Campus Rape Frenzy: The Attack on Due Process at America's Universities*. New York: Encounter Books.

Johnson, Merri Lisa (2002). *Jane Sexes It Up: True Confessions of Feminist Desire*. New York: Four Walls Eight Windows.

Johnson, Scott, and Stephen Galloway (2017). 'Young Harvey Weinstein: The making of a monster.' *The Hollywood Reporter*, 28 February, <https://www.hollywoodreporter.com/features/young-harvey-weinstein-making-a-monster-1089069> (last accessed 25 March 2021).

Johnson, Ted (2020). 'Harvey Weinstein trial: Jurors see clip of Annabella Sciorra's "Letterman" appearance in which she talks of "lying" in press interviews.' *Deadline*, 23 January, <https://deadline.com/2020/01/harvey-weinstein-annabella-sciorra-rape-trial-1202838739> (last accessed 25 March 2021).

Johnston, Matthew S., Ryan Coulling and Jennifer M. Kilty (2020). 'Digital knowledge divides: Sexual violence and collective emotional responses to the Jian Ghomeshi verdict on Twitter.' *Annual Review of Interdisciplinary Justice Research* 9: 167–205.

Johnstone, Albert A. (1992). 'The bodily nature of the self or what Descartes should have conceded Princess Elizabeth of Bohemia.' In Maxine Sheets-Johnstone (ed.), *Giving the Body its Due*. Albany: State University of New York Press, pp. 16–47.

Johnstone, Dusty Jane (2013). 'Voices from liminal spaces: Narratives of unacknowledged rape.' Doctoral dissertation, University of Windsor, <http://scholar.uwindsor.ca/etd/4947> (last accessed 25 March 2021).

Jolly, Susie, Andrea Cornwall and Kate Hawkins (eds) (2013). *Women, Sexuality and the Political Power of Pleasure*. London: Zed Books Ltd.

Jordan, Jan (2004). 'Beyond belief? Police, rape and women's credibility.' *Criminal Justice* 4, no. 1: 29–59.

Jozkowski, Kristen N., Tiffany L. Marcantonio and Mary E. Hunt (2017).

'College students' sexual consent communication and perceptions of sexual double standards: A qualitative investigation.' *Perspectives on Sexual and Reproductive Health* 49, no. 4: 237–44.

Judd, Ashley (2020). Twitter post, 24 February, 5.33 pm, <https://twitter.com/AshleyJudd/status/1231995493888266242> (last accessed 25 March 2021).

Jülich, Shirley, John Buttle, Christine Cummins and Erin V. Freeborn (2010). *Project Restore: An Exploratory Study of Restorative Justice and Sexual Violence*. Auckland: Auckland University of Technology.

Jülich, Shirley, and Natalie Thorburn (2017). 'Sexual violence and substantive equality: Can restorative justice deliver?' *Journal of Human Rights and Social Work* 2, nos. 1–2: 34–44.

Jurasz, Olga, and Kim Barker (2019). 'Online misogyny: A challenge for digital feminism?' *Journal of International Affairs* 72, no. 2: 95–114, <https://www.jstor.org/stable/26760834> (last accessed 25 March 2021).

Kaijser, Anna, and Annica Kronsell (2014). 'Climate change through the lens of intersectionality.' *Environmental Politics* 23, no. 3: 417–33.

Kalmbacher, Colin (2018). 'Aziz Ansari's apology opens him up to criminal prosecution.' *Law & Crime*, 15 January, <https://lawandcrime.com/legal-analysis/aziz-ansaris-apology-opens-him-up-to-criminal-prosecution> (last accessed 25 March 2021).

Kane, Laura (2014). 'Lawyers for Jian Ghomeshi file lawsuit against CBC.' *CTV News*, 27 October, <https://www.ctvnews.ca/canada/lawyers-for-jian-ghomeshi-file-lawsuit-against-cbc-1.2072843> (last accessed 25 March 2021).

Kant, Immanuel (1996). *The Metaphysics of Morals*, ed. Mary Gregor. Cambridge: Cambridge University Press.

Kant, Immanuel (2001). *Lectures on Ethics*. Vol. 2. Cambridge: Cambridge University Press.

Kantor, Jodi, and Megan Twohey (2017). 'Harvey Weinstein paid off sexual harassment accusers for decades.' *The New York Times*, 5 October, <https://www.nytimes.com/2017/10/05/us/harvey-weinstein-harassment-allegations.html> (last accessed 25 March 2021).

Karaian, Lara (2013). 'The troubled relationship of feminist and queer legal theory to strategic essentialism: Theory/praxis, queer porn, and Canadian anti-discrimination law.' In Martha Albertson Fineman, Jack E. Jackson and Adam P. Romero (eds), *Feminist and Queer Legal Theory: Intimate Encounters, Uncomfortable Conversations*. Farnham: Ashgate, pp. 375–94.

Karp, David, and Lynne Walther (2001). 'Community reparative boards in Vermont.' In Gordon Bazemore and Mara Schiff (eds), *Restorative Community Justice: Repairing Harm and Transforming Communities*. Cincinnati: Anderson Publishing, pp. 199–218.

Kassam, Ashifa (2016). 'Jian Ghomeshi acquitted of all charges in sexual assault trial.' *The Guardian*, 24 March, <https://www.theguardian.com/world/2016/mar/24/jian-ghomeshi-acquitted-sexual-assault-trial> (last accessed 25 March 2021).

Kattari, Shanna K. (2015). '"Getting it": Identity and sexual communication for sexual and gender minorities with physical disabilities.' *Sexuality & Culture* 19, no. 4: 882–99.

Kavka, Misha (2020). 'Taking down the sacred: Fuck-me vs. fuck-you celebrity.' *Celebrity Studies* 11, no. 1: 8–24.

Keenan, Marie (2018). 'Training for restorative justice practice in sexual violence cases.' *The International Journal of Restorative Justice* 1, no. 2: 291–302.

Keller, Jessalynn, Kaitlynn Mendes and Jessica Ringrose (2018). 'Speaking "unspeakable things": Documenting digital feminist responses to rape culture.' *Journal of Gender Studies* 27, no. 1: 236–46.

Kennedy, Joseph L. D., Antover P. Tuliao, KayLee N. Flower, Jessie J. Tibbs and Dennis E. McChargue (2019). 'Long-term effectiveness of a brief restorative justice intervention.' *International Journal of Offender Therapy and Comparative Criminology* 63, no. 1: 3–17.

Khan, Ummni (2014). *Vicarious Kinks: S/M in the Socio-Legal Imaginary*. Toronto: University of Toronto Press.

Khoja-Moolji, Shenila (2015). 'Becoming an "intimate publics": Exploring the affective intensities of hashtag feminism.' *Feminist Media Studies* 15, no. 2: 347–50.

Kiefer, Amy K., and Diana T. Sanchez (2007). 'Scripting sexual passivity: A gender role perspective.' *Personal Relationships* 14, no. 2: 269–90.

Kilbourne, Jean (1999). *Deadly Persuasion: Why Women and Girls Must Fight the Addictive Power of Advertising*. New York: Free Press.

Kim, Mimi E. (2018). 'From carceral feminism to transformative justice: Women-of-color feminism and alternatives to incarceration.' *Journal of Ethnic & Cultural Diversity in Social Work* 27, no. 3: 219–33.

Kimmes, Jonathan G., Allen B. Mallory, Charlotte Cameron and Özlem Köse (2015). 'A treatment model for anxiety-related sexual dysfunctions using mindfulness meditation within a sex-positive framework.' *Sexual and Relationship Therapy* 30, no. 2: 286–96.

King, Christina (2017). 'Different patriarchies, same feminism: The struggle to achieve and maintain intersectionality.' *SOCIAL EYES*: 16.

Kingston, Anne (2018). 'Inside the first year of #MeToo.' *CityNews*, 7 October, <https://winnipeg.citynews.ca/2018/10/07/inside-the-first-year-of-metoo> (last accessed 25 March 2021).

Kinser, Amber E. (2004). 'Negotiating spaces for/through third-wave feminism.' *NWSA Journal*: 124–53.

Kitrosser, Heidi (1996). 'Meaningful consent: Toward a new generation of statutory rape laws.' *Virginia Journal of Social Policy & the Law* 4: 287.

Kitzinger, Celia, and Hannah Frith (1999). 'Just say no? The use of conversation analysis in developing a feminist perspective on sexual refusal.' *Discourse & Society* 10, no. 3: 293–316.

Know Your IX (2020). 'Why schools handle sexual assault reports.' *Know Your IX*, 22 May, <https://www.knowyourix.org/issues/schools-handle-sexual-violence-reports> (last accessed 25 March 2021).

Knutson, Kristine, and Caitlin Miller (2018). 'Education and the communication of consent.' *Minds@UW*, <https://minds.wisconsin.edu/handle/1793/78956> (last accessed 25 March 2021).

Kornhaber, Spencer (2019). 'Kevin Spacey is not vindicated.' *The Atlantic*, 18 July, <https://www.theatlantic.com/entertainment/archive/2019/07/kevin-spacey-not-vindicated-despite-court-win/594292> (last accessed 25 March 2021).

Koss, Mary P. (2010). 'Restorative justice for acquaintance rape and misdemeanor sex crimes.' In James Ptacek (ed.), *Restorative Justice and Violence against Women*. Oxford: Oxford University Press, pp. 218–38.

Koss, Mary P. (2014). 'The RESTORE program of restorative justice for sex crimes: Vision, process, and outcomes.' *Journal of Interpersonal Violence* 29, no. 9: 1,623–60.

Koss, Mary, and Mary Achilles (2008). 'Restorative justice responses to sexual assault.' National Online Resource Center on Violence against Women, <https://vawnet.org/material/restorative-justice-responses-sexual-assault> (last accessed 8 April 2021).

Koss, Mary P., Karen J. Bachar and C. Quince Hopkins (2003). 'Restorative justice for sexual violence: Repairing victims, building community, and holding offenders accountable.' *Annals of the New York Academy of Sciences* 989, no. 1: 384–96.

Kotef, Hagar (2009). 'On abstractness: First wave liberal feminism and the construction of the abstract woman.' *Feminist Studies* 35, no. 3: 495–522.

Krishnan, Manisha (2017). 'Jian Ghomeshi is back with a new project and people are angry about it.' *Vice*, 10 April, <https://www.vice.com/en_ca/article/z49j74/jian-ghomeshi-is-back-with-a-new-project-and-people-are-angry-about-it> (last accessed 25 March 2021).

Kristeva, Julia (1982). *Powers of Horror*. New York: Columbia University Press.

Kristeva, Julia (2002). *The Portable Kristeva*. New York: Columbia University Press.

Kruks, Sonia (2001). *Retrieving Experience: Subjectivity and Recognition in Feminist Politics*. Ithaca, NY: Cornell University Press.

Kukla, Rebecca (2018). 'That's what she said: The language of sexual negotiation.' *Ethics* 129, no. 1: 70–97.

Kurtz, Judy (2018). 'Norm Macdonald: There's "no forgiveness" in #MeToo.' *The Hill*, 11 September, <https://thehill.com/blogs/in-the-know/in-the-know/406052-norm-macdonald-theres-no-forgiveness-in-metoo> (last accessed 25 March 2021).

Kyrölä, Katariina (2019). 'Negotiating vulnerability in the trigger warning debates.' In Anne Graefer (ed.), *Media and the Politics of Offence*. Cham: Palgrave Macmillan, pp. 207–32.

Lacey, Nicola (1998a). *Unspeakable Subjects: Feminist Essays in Legal and Social Theory*. Oxford: Hart Publishing.

Lacey, Nicola (1998b). 'Unspeakable subjects, impossible rights: Sexuality, integrity and criminal law.' *Canadian Journal of Law and Jurisprudence* 11: 47–68.

Lamb, Sharon (ed.) (1999). *New Versions of Victims: Feminists Struggle with the Concept*. New York: New York University Press.

Lamont, Ellen (2017). '"We can write the scripts ourselves": Queer challenges to heteronormative courtship practices.' *Gender & Society* 31, no. 5: 624–46.

Laplanche, Jean (1976). *Life and Death in Psychoanalysis*. Baltimore: Johns Hopkins University Press.

Larcombe, Wendy (2002). 'The "ideal" victim v successful rape complainants: Not what you might expect.' *Feminist Legal Studies* 10, no. 2: 131–48.

LaRocque, Emma (1997). 'Re-examining culturally appropriate models in criminal justice applications.' In Michael Asch (ed.), *Aboriginal and Treaty Rights in Canada: Essays on Law, Equality, and Respect for Difference*. Vancouver: University of British Columbia Press, pp. 75–96.

LaRocque, Emma. 'Re-examining culturally appropriate models in criminal

Latimer, Jeff, Craig Dowden and Danielle Muise (2005). 'The effectiveness of restorative justice practices: A meta-analysis.' *The Prison Journal* 85, no. 2: 127–44.

Legal Information Institute (2020). 10 US Code 920 – Art. 120. Rape and sexual assault generally. Cornell University Law School, <https://www.law.cornell.edu/uscode/text/10/920> (last accessed 25 March 2021).

Leiter Reports (2018). 'Blaming the victim is apparently OK when the accused in a Title IX proceeding is a feminist literary theorist.' *Leiter Reports*, June, <https://leiterreports.typepad.com/blog/2018/06/blaming-the-victim-is-apparently-ok-when-the-accused-is-a-feminist-literary-theorist.html> (last accessed 25 March 2021).

LeMaire, Kelly L., Debra L. Oswald and Brenda L. Russell (2016). 'Labeling sexual victimization experiences: The role of sexism, rape myth acceptance, and tolerance for sexual harassment.' *Violence and Victims* 31, no. 2: 332–46.

Lemke, Thomas (2015). 'New materialisms: Foucault and the "government of things".' *Theory, Culture & Society* 32, no. 4: 3–25.

Leung, Rebecca, and Robert Williams (2019). '#MeToo and intersectionality: An examination of the #MeToo movement through the R. Kelly scandal.' *Journal of Communication Inquiry* 43, no. 4: 349–71.

Levand, Mark A., and Nicolle Zapien (2019). 'Sexual consent as transcendence: A phenomenological understanding.' *The International Journal of Transpersonal Studies* 38, no. 1: 154–65.

Levenson, Eric, and Aaron Cooper (2018). 'Bill Cosby guilty on all three counts in indecent assault trial.' *CNN*, 27 April, <https://edition.cnn.com/2018/04/26/us/bill-cosby-trial/index.html> (last accessed 25 March 2021).

Levinas, Emmanuel (1998). *Entre nous: Thinking-of-the-Other*. New York: Columbia University Press.

Levine, Judith (2017). 'Will feminism's past mistakes haunt #MeToo?' *Boston Review*, 8 December, <http://bostonreview.net/gender-sexuality/judith-levine-will-feminisms-past-mistakes-haunt-metoo> (last accessed 25 March 2021).

Lewis, Desiree (2020). 'Governmentality and South Africa's edifice of gender and sexual rights.' Women's and Gender Studies Department, University of the Western Cape, <https://www.researchgate.net/profile/Desiree_Lewis/publication/340136597_Governmentality_and_South_Africa's_Edifice_of_Gender_and_Sexual_Rights> (last accessed 25 March 2021).

Li, Anita (2014). 'At least 8 women now accuse former CBC host Jian Ghomeshi of sexual abuse.' *Mashable*, 30 October, <https://mashable.

com/2014/10/30/jian-ghomeshi-sexual-abuse/?europe=true> (last accessed 25 March 2021).

Liberman, Alida (2018). 'Disability, sex rights and the scope of sexual exclusion.' *Journal of Medical Ethics* 44, no. 4: 253–6.

Lifshutz, Hannah (2019). 'Louis C.K. addresses sexual harassment allegations and Parkland jokes in standup routine.' *Complex*, 17 January, <https://www.complex.com/pop-culture/2019/01/louis-ck-addresses-sexual-harassment-allegations-and-parkland-jokes-in-standup-routine> (last accessed 25 March 2021).

Lin, Zhongxuan, and Liu Yang (2019). '"Me too!": Individual empowerment of disabled women in the #MeToo movement in China.' *Disability & Society* 34, no. 5: 842–7.

Lindin, Emily (EmilyLindin) (2017). Twitter post, 21 November, 12.45 pm, 'Here's an unpopular opinion: I'm actually not at all concerned about innocent men losing their jobs over false sexual assault/harassment allegations.'

Lisak, David, Lori Gardinier, Sarah C. Nicksa and Ashley M. Cote (2010). 'False allegations of sexual assault: An analysis of ten years of reported cases.' *Violence Against Women* 16, no. 12: 1,318–34.

Little, Nicholas J. (2005). 'From no means no to only yes means yes: The rational results of an affirmative consent standard in rape law.' *Vanderbilt Law Review* 58: 1,321.

Liu, Heidi (2017). 'When whispers enter the cloud: Evaluating technology to prevent and report sexual assault.' *Harvard Journal of Law & Technology* 31, no. 2: 939–63.

Livingstone, Josephine (2018). 'Asia Argento, Avital Ronell, and the integrity of #MeToo.' *The New Republic*, 21 August, <https://newrepublic.com/article/150791/asia-argento-avital-ronell-integrity-metoo> (last accessed 25 March 2021).

Lodhia, Sharmila (2015). 'From "living corpse" to India's daughter: Exploring the social, political and legal landscape of the 2012 Delhi gang rape.' *Women's Studies International Forum* 50: 89–101.

Logan, Brian (2020). 'Sincerely Louis CK review – standup returns with not-quite apology.' *The Guardian*, 7 April, <https://www.theguardian.com/stage/2020/apr/07/sincerely-louis-ck-review-standup-comedy-me-too> (last accessed 25 March 2021).

Loick, Daniel (2020). '". . . as if it were a thing." A feminist critique of consent.' *Constellations* 27, no. 3: 412–22.

Lonsway, Kimberly A., and Joanne Archambault (2012). 'The "justice gap" for sexual assault cases: Future directions for research and reform.' *Violence Against Women* 18, no. 2: 145–68.

Lopes-Baker, Aliza, Mathew McDonald, Jessica Schissler and Victor Pirone (2017). 'Canada and United States: Campus sexual assault law & policy comparative analysis.' *Canada–United States Law Journal* 41: 156.

López-Fernández, Andrée Marie (2020). 'Stakeholder influence on decision making: From e-movements (#metoo) to corporate social responsibility policy.' In Rajagopal and Ramesh Behl (eds), *Innovation, Technology, and Market Ecosystems*. Cham: Palgrave Macmillan, pp. 161–86.

Lukose, Ritty (2018). 'Decolonizing feminism in the #MeToo era.' *The Cambridge Journal of Anthropology* 36, no. 2: 34–52.

Lunceford, Brett (2012). *Naked Politics: Nudity, Political Action, and the Rhetoric of the Body*. Lanham, MD: Lexington Books.

Lynch, John (2017). 'All the women who have accused Louis C.K. of sexual misconduct.' *Business Insider*, 10 November, <https://www.businessinsider.com/list-of-women-who-have-accused-louis-ck-of-sexual-misconduct-2017-11?r=US&IR=T> (last accessed 25 March 2021).

Lyng, Stephen (2004). *Edgework: The Sociology of Risk-Taking*. New York: Routledge.

McCann, Hannah (2018). 'Big reputations: Who has the power to speak #MeToo?' *Australian Humanities Review* 63: 185–9.

McCormick, Tyler H., Hedwig Lee, Nina Cesare, Ali Shojaie and Emma S. Spiro (2017). 'Using Twitter for demographic and social science research: Tools for data collection and processing.' *Sociological Methods & Research* 46, no. 3: 390–421.

McCracken, Jill (2013). *Street Sex Workers' Discourse: Realizing Material Change through Agential Choice*. New York: Routledge.

McDonald, Aubri F. (2019). 'Framing #MeToo: Assessing the power and unintended consequences of a social media movement to address sexual assault.' In William O'Donohue and Paul A. Schewe (eds), *Handbook of Sexual Assault and Sexual Assault Prevention*. Cham: Springer, pp. 79–107.

McFadden, Patricia (1992). 'Nationalism and gender issues in South Africa.' *Journal of Gender Studies* 1, no. 4: 510–20.

McGinley, Ann C. (2019). 'The masculinity mandate: #MeToo, Brett Kavanaugh, and Christine Blasey Ford.' *Employee Rights and Employment Policy Journal* 23, no. 1: 59–83.

McGlynn, Clare (2011). 'Feminism, rape and the search for justice.' *Oxford Journal of Legal Studies* 31, no. 4: 825–42.

Macharia, Keguro (2018). 'kburd: Caliban responds.' *The New Inquiry*, 22 August, <https://thenewinquiry.com/blog/kburd-caliban-responds> (last accessed 25 March 2021).

Mack, Ashley Noel, and Bryan J. McCann (2018). 'Critiquing state and gendered violence in the age of #MeToo.' *Quarterly Journal of Speech* 104, no. 3: 329–44.

Mackenzie, Catriona (2006). 'Relational autonomy, sexual justice and cultural pluralism.' In Barbara Arneil, Monique Deveaux, Rita Dhamoon and Avigail Eisenberg (eds), *Sexual Justice/Cultural Justice*. London: Routledge, pp. 113–31.

Mackenzie, Catriona, and Natalie Stoljar (eds) (2000). *Relational Autonomy: Feminist Perspectives on Autonomy, Agency, and the Social Self*. Oxford: Oxford University Press.

McKibbin, Gemma, Rachael Duncan, Bridget Hamilton, Cathy Humphreys and Connie Kellett (2015). 'The intersectional turn in feminist theory: A response to Carbin and Edenheim (2013).' *European Journal of Women's Studies* 22, no. 1: 99–103.

McKinney, Kathleen, and Susan Sprecher (eds) (2014). *Sexuality in Close Relationships*. New York: Psychology Press.

MacKinnon, Catharine A. (1987). *Feminism Unmodified: Discourses on Life and Law*. Cambridge, MA: Harvard University Press.

MacKinnon, Catharine A. (1989). *Toward a Feminist Theory of the State*. Cambridge, MA: Harvard University Press.

MacKinnon, Catharine A. (1997). 'Rape: On coercion and consent.' In Katie Conboy, Nadia Medina and Sarah Stanbury (eds), *Writing on the Body: Female Embodiment and Feminist Theory*. New York: Columbia University Press, pp. 42–58.

MacKinnon, Catharine A. (2019). 'Where #MeToo came from, and where it's going.' *The Atlantic*, 24 March, <https://www.theatlantic.com/ideas/archive/2019/03/catharine-mackinnon-what-metoo-has-changed/585313> (last accessed 25 March 2021).

Maclaran, Pauline (2015). 'Feminism's fourth wave: A research agenda for marketing and consumer research.' *Journal of Marketing Management* 31, nos. 15–16: 1,732–8.

Maclean's (2016). 'Read the judge's ruling in the Jian Ghomeshi case.' *Maclean's*, 25 March, <https://www.macleans.ca/news/canada/read-the-judges-ruling-in-the-jian-ghomeshi-case> (last accessed 25 March 2021).

McRobbie, Angela (2004). 'Post-feminism and popular culture.' *Feminist Media Studies* 4, no. 3: 255–64.

McSherry, Bernadette, and Patrick Keyzer (eds) (2011). *Dangerous People: Policy, Prediction, and Practice*. New York: Routledge.

McWhorter, Ladelle (2004). 'Sex, race, and biopower: A Foucauldian genealogy.' *Hypatia* 19, no. 3: 38–62.

Madsen, Karin Sten (2004). 'Mediation as a way of empowering women exposed to sexual coercion.' *NORA – Nordic Journal of Feminist and Gender Research* 12, no. 1: 58–61.

Mallenbaum, Carly, Patrick Ryan and Maria Puente (2018). 'A complete list of the 60 Bill Cosby accusers and their reactions to his prison sentence.' *USA Today*, 27 April, <https://eu.usatoday.com/story/life/people/2018/04/27/bill-cosby-full-list-accusers/555144002> (last accessed 25 March 2021).

Mandell, Nancy, and Jennifer Lesley Johnson (eds) (1995). *Feminist Issues: Race, Class and Sexuality*. Toronto: Prentice-Hall Canada.

Mann, Susan Archer, and Douglas J. Huffman (2005). 'The decentering of second wave feminism and the rise of the third wave.' *Science & Society* 69, no. 1: 56–91.

Manne, Kate (2017). *Down Girl: The Logic of Misogyny*. Oxford: Oxford University Press.

Manne, Kate (2020). *Entitled: How Male Privilege Hurts Women*. New York: Crown.

Marino, Patricia (2019). *Philosophy of Sex and Love: An Opinionated Introduction*. New York: Routledge.

Marsh, Francesca, and Nadia M. Wager (2015). 'Restorative justice in cases of sexual violence: Exploring the views of the public and survivors.' *Probation Journal* 62, no. 4: 336–56.

Marshall, Tony F. (1998). *Restorative Justice: An Overview*. St. Paul, MN: Center for Restorative Justice & Mediation.

Martin, Elaine K., Casey T. Taft and Patricia A. Resick (2007). 'A review of marital rape.' *Aggression and Violent Behavior* 12, no. 3: 329–47.

Martinelli, Marissa (2018). 'Dan Harmon acknowledges that he sexually harassed *Community* writer Megan Ganz in a seven-minute podcast monologue.' *Slate*, 11 January, <https://slate.com/arts/2018/01/dan-harmon-apologizes-to-community-writer-megan-ganz-on-harmontown.html> (last accessed 25 March 2021).

Maruna, Shadd, and Brunilda Pali (2020). 'From victim blaming to reintegrative shaming: The continuing relevance of crime, shame and reintegration in the era of #MeToo.' *The International Journal of Restorative Justice* 3, no. 1: 38–44.

Maruska, Jennifer Heeg (2010). 'Feminist ontologies, epistemologies, methodologies, and methods in international relations.' In *Oxford Research Encyclopedia of International Studies*. Oxford: Oxford University Press.

Marwick, Alice E. (2014). 'Ethnographic and qualitative research on Twitter.' *Twitter and Society* 89: 109–21.

Matthews, Nancy A. (2005). *Confronting Rape: The Feminist Anti-Rape Movement and the State*. New York: Routledge.

Matthis, Iréne (2018). *Dialogues on Sexuality, Gender and Psychoanalysis*. Abingdon: Routledge.

Maxwell, Gabrielle, and Hennessey Hayes (2006). 'Restorative justice developments in the Pacific region: A comprehensive survey.' *Contemporary Justice Review* 9, no. 2: 127–54.

Maxwell, Zerlina (2014). 'Rape culture is real.' *Time*, 27 March, <https://time.com/40110/rape-culture-is-real> (last accessed 25 March 2021).

Mayer, Melissa (2018). *Coping with Date Rape and Acquaintance Rape*. New York: Rosen Publishing Group, Inc.

Me Too (2019). 'A love letter to Dr. Christine Blasey Ford.' *Me Too*, <https://metoomvmt.org> (last accessed 25 March 2021).

Me Too (2020). 'Masculinity, Male Privilege & Consent Toolkit.' *Me Too*, 31 May, <https://metoomvmt.org/wp-content/uploads/2020/05/1.5.3_Masculinity-Male-Privilege-Consent-Toolkit_TOOLKIT_V2.pdf> (last accessed 25 March 2021).

Megale, Elizabeth (2011). 'The invisible man: How the sex offender registry results in social death.' *Journal of Law and Social Deviance* 2: 92–157.

Meiners, Erica R. (2009). 'Never innocent: Feminist trouble with sex offender registries and protection in a prison nation.' *Meridians* 9, no. 2: 31–62.

Milano, Alyssa (AlyssaMilano) (2017). Twitter post, 15 October, 'If all the women who have been sexually harassed or assaulted wrote "Me too." as a status, we might give people a sense of the magnitude of the problem.'

Miller, Adam (2016). 'Trailer Park Boys actress wrote "love letter" to Jian Ghomeshi days after alleged attack.' *Global News*, 5 February, <https://globalnews.ca/news/2499830/ghomeshi-defence-lawyer-hints-at-new-information-as-cross-examination-of-lucy-decoutere-resumes> (last accessed 25 March 2021).

Miller, Peggy, and Nancy Biele (1993). 'Twenty years later: The unfinished revolution.' In Emilie Buchwald, Pamela Fletcher and Martha Roth (eds), *Transforming a Rape Culture*. Minneapolis: Milkweed Editions, pp. 47–54.

Miller, Sarah (2019). 'Beyond silence, towards refusal: The epistemic possibilities of #MeToo.' *The American Philosophical Association* 19, no. 1: 12–16.

Millett, Kate (1977). *Sexual Politics*. London: Virago.

Mills, Linda G., Briana Barocas and Barak Ariel (2013). 'The next generation of court-mandated domestic violence treatment: A comparison study of batterer intervention and restorative justice programs.' *Journal of Experimental Criminology* 9, no. 1: 65–90.

Moghadam, Valentine M. (ed.) (2019). *Identity Politics and Women: Cultural Reassertions and Feminisms in International Perspective*. New York: Routledge.

Mohacsy, Ildiko (2004). 'Artemisia Gentileschi and her world.' *Journal of the American Academy of Psychoanalysis and Dynamic Psychiatry* 32, no. 1 (special issue): 153–76.

Monk, Judi Shade (2020). 'Black box | White palace | #MeToo: Workplace sexual assault at the hands of a professional hero.' *Journal of Architectural Education* 74, no. 1: 10–13.

Moore, Suzanne (2017). 'It's not just one monster: "MeToo" reveals the ubiquity of sexual assault.' *The Guardian*, 16 October, <https://www.theguardian.com/commentisfree/2017/oct/16/harvey-weinstein-women-sexual-assault-me-too> (last accessed 25 March 2021).

Mortimer-Sandilands, Catriona, and Bruce Erickson (2010). *Queer Ecologies: Sex, Nature, Politics, Desire*. Bloomington: Indiana University Press.

Moyle, Paora, and Juan Marcellus Tauri (2016). 'Māori, family group conferencing and the mystifications of restorative justice.' *Victims & Offenders* 11, no. 1: 87–106.

Mullet, Judy Hostetler (2014). 'Restorative discipline: From getting even to getting well.' *Children & Schools* 36, no. 3: 157–62.

Mumford, Gwilym (2017). 'Actor Terry Crews: I was sexually assaulted by Hollywood executive.' *The Guardian*, 11 October, <https://www.theguardian.com/film/2017/oct/11/actor-terry-crews-sexually-assaulted-by-hollywood-executive> (last accessed 25 March 2021).

Munro, Ealasaid (2013). 'Feminism: A fourth wave?' *Political Insight* 4, no. 2: 22–5.

Munro, Vanessa E. (2008). 'Constructing consent: Legislating freedom and legitimating constraint in the expression of sexual autonomy.' *Akron Law Review* 41: 923–55.

Murray, Andrew Hunter (2018). 'Generation snowflake?' *RSA Journal* 164, no. 4 (5576): 44–7.

Murray, Daisy (2017). '"Empowerment through empathy" – we spoke to Tarana Burke, the woman who really started the "Me Too" movement.' *Elle Magazine*, 23 October, <https://www.elle.com/uk/life-and-culture/culture/news/a39429/empowerment-through-empathy-tarana-burke-me-too> (last accessed 25 March 2021).

Musser, Amber Jamilla (2018). *Sensual Excess: Queer Femininity and Brown Jouissance*. New York: New York University Press.

Na, Ali (2019). '#AzizAnsariToo? Desi masculinity in America and performing funny cute.' *Women's Studies in Communication* 42, no. 3: 308–26.

Nachescu, Voichita (2009). 'Radical feminism and the nation: History and space in the political imagination of second-wave feminism.' *Journal for the Study of Radicalism* 3, no. 1: 29–59.

Nash, Jennifer C. (2008). 'Re-thinking intersectionality.' *Feminist Review* 89: 1–15.

Nash, Jennifer C. (2014). *The Black Body in Ecstasy: Reading Race, Reading Pornography*. Durham, NC: Duke University Press.

Nathan, Debbie (2018). 'Black men disproportionately represented on sex offender registries.' *The Appeal*, 15 November, <https://theappeal.org/black-men-disproportionately-represented-on-sex-offender-registries> (last accessed 25 March 2021).

National Research Council (2014). *Estimating the Incidence of Rape and Sexual Assault*. Washington, DC: The National Academies Press.

Nedelsky, Jennifer (1989). 'Reconceiving autonomy: Sources, thoughts and possibilities.' *Yale Journal of Law and Feminism* 1: 7–36.

Nedelsky, Jennifer (1996). 'Violence against women: Challenges to the liberal state and relational feminism.' *Nomos* 38: 454–97.

Nedelsky, Jennifer (2011). *Law's Relations: A Relational Theory of Self, Autonomy, and Law*. New York: Oxford University Press.

Neustaeter, Brooklyn (2019). '"I do forgive him as a human": Rape victim confronts her attacker in restorative justice process.' *CTV News*, 1 November, <https://www.ctvnews.ca/canada/i-do-forgive-him-as-a-human-rape-victim-confronts-her-attacker-in-restorative-justice-process-1.4665519> (last accessed 25 March 2021).

New Yorker, The (2017). 'Read: Two settlements that Harvey Weinstein reached with his accusers.' *The New Yorker*, <https://www.newyorker.com/sections/news/read-the-settlements-that-harvey-weinstein-used-to-silence-accusers> (last accessed 25 March 2021).

Newberry, Laura, and James Queally (2020). 'Harvey Weinstein found guilty of rape in sexual assault trial.' *Los Angeles Times*, 24 February,

<https://www.latimes.com/california/story/2020-02-24/harvey-weinstein-trial-verdict-sexual-assault> (last accessed 25 March 2021).

Newman, Christy E., and Bridget Haire (2019). '"A reckoning that is long overdue": Reconfiguring the work of progressive sex advice post #MeToo.' In Bianca Fileborn and Rachel Loney-Howes (eds), *#MeToo and the Politics of Social Change*. Cham: Palgrave Macmillan, pp. 235–50.

Nguyen, Hanh (2017). 'Louis C.K.'s statement follows in the footsteps of self-indulgent so-called apologies.' *IndieWire*, 10 November, <https://www.indiewire.com/2017/11/louis-ck-apology-self-indulgent-masturbation-weinstein-spacey-1201896354> (last accessed 25 March 2021).

Nickolai, Nate (2018). 'Sarah Silverman says Louis C.K. masturbated in front of her with her consent.' *Variety*, 22 October, <https://variety.com/2018/tv/news/sarah-silverman-louis-ck-masturbated-1202988208> (last accessed 25 March 2021).

Nielsen, Morten Ebbe Juul (2010). 'Safe, sane, and consensual – consent and the ethics of BDSM.' *International Journal of Applied Philosophy* 24, no. 2: 265–88.

Noble, Safiya Umoja (2016). 'A future for intersectional Black feminist studies.' *Scholar & Feminist Online* 13, no. 3: 1–8.

North, Anna (2019a). 'Aziz Ansari has addressed his sexual misconduct allegation. But he hasn't publicly apologized.' *Vox*, 12 July, <https://www.vox.com/identities/2019/7/12/20690303/aziz-ansari-sexual-misconduct-accusation-right-now> (last accessed 25 March 2021).

North, Anna (2019b). 'What's next for #MeToo? This college might have the answer.' *Vox*, 10 October, <https://www.vox.com/identities/2019/10/10/20885824/me-too-movement-sexual-assault-college-campus> (last accessed 25 March 2021).

NPR (2018). 'The fine line between a bad date and sexual assault: 2 views on Aziz Ansari.' *NPR: All Things Considered*, 16 January, <https://www.npr.org/2018/01/16/578422491/the-fine-line-between-a-bad-date-and-sexual-assault-two-views-on-aziz-ansari> (last accessed 25 March 2021).

Nussbaum, Martha C. (2003). *Upheavals of Thought: The Intelligence of Emotions*. Cambridge: Cambridge University Press.

Nye, Andrea (2013). *Feminist Theory and the Philosophies of Man*. New York: Routledge.

Nyseth Brehm, Hollie, and Shannon Golden (2017). 'Centering survivors in local transitional justice.' *Annual Review of Law and Social Science* 13: 101–21.

O'Byrne, Rachael, Susan Hansen and Mark Rapley (2008). '"If a girl doesn't say 'no'. . .": young men, rape and claims of "insufficient knowledge".' *Journal of Community & Applied Social Psychology* 18, no. 3: 168–93.

O'Connor, Maureen (2020). '"You take on a role, correct?" How an actress accuser revealed the true theatrics of the Harvey Weinstein trial.' *Vanity Fair*, 27 January, <https://www.vanityfair.com/hollywood/2020/01/harvey-weinstein-trial-annabella-sciorra-testimony> (last accessed 25 March 2021).

O'Hehir, Andrew (2018). 'When a woman is accused of sexual misconduct: The strange case of Avital Ronell.' *Salon*, 18 August, <https://www.salon.com/2018/08/18/when-a-woman-is-accused-of-sexual-misconduct-the-strange-case-of-avital-ronell> (last accessed 25 March 2021).

Ogden, Charles Kay, and Ivor Armstrong Richards (1923). *The Meaning of Meaning: A Study of the Influence of Language upon Thought and of the Science of Symbolism*. Vol. 29. London: Kegan Paul, Trench, Trübner & Co. Ltd.

Okin, Susan (1994). 'Political liberalism, justice and gender.' *Ethics* 105: 23–43.

Oliver, Kelly (1996). 'Party rape, "nonconsensual sex," and affirmative consent policies.' *Americana* 3: 19.

Olsen, Frances (1993). 'Constitutional law: Feminist critiques of the public/private distinction.' *Constitutional Commentary* 10: 319–27.

Onwuachi-Willig, Angela (2018). 'What about #UsToo: The invisibility of race in the #MeToo movement.' *Yale Law Journal Forum* 128: 105–20.

Orgad, Shani, and Rosalind Gill (2019). 'Safety valves for mediated female rage in the #MeToo era.' *Feminist Media Studies* 19, no. 4: 596–603.

Ortmann, David M., and Richard A. Sprott (2012). *Sexual Outsiders: Understanding BDSM Sexualities and Communities*. Lanham, MD: Rowman & Littlefield.

Out in the Open (2016), '"People were so angry": The public – and the very personal – impact of the Jian Ghomeshi trial.' *CBC*, 23 December, <https://www.cbc.ca/radio/outintheopen/see-ya-2016-1.3909897/people-were-so-angry-the-public-and-the-very-personal-impact-of-the-jian-ghomeshi-trial-1.3909903> (last accessed 25 March 2021).

Owens, Christina D. (2016). '*East Meets Black: Asian and Black Masculinities in the Post-Civil Rights Era* by Chong Chon-Smith.' *Journal of Asian American Studies* 19, no. 2: 270–2.

Paechter, Carrie (2006). 'Reconceptualizing the gendered body: Learning and constructing masculinities and femininities in school.' *Gender and Education* 18, no. 2: 121–35.

Page, Allison, and Jacquelyn Arcy (2020). '#MeToo and the politics of collective healing: Emotional connection as contestation.' *Communication, Culture and Critique* 13, no. 3: 333–48.

Paiva, Raquel (2019). '#MeToo, feminism and femicide in Brazil.' *Interactions: Studies in Communication & Culture* 10, no. 3: 241–55.

Pali, Brunilda, and Madsen Karin Sten (2011). 'Dangerous liaisons? A feminist and restorative approach to sexual assault.' *Temida* 14, no. 1: 49–65.

Papendick, Michael, and Gerd Bohner (2017). '"Passive victim – strong survivor"? Perceived meaning of labels applied to women who were raped.' *PLoS ONE* 12, no. 5: e0177550.

Parks, Fayth M., Gregory S. Felzien and Sally Jue (eds) (2017). *HIV/AIDS in Rural Communities: Research, Education, and Advocacy*. Cham: Springer.

Pastor, Nola (2014). 'Beyond consent: Exploring sexual violence prevention at Macalester through a framework of sexual subjectivity and sexual ethics.' Macalester College, <https://core.ac.uk/download/pdf/46725375.pdf> (last accessed 7 April 2021).

Pastras, Thea (2018). 'Us too? The #MeToo movement and its critics.' *CIE Essay Writing Contest* 3, <https://digitalcommons.ursinus.edu/cie_essay/3> (last accessed 25 March 2021).

Pateman, Carole (2016). 'Sexual contract.' *The Wiley Blackwell Encyclopedia of Gender and Sexuality Studies*: 1–3.

Pearl, Sharrona (2018). 'When a queer feminist professor is accused of harassment.' *The Lilith Blog*, 22 August, <https://www.lilith.org/blog/2018/08/when-a-queer-feminist-professor-is-accused-of-harassment> (last accessed 25 March 2021).

Pellegrini, Ann (2018). '#MeToo: Before and after.' *Studies in Gender and Sexuality* 19, no. 4: 262–4.

Pereboom, Derk (2014). *Free Will, Agency, and Meaning in Life*. Oxford: Oxford University Press.

Pereira, Charmaine (2009). 'Interrogating norms: Feminists theorizing sexuality, gender and heterosexuality.' *Development* 52, no. 1: 18–24.

Pettit, Becky, and Bruce Western (2004). 'Mass imprisonment and the life course: Race and class inequality in US incarceration.' *American Sociological Review* 69, no. 2: 151–69.

Phillips, Anne (1987). *Feminism and Equality*. Oxford: Basil Blackwell.

Phillips, Anne (2013). *Our Bodies, Whose Property?* Princeton: Princeton University Press.

Phillips, Nelson, and Cliff Oswick (2012). 'Organizational discourse:

Domains, debates, and directions.' *Academy of Management Annals* 6, no. 1: 435–81.

Phillips, Nickie D. (2016). *Beyond Blurred Lines: Rape Culture in Popular Media*. Lanham, MD: Rowman & Littlefield.

Phipps, Alison (2020). *Me, Not You: The Trouble with Mainstream Feminism*. Manchester: Manchester University Press.

Pickens, Josie (2013). 'Black Wall Street and the destruction of an institution.' *Ebony*, <http://www.ebony.com/black-history/the-destruction-of-black-wall-street-405#axzz3ciwo5htv> (last accessed 25 March 2021).

Pilkington, Ed (2020a). 'Harvey Weinstein hired Black Cube to block New York Times article, jury hears.' *The Guardian*, 30 January, <https://www.theguardian.com/film/2020/jan/30/harvey-weinstein-black-cube-new-york-times> (last accessed 25 March 2021).

Pilkington, Ed (2020b). 'Weinstein's enablers: How associates helped him silence accusers for years.' *The Guardian*, 25 February, <https://www.theguardian.com/world/2020/feb/25/harvey-weinstein-trial-helpers-ena blers> (last accessed 25 March 2021).

Pineau, Lois (1989). 'Date rape: A feminist analysis.' *Law and Philosophy* 8, no. 2: 217–43.

Piper, Melanie (2020). 'Louis CK's time's up time out: Rereading persona post-scandal.' *Celebrity Studies* 11, no. 2: 264–6.

Pipyrou, Stavroula (2018). '#MeToo: #MeToo is little more than mob rule // vs // #MeToo is a legitimate form of social justice.' *HAU: Journal of Ethnographic Theory* 8, no. 3: 415–19.

Pitagora, Dulcinea (2013). 'Consent vs. coercion: BDSM interactions highlight a fine but immutable line.' *The New School Psychology Bulletin* 10, no. 1: 27–36.

Pitts-Taylor, Victoria (ed.) (2016). *Mattering: Feminism, Science, and Materialism*. Vol. 1. New York: New York University Press.

Pollard, Alexandra (2019). 'Aziz Ansari should try taking responsibility for actions that left a woman feeling violated.' *The Independent*, 12 July, <https://www.independent.co.uk/arts-entertainment/tv/aziz-ansari-netf lix-stand-special-sexual-misconduct-apology-louis-ck-statement-dan-har mon-a9002031.html> (last accessed 25 March 2021).

Powell, Anastasia (2010). *Sex, Power and Consent: Youth Culture and the Unwritten Rules*. Cambridge: Cambridge University Press.

Pranis, Kay (2005). *The Little Book of Circle Processes: A New/Old Approach to Peacebuilding*. Intercourse, PA: Good Books.

Press, Alex (2018). '#MeToo must avoid "carceral feminism".' *Vox*, 1

February, <https://www.vox.com/the-big-idea/2018/2/1/16952744/me-too-larry-nassar-judge-aquilina-feminism> (last accessed 25 March 2021).

Proulx, Craig (1998). 'Justice as healing: Current critiques.' *Algonquian Papers – Archive* 29, <https://ojs.library.carleton.ca/index.php/ALGQP/article/view/486/388> (last accessed 25 March 2021).

Ptacek, James (ed.) (2010), *Restorative Justice and Violence against Women*. Oxford: Oxford University Press.

Puar, Jasbir K. (2018). *Terrorist Assemblages: Homonationalism in Queer Times*. Durham, NC: Duke University Press.

Puente, Maria (2019). 'Louis C.K. hit with multiple sexual misconduct claims.' *USA Today*, 14 December, <https://eu.usatoday.com/story/life/2017/11/09/louis-c-k-hit-multiple-sexual-misconduct-claims/848785001> (last accessed 25 March 2021).

Quatrella, Lucy A., and Diane Keyser Wentworth (1995). 'Students' perceptions of unequal status dating relationships in academia.' *Ethics & Behavior* 5, no. 3: 249–59.

Quintero Johnson, Jessie M., and Bonnie Miller (2016). 'When women "snap": The use of mental illness to contextualize women's acts of violence in contemporary popular media.' *Women's Studies in Communication* 39, no. 2: 211–27.

Quixley, Petra (2018). 'A Response to MeToo.' *Literary Cultures* 1, no. 2.

RAINN (2020a). 'The criminal justice system: Statistics.' *RAINN*, <https://www.rainn.org/statistics/criminal-justice-system> (last accessed 25 March 2021).

RAINN (2020b). 'What consent looks like.' *RAINN*, <https://www.rainn.org/articles/what-is-consent> (last accessed 25 March 2021).

Rampton, Martha (2015). 'Four waves of feminism.' Pacific University Oregon, <https://www.pacificu.edu/about/media/four-waves-feminism> (last accessed 8 April 2021).

Randall, Melanie (2010). 'Sexual assault law, credibility, and "ideal victims": Consent, resistance, and victim blaming.' *Canadian Journal of Women and the Law* 22, no. 2: 397–433.

Randall, Melanie (2013). 'Restorative justice and gendered violence? From vaguely hostile skeptic to cautious convert: Why feminists should critically engage with restorative approaches to law.' *Dalhousie Law Journal* 36: 461–99.

Rao, Sonia (2019). 'Aziz Ansari addresses his sexual misconduct allegations in a new Netflix comedy special.' *The Washington Post*, 9 July, <https://www.washingtonpost.com/arts-entertainment/2019/07/09/aziz-ansari-

addresses-his-sexual-misconduct-allegations-new-netflix-comedy-special> (last accessed 25 March 2021).

Redden, Molly (2016). 'Ghomeshi accuser tells court she wanted sex a day after alleged assault.' *The Guardian*, 5 February, <https://www.theguardian.com/world/2016/feb/05/jian-ghomeshi-trial-toronto-lucy-decoutere-testimony-alleged-assault> (last accessed 25 March 2021).

Reece, Helen (2013). 'Rape myths: Is elite opinion right and popular opinion wrong?' *Oxford Journal of Legal Studies* 33, no. 3: 445–73.

Reese, Hope, and Stephanie Coontz (2018). '#MeToo is powerful but will fail unless we do more.' In *Where Freedom Starts: Sex Power Violence #MeToo: A Verso Report*. London: Verso, pp. 35–49.

Reiss, Timothy J. (2002). *Against Autonomy: Global Dialectics of Cultural Exchange*. Stanford: Stanford University Press.

Reitman, Nimrod (2018). 'Nimrod Reitman against Avital Ronell and New York University.' Supreme Court of the State of New York, County of New York, 16 August, <https://blog.simplejustice.us/wp-content/uploads/2018/08/FINAL-Complaint-Reitman-v.-Ronell-and-NYU.pdf> (last accessed 25 March 2021).

Reskin, Barbara F. (1988). 'Bringing the men back in: Sex differentiation and the devaluation of women's work.' *Gender & Society* 2, no. 1: 58–81.

Rhode, Deborah L. (2019). '#MeToo: Why now? What next?' *Duke Law Journal* 69: 377–428.

Richardson, Diane (1998). 'Sexuality and citizenship.' *Sociology* 32, no. 1: 83–100.

Richardson, Diane (2000). 'Constructing sexual citizenship: Theorizing sexual rights.' *Critical Social Policy* 20, no. 1: 105–35.

Richardson, Diane (2004). 'Locating sexualities: From here to normality.' *Sexualities* 7, no. 4: 391–411.

Ringrose, Jessica, Sophie Whitehead, Kaitlyn Regehr and Amelia Jenkinson (2019). 'Play-Doh vulvas and felt tip dick pics: Disrupting phallocentric matter(s) in sex education.' *Reconceptualizing Educational Research Methodology* 10, nos. 2–3: 259–91.

Rivers, Nicola (2017). *Postfeminism(s) and the Arrival of the Fourth Wave: Turning Tides*. Cham: Springer.

Robinson, Paul H., and Tyler Scot Williams (2017). 'Mapping American criminal law: Variations across the 50 states: Ch. 20 statutory rape.' *Faculty Scholarship at Penn Law*, <https://scholarship.law.upenn.edu/faculty_scholarship/1714> (last accessed 25 March 2021).

Rodino-Colocino, Michelle (2018). 'Me too, #MeToo: Countering cruelty with empathy.' *Communication and Critical/Cultural Studies* 15, no. 1: 96–100.

Rodriguez, Favianna, and Leah Lakshmi Piepzna-Samarasinha (2019). *Pleasure Activism: The Politics of Feeling Good*. Chico, CA: AK Press.

Rogers, Katie (2015). 'Bill Cosby: The latest from his accusers and defenders.' *The New York Times*, 8 July, <https://www.nytimes.com/2015/07/09/business/media/bill-cosby-the-latest-from-his-accusers-and-defenders.html> (last accessed 25 March 2021).

Rogers, Richard (2020). 'Deplatforming: Following extreme Internet celebrities to Telegram and alternative social media.' *European Journal of Communication* 35, no. 3: 213–29.

Roiphe, Katie (1993). *The Morning After: Sex, Fear, and Feminism on Campus*. Boston: Little, Brown and Company.

Roiphe, Katie (2018). 'The other whisper network: How Twitter feminism is bad for women.' *Harper's Magazine*, March, <https://harpers.org/archive/2018/03/the-other-whisper-network-2> (last accessed 25 March 2021).

Ronell, Avital (2018). 'Press release on behalf of Professor Avital Ronell.' <https://pdffox.com/ronell-press-release-2018-pdf-free.html> (last accessed 15 April 2021).

Rosenau, Pauline Marie (1991). *Post-Modernism and the Social Sciences: Insights, Inroads, and Intrusions*. Princeton: Princeton University Press.

Rosenberg, Rebecca (2019). 'Harvey Weinstein: I deserve pat on back when it comes to women.' *Page Six*, 15 December, <https://pagesix.com/2019/12/15/harvey-weinstein-i-deserve-pat-on-back-when-it-comes-to-women> (last accessed 25 March 2021).

Rosenthal, Lisa (2016). 'Incorporating intersectionality into psychology: An opportunity to promote social justice and equity.' *American Psychologist* 71, no. 6: 474–85.

Ross, Josephine (2018). 'What the #MeToo campaign teaches about stop and frisk.' *Idaho Law Review* 54, no. 2: 543–61.

Rowland, Robyn, and Renate Klein (1996). 'Radical feminism: History, politics, action.' In Diane Bell and Renate Klein (eds), *Radically Speaking: Feminism Reclaimed*. Melbourne: Spinifex Press, pp. 9–36.

Roy, Srila (2016). 'Breaking the cage.' *Dissent*, Fall, <https://www.dissentmagazine.org/article/breaking-cage-india-feminism-sexual-violence-public-space> (last accessed 25 March 2021).

Rubenfeld, Jed (2013). 'The riddle of rape-by-deception and the myth of sexual autonomy.' *Yale Law Journal* 122, no. 6: 1,372–443.

Rubin, Gayle S. (1993). 'Thinking sex: Notes for a radical theory of the politics of sexuality.' In Henry Abelove, Michèle Aina Barale and David M. Halperin (eds), *The Lesbian and Gay Studies Reader*. New York: Routledge, pp. 3–44.

Rubin, Gayle S. (1998). 'Thinking sex: Notes for a radical theory of the politics of sexuality.' In Peter M. Nardi and Beth E. Schneider (eds), *Social Perspectives in Lesbian and Gay Studies: A Reader*. London: Routledge, pp. 100–33.

Rubin, Gayle (2011). 'Blood under the bridge: Reflections on "Thinking sex".' *GLQ: A Journal of Lesbian and Gay Studies* 17, no. 1: 15–48.

Ruppert, Brenna (2013). 'The 15 best one-liners of Louis C.K.' *Phoenix New Times*, 12 February, <https://www.phoenixnewtimes.com/arts/the-15-best-one-liners-of-louis-ck-6555700> (last accessed 15 April 2021).

Russell, Emma, and Bree Carlton (2013). 'Pathways, race and gender responsive reform: Through an abolitionist lens.' *Theoretical Criminology* 17, no. 4: 474–92.

Ryzik, Melena, Cara Buckley and Jodi Kantor (2017). 'Louis C.K. is accused by 5 women of sexual misconduct.' *The New York Times*, 9 November, <https://www.nytimes.com/2017/11/09/arts/television/louis-ck-sexual-misconduct.html> (last accessed 15 April 2021).

Saad, Nardine (2019). 'Here's what Aziz Ansari said about his sexual misconduct scandal in his Netflix special.' *Los Angeles Times*, 9 July, <https://www.latimes.com/entertainment/tv/la-et-st-aziz-ansari-right-now-mis conduct-netflix-20190709-story.html> (last accessed 25 March 2021).

Saad-Filho, Alfredo, and Deborah Johnston (2005). *Neoliberalism: A Critical Reader*. Chicago: University of Chicago Press.

Saketopoulou, Avgi (2019). 'The draw to overwhelm: Consent, risk, and the retranslation of enigma.' *Journal of the American Psychoanalytic Association* 67, no. 1: 133–67.

Sanchez, Diana T., Jennifer Crocker and Karlee R. Boike (2005). 'Doing gender in the bedroom: Investing in gender norms and the sexual experience.' *Personality and Social Psychology Bulletin* 31, no. 10: 1, 445–55.

Sandoval, Eric (2019). 'The case for an affirmative consent provision in rape law.' *North Dakota Law Review* 94: 455–80.

Savigny, Heather (2020). *Cultural Sexism: The Politics of Feminist Rage in the #MeToo Era*. Bristol: Bristol University Press.

Sayej, Nadja (2017). 'Alyssa Milano on the #MeToo movement: "We're not going to stand for it any more."' *The Guardian*, 1 December, <https://

www.theguardian.com/culture/2017/dec/01/alyssa-milano-mee-too-sexual-harassment-abuse> (last accessed 25 March 2021).

Schippers, Mimi (2007). 'Recovering the feminine other: Masculinity, femininity, and gender hegemony.' *Theory and Society* 36, no. 1: 85–102.

Schulhofer, Stephen J. (1992). 'Taking sexual autonomy seriously: Rape law and beyond.' *Law and Philosophy* 11: 35–94.

Schulhofer, Stephen J. (1998). *Unwanted Sex: The Culture of Intimidation and the Failure of Law*. Vol. 99. Cambridge, MA: Harvard University Press.

Schulhofer, Stephen J. (2015). 'Consent: What it means and why it's time to require it.' *University of the Pacific Law Review* 47, no. 4: 665–81.

Schwendinger, Julia R., and Herman Schwendinger (1983). *Rape and Inequality*. Beverly Hills: Sage.

Scorcia-Popescu, Rebeca (2017). 'Towards restorative justice or relapse prevention – probation perspective.' *Revista de Asistență Socială* 3: 63–70.

Scott, David (ed.) (2013). *Why Prison?* Cambridge: Cambridge University Press.

Searles, Patricia (2018). *Rape and Society: Readings on the Problem of Sexual Assault*. New York: Routledge.

Sebring, J. H. (2019). 'Hashtag feminism: Examining contemporary feminist concerns and social justice activism in a social media age.' *Crossings* 3: 49–62.

Sedgwick, Eve Kosofsky (1993). *Tendencies*. Durham, NC: Duke University Press.

Sedgwick, Eve Kosofsky (2003). *Touching Feeling: Affect, Pedagogy, Performativity*. Durham, NC: Duke University Press.

Sedgwick, Eve Kosofsky (2008). *Epistemology of the Closet*. Berkeley: University of California Press.

Sedgwick, Eve Kosofsky (2013). 'Queer and now.' In Donald E. Hall and Annamarie Jagose (eds), *The Routledge Queer Studies Reader*. New York: Routledge, pp. 3–17.

Seidman, Ilene, and Susan Vickers (2004). 'The second wave: An agenda for the next thirty years of rape law reform.' *Suffolk University Law Review* 38: 467–91.

Selter, Brian (2014). 'Bill Cosby's attorney calls rape allegations "decade-old" and "discredited".' *CNN Business*, 16 November, <https://money.cnn.com/2014/11/15/media/bill-cosby-rape-allegations> (last accessed 25 March 2021).

Shams, Tahseen (2019). 'Successful yet precarious: South Asian Muslim

Americans, Islamophobia, and the model minority myth.' *Sociological Perspectives* 63, no. 4: 653–69.

Sharma, Nitasha (2016). 'Racialization and resistance: The double bind of post-9/11 Brown.' In Aparajita De (ed.), *South Asian Racialization and Belonging after 9/11: Masks of Threat*. Lanham, MD: Lexington Books, pp. 137–48.

Showden, Carisa R. (2016). 'Feminist sex wars.' In *The Wiley Blackwell Encyclopedia of Gender and Sexuality Studies*: 1–3.

Shusterman, Richard (1999). 'Somaesthetics: A disciplinary proposal.' *The Journal of Aesthetics and Art Criticism* 57, no. 3: 299–313.

Sicari, Anna (2018). 'Centering the conversation: Patriarchy, academic culture, and #MeToo.' *Composition Studies* 46, no. 2: 200–38.

Simien, Evelyn M. (2007). 'Doing intersectionality research: From conceptual issues to practical examples.' *Politics & Gender* 3, no. 2: 264–71.

Singleton, Tyra (2017). 'Conflicting definitions of sexual assault and consent: The ramifications of the Title IX male gender discrimination claims against college campuses.' *Hastings Women's Law Journal* 28, no. 2: 155.

Skelton, Ann, and Mike Batley (2006). *Charting Progress, Mapping the Future: Restorative Justice in South Africa*. Pretoria: Restorative Justice Centre and Institute for Security Studies.

Slatton, Brittany C., and April L. Richard (2020). 'Black women's experiences of sexual assault and disclosure: Insights from the margins.' *Sociology Compass* 14: 1–12.

Small, Tamara A. (2020). 'The promises and perils of hashtag feminism.' In Fiona MacDonald and Alexandra Dobrowolsky (eds), *Turbulent Times, Transformational Possibilities? Gender and Politics Today and Tomorrow*. Toronto: University of Toronto Press, pp. 177–98.

Small, Zachary (2018). 'When famous academics would rather condemn #MeToo than support queer victims.' *Hyperallergic*, 28 August, <https://hyperallergic.com/456807/when-famous-academics-would-rather-condemn-metoo-than-support-queer-victims> (last accessed 25 March 2021).

Smart, C. (2002). *Feminism and the Power of Law*. London: Routledge.

Smiley, CalvinJohn, and David Fakunle (2016). 'From "brute" to "thug": The demonization and criminalization of unarmed Black male victims in America.' *Journal of Human Behavior in the Social Environment* 26, nos. 3–4: 350–66.

Smith, Elizabeth Alison (1990). 'Charged with sexuality: Feminism, liberalism, and pornography, 1970–1982.' Dissertation, University of Pennsylvania.

Smith, Evan (2020). *No Platform: A History of Anti-Fascism, Universities and the Limits of Free Speech*. New York: Routledge.

Smith, Jennifer (2019). 'Rose McGowan lashes out at "prolific rapist" Harvey Weinstein after he complained that he is a "forgotten man" who "pioneered" women in film making.' *Mail Online*, 16 December, <https://www.dailymail.co.uk/news/article-7797137/Weinsteins-accusers-disgusted-bizarre-hospital-room-interview.html> (last accessed 25 March 2021).

Smith, Tovia (2019). 'This chef says he's faced his #MeToo offenses. Now he wants a second chance.' *NPR*, 7 October, <https://www.npr.org/2019/10/07/767901018/this-chef-says-hes-faced-his-metoo-offenses-now-he-wants-a-second-chance> (last accessed 25 March 2021).

Snitow, Ann, Christine Stansell and Sharon Thompson (eds) (1983). *Powers of Desire: The Politics of Sexuality*. New York: Monthly Review Press.

Sobchack, Vivian (2004). *Carnal Thoughts: Embodiment and Moving Image Culture*. Berkeley: University of California Press.

Solnit, Rebecca (2018). 'Feminists have slowly shifted power. There's no going back.' *The Guardian*, 8 May, <https://www.theguardian.com/commentisfree/2018/mar/08/feminists-power-metoo-timesup-rebecca-solnit> (last accessed 25 March 2021).

Sood, Reema (2018). 'Biases behind sexual assault: A Thirteenth Amendment solution to under-enforcement of the rape of Black women.' *University of Maryland Law Journal of Race, Religion, Gender and Class* 18, no. 2: 405–28.

Sorensen, Anna (2018). 'Finding feminism: Millennial activists and the unfinished gender revolution.' *Feminist Media Studies* 18, no 1: 152–4.

Sovdi, Karissa (2016). 'Asking for it: The sexualized violence of Jian Ghomeshi as depicted by four traditional journalistic media sources.' PhD dissertation, City University of Seattle.

Spacks, Patricia Meyer (2012). *Gossip*. New York: Knopf.

Spade, Dean (2013). 'Intersectional resistance and law reform.' *Signs: Journal of Women in Culture and Society* 38, no. 4: 1,031–55.

Spalding, Amanda (2019). 'The "cool girl" strikes back? A socio-legal analysis of *Gone Girl*.' In Dimitris Akrivos and Alexandros K. Antoniou (eds), *Crime, Deviance and Popular Culture*. London: Palgrave Macmillan, pp. 121–45.

Spear, Richard E. (2000). 'Artemisia Gentileschi: Ten years of fact and fiction.' *The Art Bulletin* 82, no. 3: 568–79.

Spencer, Chelsea, Allen Mallory, Michelle Toews, Sandra Stith and Leila Wood (2017). 'Why sexual assault survivors do not report to universities: A feminist analysis.' *Family Relations* 66, no. 1: 166–79.

Spencer, Ruth (2016). 'Lucy DeCoutere on the trauma of the Jian Ghomeshi trial: "After everything I went through, Jian is free."' *The Guardian*, 25 March, <https://www.theguardian.com/world/2016/mar/25/jian-ghomeshi-trial-lucy-de-coutere-interview> (last accessed 25 March 2021).

Spencer, Ruth (2018). 'What I know about Jian Ghomeshi.' *The Cut*, 15 September, <https://www.thecut.com/2018/09/jian-ghomeshi-new-york-review-of-books-essay.html> (last accessed 25 March 2021).

Spivak, Gayatri Chakravorty (1990). 'Practical politics of the open end.' In *The Post-Colonial Critic: Interviews, Strategies, Dialogues*. New York: Routledge, pp. 95–112.

Spohn, Cassia C. (1999). 'The rape reform movement: The traditional common law and rape law reforms.' *Jurimetrics* 39: 119–30.

Spratt, Vicky (2018). 'The Aziz Ansari consent debate isn't the same as #MeToo, but it's just as important.' *Grazia*, 10 January, <https://graziadaily.co.uk/life/real-life/aziz-ansari-consent-me-too> (last accessed 25 March 2021).

Spry, Tami (1995). 'In the absence of word and body: Hegemonic implications of "victim" and "survivor" in women's narratives of sexual violence.' *Women and Language* 18, no. 2: 27–33.

Stabile, Bonnie, Aubrey Grant, Hemant Purohit and Mohammad Rama (2019). '"She lied": Social construction, rape myth prevalence in social media, and sexual assault policy.' *Sexuality, Gender & Policy* 2, no. 2: 80–96.

Stanley, Liz, and Sue Wise (1992). 'Feminist epistemology and ontology: Recent debates in feminist social theory.' *Indian Journal of Social Work* 53: 343–65.

Starkey, Jesse C., Amy Koerber, Miglena Sternadori and Bethany Pitchford (2019). '#MeToo goes global: Media framing of silence breakers in four national settings.' *Journal of Communication Inquiry* 43, no. 4: 437–61.

Stein, Ruth (2008). 'The otherness of sexuality: Excess.' *Journal of the American Psychoanalytic Association* 56, no. 1: 43–71.

Stevens, Bethany (2011). 'Structural barriers to sexual autonomy for disabled people.' *Human Rights Law Review* 38: 14.

Stewart, Nora (2018). 'The light we shine into the grey: A restorative #MeToo solution and an acknowledgement of those #MeToo leaves in the dark.' *Fordham Law Review* 87, no. 4: 1,693–1,720.

Stites, M. Cynara (1996). 'What's wrong with faculty-student consensual sexual relationships?' In Michele A. Paludi (ed.), *Sexual Harassment on College Campuses: Abusing the Ivory Power*. Albany: State University of New York Press, pp. 115–39.

Stoeffel, Kat (2014). 'Jian Ghomeshi isn't the first alleged abuser to cite the right to BDSM sexuality.' *The Cut*, 28 October, <https://www.thecut.com/2014/10/jian-ghomeshi-and-the-right-to-bdsm-sexuality.html> (last accessed 25 March 2021).

Stone, Meighan, and Rachel Vogelstein (2019). 'Celebrating #MeToo's global impact: In countries around the world, progress defies the backlash.' *Foreign Policy*, 2 March, <https://foreignpolicy.com/2019/03/07/metooglobalimpactinternationalwomens-day> (last accessed 25 March 2021).

Strait, Naomi (2020). 'Justice, Prevention, Respect: A Critical Investigation of Sexual Violence on College Campuses; and a Denunciation of Carceral Feminism.' *American Studies Honors Projects* 16.

Strang, Heather, and John Braithwaite (eds) (2017). *Restorative Justice: Philosophy to Practice*. New York: Routledge.

Straussman-Pflanzer, Eve, and Art Institute of Chicago (2013). *Violence and Virtue: Artemisia Gentileschi's 'Judith Slaying Holofernes'*. Chicago: Art Institute of Chicago.

Stubbs, Julie (2007). 'Beyond apology? Domestic violence and critical questions for restorative justice.' *Criminology & Criminal Justice* 7, no. 2: 169–87.

Stubbs, Julie (2010). 'Restorative justice, gendered violence, and Indigenous women.' In James Ptacek (ed.), *Restorative Justice and Violence against Women*. Oxford: Oxford University Press, pp. 103–22.

Subotnik, Dan (2006). 'Hands off: Sex, feminism, affirmative consent, and the law of foreplay.' *Southern California Review of Law and Social Justice* 16: 249.

Subotnik, Dan (2008). 'Copulemus in pace: A mediation on rape, affirmative consent to sex, and sexual autonomy.' *Akron Law Review* 41: 847.

Sullivan, Lynne E., and James R. P. Ogloff (1998). 'Appropriate supervisor–graduate student relationships.' *Ethics & Behavior* 8, no. 3: 229–48.

Supreme Court of the State of New York (2018). 'Complaint.' Supreme Court of the State of New York, County of New York, 16 August, <https://blog.simplejustice.us/wp-content/uploads/2018/08/FINAL-Complaint-Reitman-v.-Ronell-and-NYU.pdf> (last accessed 25 March 2021).

SWOP (Sex Workers Outreach Project) (2018). 'Submission to the NSW

Law Reform Commission: Review of consent in relation to sexual offences'. <https://www.lawreform.justice.nsw.gov.au/Documents/Current-projects/Consent/Preliminary-submissions/PCO103.pdf> (last accessed 25 March 2021).

Tamarit, Josep, and Eulalia Luque (2016). 'Can restorative justice satisfy victims' needs? Evaluation of the Catalan victim–offender mediation programme.' *Restorative Justice* 4, no. 1: 68–85.

Tambe, Ashwini (2018). 'Reckoning with the silences of #MeToo.' *Feminist Studies* 44, no. 1: 197–203.

Tasker, Yvonne, and Diane Negra (2007). 'Introduction: Feminist politics and postfeminist culture.' In Yvonne Tasker and Diane Negra (eds), *Interrogating Postfeminism*. Durham, NC: Duke University Press, pp. 1–26.

Tauri, Juan M. (2014). 'An Indigenous commentary on the globalisation of restorative justice.' *British Journal of Community Justice* 12, no. 2: 35–55.

Taylor, Affrica, and Mindy Blaise (2017). 'Queer departures into more-than-human worlds.' In Louisa Allen and Mary Lou Rasmussen (eds), *The Palgrave Handbook of Sexuality Education*, London: Palgrave Macmillan, pp. 591–609.

Taylor, Chloë (2014). 'Biopower.' In Dianna Taylor (ed.), *Michel Foucault: Key Concepts*. New York: Routledge, pp. 49–62.

Taylor, Chloë (2018). 'Anti-carceral feminism and sexual assault – a defense in advance: A critique of the critique of the critique of carceral feminism.' *Social Philosophy Today* 34: 29–49.

Ter Bogt, Tom F. M., Rutger C. M. E. Engels, Sanne Bogers and Monique Kloosterman (2010). '"Shake it baby, shake it": Media preferences, sexual attitudes and gender stereotypes among adolescents.' *Sex Roles* 63, nos. 11–12: 844–59.

Tharp, A. T., K. Swartout, M. P. Koss, S. DeGue, K. C. Basile, J. White and M. Thompson (2015). *Key Findings: Rethinking Serial Perpetration*. Harrisburg, PA: National Sexual Violence Resource Center.

Theixos, Heleana (2018). 'Feminist perspectives on the apology of Louis CK and the #MeToo and #TimesUp movements.' *Media Watch* 9, no. 3: 267–77.

Thiessen, Brock (2020). 'Jian Ghomeshi launches another new podcast.' *Exclaim!*, 13 May, <http://exclaim.ca/music/article/jian_ghomeshi_has_launched_another_new_podcast> (last accessed 25 March 2021).

Thompson, Denise (2001). *Radical Feminism Today*. London: Sage.

Tiffany, Kaitlyn (2018). 'The Aziz Ansari story is a mess, but so are the arguments against it.' *The Verge*, 17 January 17, <https://www.theverge.com/2018/1/17/16893896/babe-aziz-ansari-sexual-misconduct-new-journalism-millennials-platform-reporting> (last accessed 25 March 2021).

Time Magazine (2019). '"Our pain is never prioritized." #MeToo founder Tarana Burke says we must listen to "untold" stories of minority women.' *Time Magazine*, 23 April, <https://time.com/5574163/tarana-burke-metoo-time-100-summit> (last accessed 25 March 2021).

Tok, Gül Ceylan (2018). 'The politicization of migration and the rise of competitive authoritarianism in Hungary.' *Akdeniz Üniversitesi İktisadi ve İdari Bilimler Fakültesi Dergisi* 18, no. 37: 88–117.

Tolentino, Jia (2017). 'The whisper network after Harvey Weinstein and "shitty media men".' *The New Yorker*, 14 October, <https://www.newyorker.com/news/news-desk/the-whisper-network-after-harvey-weinstein-and-shitty-media-men> (last accessed 25 March 2021).

Tong, Rosemarie (1989). *Feminist Thought: A Comprehensive Introduction*. Boulder: Westview.

Toronto Star (2014). 'Jian Ghomeshi's full Facebook post: "a campaign of false allegations" at fault.' *Toronto Star*, 27 October, <https://www.thestar.com/news/gta/2014/10/27/jian_ghomeshis_full_facebook_post_a_campaign_of_false_allegations_at_fault.html> (last accessed 25 March 2021).

Tracy, Carol E., Terry L. Fromson, Jennifer Gentile Long and Charlene Whitman (2012). *Rape and Sexual Assault in the Legal System*. National Research Council of the National Academies Panel on Measuring Rape and Sexual Assault in the Bureau of Justice Statistics Household Surveys Committee on National Statistics.

Traister, Rebecca (2018). *Good and Mad: The Revolutionary Power of Women's Anger*. New York: Simon & Schuster.

Traister, Rebecca (2020). '"You believe he's lying?" The latest debate captured Americans' exhausting tendency to mistrust women.' *The Cut*, 26 February, <https://www.thecut.com/2020/02/chris-matthews-elizabeth-warren-believe-women.html> (last accessed 25 March 2021).

Triggs, Sue (2005). 'New Zealand court-referred restorative justice pilot.' Ministry of Justice, <https://www.ojp.gov/ncjrs/virtual-library/abstracts/new-zealand-court-referred-restorative-justice-pilot-evaluation> (last accessed 8 April 2021).

Troost, Hazel/Cedar (2008). 'Reclaiming touch: Rape culture, explicit verbal consent, and body sovereignty.' In Jaclyn Friedman and Jessica Valenti (eds), *Yes Means Yes: Visions of Female Sexual Power and a World without Rape*. Berkeley: Seal Press, pp. 171–8.

Truscott, Carol (1991). 'S/M: Some questions and a few answers.' In Mark Thompson (ed.), *Leatherfolk: Radical Sex, People, Politics, and Practice*. Los Angeles: Daedalus Publishing, pp. 15–36.

Tsing, Anna Lowenhaupt (2015). *The Mushroom at the End of the World: On the Possibility of Life in Capitalist Ruins*. Princeton: Princeton University Press.

Tuana, Nancy (1983). 'Re-fusing nature/nurture.' *Women's Studies International Forum*, 6, no. 6: 621–32.

Tuerkheimer, Deborah (2015). 'Affirmative consent.' *Ohio State Journal of Criminal Law* 13, no. 2: 441–68.

Tuerkheimer, Deborah (2019a). 'Beyond #MeToo.' *New York University Law Review* 94, no. 5: 1,146–208.

Tuerkheimer, Deborah (2019b). 'Unofficial reporting in the #MeToo era.' *University of Chicago Legal Forum*: 273–98.

Turner, William Benjamin, and Sir William Turner (2000). *A Genealogy of Queer Theory*. Vol. 12. Philadelphia: Temple University Press.

Umbreit, Mark S., Robert B. Coates and Boris Kalanj (1994). *Victim Meets Offender: The Impact of Restorative Justice and Mediation*. Monsey, NY: Criminal Justice Press.

University of Michigan (2019). 'Policy and procedures on student sexual and gender-based misconduct and other forms of interpersonal violence.' <https://hr.umich.edu/sites/default/files/um-policy-and-procedures-on-student-sexual-misconduct-and-other-forms-of-interpersonal-violence.pdf> (last accessed 8 April 2021).

Valenti, Jessica (JessicaValenti) (2018). Twitter post, 14 January, 'A lot of men will read that post about Aziz Ansari and see an everyday, reasonable sexual interaction. But part of what women are saying right now is that what the culture considers "normal" sexual encounters are not working for us, and are oftentimes harmful.'

Van Camp, Tinneke, and Jo-Anne Wemmers (2013). 'Victim satisfaction with restorative justice: More than simply procedural justice.' *International Review of Victimology* 19, no. 2: 117–43.

Van Dijk, Teun A. (2001). 'Multidisciplinary CDA: A plea for diversity.' *Methods of Critical Discourse Analysis* 1: 95–120.

Van Ness, Daniel W., and Karen Heetdersks Strong (2014). *Restoring Justice: An Introduction to Restorative Justice*. New York: Routledge.

Van Wormer, Katherine (2009). 'Restorative justice as social justice for victims of gendered violence: A standpoint feminist perspective.' *Social Work* 54, no. 2: 107–16.

Vance, Carole S. (1984). 'Pleasure and danger: Toward a politics of sexuality.' *Pleasure and Danger: Exploring Female Sexuality* 1, no. 3.

Vance, Carole S. (1993). 'More danger, more pleasure: A decade after the Barnard sexuality conference.' *New York Law School Law Review* 38: 289, <https://heinonline.org/HOL/LandingPage?handle=hein.journals/nyls38&div=23&id=&page=> (last accessed 25 March 2021).

Vandervort, Lucinda (2019). '"Reasonable steps": Amending Section 273.2 to reflect the jurisprudence.' *Criminal Law Quarterly* 66, no. 4: 376–87.

VanHaitsma, Pamela (2016). 'Gossip as rhetorical methodology for queer and feminist historiography.' *Rhetoric Review* 35, no. 2: 135–47.

Variety (2018). 'Aziz Ansari responds to sexual misconduct allegation: "I was surprised and concerned."' *Variety*, 24 January, <https://variety.com/2018/film/news/aziz-ansari-responds-to-sexual-misconduct-allegation-i-was-surprised-and-concerned-1202664264/#article-comments> (last accessed 25 March 2021).

Verbruggen, Robert (2019). 'Aziz Ansari returns, chastened – and funnier.' *National Review*, 10 July, <https://www.nationalreview.com/2019/07/aziz-ansari-netflix-special-right-now-chastened-funnier> (last accessed 25 March 2021).

Vogel, Howard J. (2006). 'The restorative justice wager: The promise and hope of a value-based, dialogue-driven approach to conflict resolution for social healing.' *Cardozo Journal of Conflict Resolution* 8: 565–609.

Vogel, Wendy (2014). 'Riding the fourth wave in a changing sea.' *The Brooklyn Rail: Critical Perspectives on Art, Politics, and Culture*, 4 September, <http://www.brooklynrail.org/2014/09/criticspage/riding-the-fourth-wave-in-a-changing-sea> (last accessed 25 March 2021).

von Hirsch, Andrew (1993). *Censure and Sanctions*. Oxford: Oxford University Press.

Vox (2020). 'Sexual harassment assault allegations.' *Vox*, 19 September, <https://www.vox.com/a/sexual-harassment-assault-allegations-list> (last accessed 25 March 2021).

Wachtel, Ted (2003). 'In pursuit of paradigm: A theory of restorative justice.' *Restorative Practices E-Forum*, 12 August, <https://biblioteca.cejamericas.org/bitstream/handle/2015/2163/paradigm.pdf?sequence=1&isAllowed=y> (last accessed 25 March 2021).

Wacquant, Loïc (2009). *Punishing the Poor: The Neoliberal Government of Social Insecurity*. Durham, NC: Duke University Press.

Wadsworth, Nancy D. (2017). 'Louis C.K.'s apology is imperfect. But it is still important.' *The Washington Post*, 14 November, <www.washingtonpost.com/news/monkey-cage/wp/2017/11/14/louis-c-k-s-apology-was-imperfect-but-it-was-still-important> (last accessed 25 March 2021).

Wall, Steve (2001). 'Review: *A Genealogy of Queer Theory*.' *H-Net Reviews*, September, <https://www.h-net.org/reviews/showpdf.php?id=5490> (last accessed 25 March 2021).

Wallerstein, Shlomit (2009). '"A drunken consent is still consent" – or is it? A critical analysis of the law on a drunken consent to sex following Bree.' *The Journal of Criminal Law* 73, no. 4: 318–44.

Wang, Esther (2018). 'What are we to make of the case of scholar Avital Ronell?' *Jezebel*, 17 August, <https://jezebel.com/what-are-we-to-make-of-the-case-of-scholar-avital-ronel-1828366966> (last accessed 25 March 2021).

Wang, W. (2006). 'Newspaper commentaries on terrorism in China and Australia: A contrastive genre study.' Unpublished PhD dissertation, University of Sydney.

Ward, L. Monique, and Kimberly Friedman (2006). 'Using TV as a guide: Associations between television viewing and adolescents' sexual attitudes and behavior.' *Journal of Research on Adolescence* 16, no. 1: 133–56.

Warner, Michael (1993). 'Introduction.' In Michael Warner (ed.), *Fear of a Queer Planet: Queer Politics and Social Theory*, Minneapolis: University of Minnesota Press, pp. vii–xxxi.

Warner, Michael (2000). *The Trouble with Normal: Sex, Politics, and the Ethics of Queer Life*. Cambridge, MA: Harvard University Press.

Washington Post, The (2020). 12 May, <https://www.washingtonpost.com> (last accessed 25 March 2021).

Way, Katie (2018). 'I went on a date with Aziz Ansari. It turned into the worst night of my life.' *Babe*, 13 January, <https://babe.net/2018/01/13/aziz-ansari-28355> (last accessed 25 March 2021).

Weed, Elizabeth, and Naomi Schor (eds) (1997). *Feminism Meets Queer Theory*. Vol. 2. Bloomington: Indiana University Press.

Weeks, Jacquilyn (2011). 'Un-/Re-productive maternal labor: Marxist feminism and chapter fifteen of Marx's *Capital*.' *Rethinking Marxism* 23, no. 1: 31–40.

Weeks, Jeffrey (2012). 'Reflections on the new frontiers in sexualities research.' In Peter Aggleton, Paul Boyce, Henrietta L. Moore and Richard Parker (eds), *Understanding Global Sexualities: New Frontiers*. New York: Routledge, pp. 247–57.

Weinstein, Harvey (2017). 'Harvey Weinstein scandal: Read his full apology.' *USA Today*, 5 October, <https://eu.usatoday.com/story/life/movies/2017/10/05/harvey-weinstein-scandal-read-his-full-apology/738093001> (last accessed 25 March 2021).

Weir, Charissa (2020). 'Narratives and the legal game: Narrative power dynamics and their reproduction in the sexual assault trial of *R. v. Ghomeshi*.' PhD dissertation, University of Ottawa, <https://ruor.uottawa.ca/bitstream/10393/40518/3/Weir_Charissa_2020_thesis.pdf> (last accessed 25 March 2021).

Weiss, Bari (2017). 'The limits of "believe all women".' *The New York Times*, 28 November, <https://www.nytimes.com/2017/11/28/opinion/metoo-sexual-harassment-believe-women.html> (last accessed 25 March 2021).

Weiss, Bari (2018). 'Aziz Ansari is guilty. Of not being a mind reader.' *The New York Times*, 15 January, <https://www.nytimes.com/2018/01/15/opinion/aziz-ansari-babe-sexual-harassment.html> (last accessed 25 March 2021).

Weiss, Margot D. (2008). 'Gay shame and BDSM pride: Neoliberalism, privacy, and sexual politics.' *Radical History Review* 100: 87–101.

Weitz, Rose, and R. Weitz (2016). 'A history of women's bodies.' In Bonnie Kime Scott, Susan E. Cayleff, Anne Donadey and Irene Lara (eds), *Women in Culture: An Intersectional Anthology for Gender and Women's Studies*. Hoboken: Wiley-Blackwell, pp. 248–55.

Welch, Shay (2012). 'Social freedom and commitment.' *Ethical Theory and Moral Practice* 15, no. 1: 117–34.

Weldon, S. Laurel (2006). 'The structure of intersectionality: A comparative politics of gender.' *Politics & Gender* 2, no. 2: 235–48.

Wente, Margaret (2016). 'The biggest losers in the Ghomeshi debacle.' *The Globe and Mail*, 12 February, <https://www.theglobeandmail.com/opinion/the-biggest-losers-in-the-ghomeshi-debacle/article28741727> (last accessed 25 March 2021).

Wertheimer, Alan (1996). 'Consent and sexual relations.' *Legal Theory* 2, no. 2: 89–112.

West, Robin (1987). 'The feminist-conservative anti-pornography alliance and the 1986 Attorney General's Commission on Pornography report.' *American Bar Foundation Research Journal* 12, no. 4: 681–711.

West, Robin L. (1993). 'Legitimating the illegitimate: A comment on "Beyond rape".' *Columbia Law Review* 93, no. 6: 1,442–59.

West, Robin L. (2000). 'The difference in women's hedonic lives: A phenomenological critique of feminist legal theory.' *Wisconsin Women's Law Journal* 15: 149.

West, Robin (2008). 'Unwelcome sex: Toward a harm-based analysis.' In Catharine A. MacKinnon and Reva B. Siegel (eds), *Directions in Sexual Harassment Law*. New Haven: Yale University Press, pp. 138–52.

West, Robin (2010). 'Sex, law, and consent.' In Franklin G. Miller and Alan Wertheimer (eds), *The Ethics of Consent: Theory and Practice*. Oxford: Oxford University Press, pp. 221–49.

West, Robin (2020). 'Consent, legitimation, and dysphoria.' *The Modern Law Review* 83, no. 1: 1–34.

Westen, Peter (2017). *The Logic of Consent: The Diversity and Deceptiveness of Consent as a Defense to Criminal Conduct*. New York: Routledge.

Westmarland, Nicole, Clare McGlynn and Clarissa Humphreys (2018). 'Using restorative justice approaches to police domestic violence and abuse.' *Journal of Gender-Based Violence* 2, no. 2: 339–58.

Wetherbee, Ben (2019). '"Redemption follows allocution": Dan Harmon and the #MeToo apology.' *Journal of Contemporary Rhetoric* 9: 112–25.

Wexler, Lesley (2018). '2018 symposium lecture: #MeToo and procedural justice.' *Richmond Public Interest Law Review* 22, no. 2: 13–24.

Wexler, Lesley (2019). '#MeToo and law talk.' *University of Chicago Legal Forum*: 343–69.

Wexler, Lesley, Jennifer K. Robbennolt and Colleen Murphy (2019). '#MeToo, Time's Up, and theories of justice.' *University of Illinois Law Review* 1: 45–111.

Whelehan, Imelda (1995). *Modern Feminist Thought: From the Second Wave to Post-Feminism*. New York: New York University Press.

Wiederman, Michael W. (2005). 'The gendered nature of sexual scripts.' *The Family Journal* 13, no. 4: 496–502.

Wiener, Jon (2018). 'Avital and Nimrod: Sexual harassment and "campy communications" at NYU.' *Los Angeles Review of Books*, 20 August, <https://blog.lareviewofbooks.org/essays/avital-nimrod-sexual-harassment-campy-communications-nyu> (last accessed 25 March 2021).

Williams, Joanna (2019). 'Christmas parties cancelled, written consent for sex and a growing hostility between men and women. In a provocative blast, a female academic argues: Yes it had noble intentions, but it's time we called time on #MeToo.' *Mail Online*, 24 October, <https://www.dailymail.co.uk/femail/article-7605893/Yes-noble-intentions-time-called-time-MeToo.html> (last accessed 25 March 2021).

Willingham, A. J. (2019). 'North Carolina's the only state with a law that says once a sexual act begins, you can't withdraw consent.' *CNN Health*, 2 June, <https://edition.cnn.com/2019/06/02/health/north-carolina-rape-consent-bill-563-trnd/index.html> (last accessed 25 March 2021).

Willis, Malachi, and Kristen N. Jozkowski (2019). 'Sexual precedent's effect on sexual consent communication.' *Archives of Sexual Behavior* 48, no. 6: 1,723–34.

Willsher, Kim (2018). 'Catherine Deneuve's claim of #MeToo witch-hunt sparks backlash.' *The Guardian*, 10 January, <https://www.theguardian.com/film/2018/jan/10/catherine-deneuve-claim-metoo-witch-hunt-backlash> (last accessed 25 March 2021).

Wilson, Laura C., and Katherine E. Miller (2016). 'Meta-analysis of the prevalence of unacknowledged rape.' *Trauma, Violence, & Abuse* 17, no. 2: 149–59.

Wilz, Kelly (2019). *Resisting Rape Culture through Pop Culture: Sex after #MeToo*. Lanham, MD: Lexington Books.

Withnall, Adam (2016). 'Russian-German girl "admits making up" claim she was raped by refugees in Berlin.' *The Independent*, 31 January, <https://www.independent.co.uk/news/world/europe/russian-german-girl-admits-making-up-claim-she-was-raped-by-refugees-in-berlin-a6845256.html> (last accessed 25 March 2021).

Witmer-Rich, Jonathan (2016). 'Unpacking affirmative consent: Not as great as you hope, not as bad as you fear.' *Texas Tech Law Review* 49: 57–88.

Wittig, Monique (1985). 'The mark of gender.' *Gender Issues* 5, no. 2: 3–12.

Wolov, Julia (2019). 'Counterpoint: I didn't consent to Louis C.K. masturbating in front of me.' *The Canadian Jewish News*, 12 November, <https://www.cjnews.com/perspectives/opinions/counterpoint-i-didnt-consent-to-louis-c-k-masturbating-in-front-of-me> (last accessed 25 March 2021).

Wong, Brian (2019). 'On the democracy of equals: An interview with Prof. Elizabeth Anderson.' *Oxford Political Review*, 25 July, <http://oxfordpoliticalreview.com/2019/07/25/on-the-democracy-of-equals-an-interview-with-prof-elizabeth-anderson> (last accessed 25 March 2021).

Woolf, Nicky (2014). 'Jian Ghomeshi: More women come forward with sexual violence allegations against ex-CBC host.' *The Guardian*, 30 October, <https://www.theguardian.com/world/2014/oct/30/jian-ghomeshi-cbc-sexual-violence-allegations> (last accessed 25 March 2021).

Worthington, Nancy (2020). 'Celebrity-bashing or #MeToo contribution? *New York Times Online* readers debate the boundaries of hashtag feminism.' *The Communication Review* 23, no. 1: 46–65.

Wriggins, Jennifer (1983). 'Rape, racism, and the law.' *Harvard Women's Law Journal* 6: 103–41.

Wriggins, Jennifer (1995). 'Rape, racism, and the law'. In Patricia Searles and Ronald J. Berger (eds), *Rape and Society: Readings on the Problem of Sexual Assault*. Boulder: Westview, pp. 215–24.

Yang, Guobin (2016). 'Narrative agency in hashtag activism: The case of #BlackLivesMatter.' *Media and Communication* 4, no. 4: 13–17.

Yeatman, Anna (2000). 'What can disability tell us about participation.' *Law in Context* 17, no. 2: 181–202.

Yoffe, Emily (2019). 'I'm radioactive.' *Reason*, October, <https://reason.com/2019/08/23/im-radioactive> (last accessed 25 March 2021).

Young, Alex (2020). 'Louis C.K. jokes about his sexual misconduct in new comedy special.' *Consequence*, 5 April, <https://consequenceofsound.net/2020/04/louis-ck-sexual-misconduct-comedy-special> (last accessed 25 March 2021).

Young, Amanda R. (2019). 'Addressing the suppressed epidemic: Violence against Indigenous women.' *Journal of Indigenous Research* 7, no. 1: 3.

Young, Cate (2018). 'Aziz Ansari and the struggle to trust the "feminist" men of Hollywood.' *Cosmopolitan*, 18 January, <https://www.cosmopolitan.com/entertainment/celebs/a15389604/aziz-ansari-allegations-master-of-none-feminism> (last accessed 25 March 2021).

Young, Toby (2020). 'Social justice isn't always just.' *The Spectator*, 24 May, <https://spectator.us/social-justice-isnt-always-just> (last accessed 25 March 2021).

Yudice, George (2018). 'Neither impugning nor disavowing whiteness does a viable politics make: The limits of identity politics.' In Christopher Newfield and Ronald Strickland (eds), *After Political Correctness: The Humanities and Society in the 1990s*. New York: Routlege, pp. 255–85.

Yuval-Davis, Nira (2006). 'Intersectionality and feminist politics.' *European Journal of Women's Studies* 13, no. 3: 193–209.

Zainal, Zaidah (2007). 'Case study as a research method.' *Jurnal Kemanusiaan*, <http://psyking.net/htmlobj-3837/case_study_as_a_research_method.pdf> (last accessed 8 April 2021).

Zinsstag, Estelle, and Marie Keenan (eds) (2017). *Restorative Responses to Sexual Violence: Legal, Social and Therapeutic Dimensions*. New York: Routledge.

Index

EU representative:
Easy Access System Europe
Mustamäe tee 50, 10621 Tallinn, Estonia
Gpsr.requests@easproject.com

www.ingramcontent.com/pod-product-compliance
Lightning Source LLC
Chambersburg PA
CBHW051959270326
41929CB00015B/2711

* 9 7 8 1 4 7 4 4 7 9 2 1 9 *